D0606169

EMPEROR OF THE EARTH

CZESLAW MILOSZ

EMPEROR OF THE EARTH

Modes of Eccentric Vision

UNIVERSITY OF CALIFORNIA PRESS
Berkeley   Los Angeles   London

University of California Press
Berkeley and Los Angeles, California
University of California Press, Ltd.
London, England
ISBN: 0-520-03302-7
Library of Congress Catalog Card Number: 76-20005
Copyright © 1977 by The Regents
of the University of California
Printed in the United States of America

Contents

Preface

"We are now like the Dalmatians in the collapsing Roman Empire. They cared when the others wouldn't give a damn." This is how a friend of mine from Poland spoke of the difference between the so-called Eastern and Western Europeans. He might have added that although we have been attracted to the great Western European centers of learning and art for generations, our admiration has never been without reserve. Yet it is true, something new has taken place in the last decades. Changed into outsiders by the political division of Europe, we began to see more clearly than before that which Western man, submerged by everyday life, has been reluctant to admit, and the spectacle appearing before our eyes did not seem very promising. In my friend's mixture of scorn and regret, regret prevailed. He would say that even if the only civilization that made possible the conquest of the planet by modern science has entered the stage of spiritual decline, this should still not be interpreted as auguring the emergence of a new civilization able to replace it. At best the vital tasks have to be taken over by the peripheries, by less illustrious nations, simply because the others have grown slack.

This conversation is well suited to introducing a collection of essays on subjects taken mostly from Slavic literatures. It is not difficult to detect in my friend's views the residue of an old love-hate relationship between the rural and industrial areas of Europe, as well as an echo of the accusations leveled by the

Slavs at the materialistic West for at least a hundred and fifty years. And yet, in the new context of this last quarter of the twentieth century, the possibility of a shift from the center to the peripheries cannot be dismissed lightly. I must abstain from conjectures, for I cannot pretend to be an impartial judge. Divergences of opinion on particular points do not make me very different from my colleagues in Poland, Czechoslovakia, or Lithuania. Even if I am skeptical of the generalizations typical of any philosophy of history, I recognize something specific in both our common heritage and our present attitudes.

Why such a concern with man's destiny, why such an obsession with the riddle of Evil active in History? Whatever the answer, most of the following pages are dedicated to authors who passionately believed that they were called to influence the future, be it through Cassandra-like warnings regarded, it seems, as a kind of magical counteraction. Intensity may easily lead to delusion, and as is often the case, intensity coupled with pessimism may result in odd ideas. Nevertheless, it is energy, and as Blake says, "Energy is Eternal Delight."

As to the composition of this book: I did not try to be scholarly where I was tempted to be personal, and traces of my wanderings through various lands and several languages and literatures are noticeable. I begin with a true story, "Brognart," where I describe facts that came to my attention when I lived in France. This story, a confession of remorse, gives a glimpse at the fate of countries situated between Germany and Russia, but in reality tells of my (our) conflict with French intellectuals. The essay on Vladimir Solovyov, "Science Fiction and the Coming of the Antichrist," was inspired by the memory of a fresco by Luca Signorelli in the cathedral of Orvieto. The piece on Stanisław Ignacy Witkiewicz—an apocalyptic visionary—links my student years in the thirties, when he fascinated me, with the present day. "Krasiński's Retreat," another return to my student readings, attempts to determine how a Polish romantic poet could write in 1833 (at the age of twenty-one) a drama on the approaching world revolution. "On Pasternak Soberly" is a polemic, not unrelated to my practice as a poet, with certain poetics of our century represented perfectly by the *oeuvre* of this Russian poet. "On Modern Russian Literature and the West" raises the old issue of two radically opposed perspectives. "The Importance of Simone Weil" is a tribute to a thinker who pushed to an extreme her disagreement with "the world" and the powers that rule over it. "Shestov, or the Purity of Despair" is about a great Russian philosopher akin to Simone Weil in his refusal to assuage the unbearable character of human existence with vain consolations; the essay also recalls a desperate young woman in Paris who took great comfort in his books. "Dostoevsky and Swedenborg" is the outcome of reflections on the great Swede who has been maligned and often treated as a madman—though not by Dostoevsky. The name in the next title, "On Thomas Mayne Reid," says nothing to the public: I relate who he was, how I discovered him in my childhood, and why he is known in Slavic countries. "Joseph Conrad's Father" sketches the biography of a poet and revolutionary. "Eastern Europe" is a vague term because we repeatedly encounter a conflict between the Russians on one hand and the remaining nationalities on the other, but the nearly exemplary life of this nineteenth-century Polish romantic should give insight into these tensions. Moreover, it throws some light upon the fate of the hero of the last chapter, "A One-Man Army: Stanisław Brzozowski." This philosopher was a major influence in my youth and is still at the center of intellectual controversies in Poland. In turn a Nietzschean, a Marxist revisionist, a self-avowed disciple of Giambattista Vico and Cardinal Newman, his spiritual itinerary is expressive not only of his own time but of ours as well.

Some sections of the present volume were written in English and some in Polish, the latter being translated by myself or others. I wish to thank those students who occasionally helped in giving final shape to my own versions, as well as my colleague professor Francis J. Whitfield for his attentive reading of the manuscript and very valuable suggestions.

Acknowledgments are due to the following magazines where the texts first appeared: to *Kultura*, Paris, for "Brognart"; *Dissent* for "Science Fiction and the Coming of the Antichrist"; *Tri-Quarterly* for the essays on Stanisław Ignacy Witkiewicz and Lev Shestov; *Books Abroad* for the essay on Boris Pasternak; *California Slavic Studies* for "On Modern Russian Literature and the West" and the first part of my study on Brzozowski; *The Slavic Review* for "Dostoevsky and Swedenborg"; and to *Kultura* and *Mosaic* for "Joseph Conrad's Father."

C. M.

I
Brognart: A Story Told Over a Drink

Once quite a while ago in the fifties, I found myself in Marles-les-Mines, a small town in Pas-de-Calais, a black coal-mining region. A wet winter. In the fields the dazzling green of winter wheat, inky waste heaps and movement in the air: the turning gears of the lifts. It rained almost incessantly in Marles; walls blighted with dampness, mud between pavement stones, skeleton trees. The first passerby I asked for directions, a miner with skin tattooed by coal dust who was returning from work carrying a lantern, answered in the language in which I addressed him. I have a sharp eye, he was a Pole; probably half the people in Marles understood Polish. The hue of light there is murky, foggy, and whenever the door of a café was opened, a gust of steam burst forth (maybe I'm unfair in transferring the smoke and the steam to the light there in general). There were bikes in front of the tiny cafés and inside, over shots of *calvados*, everyone was talking about Brognart. And there in Marles, the matter gripped and moved me.

I'm not the one to say how the scales of my good and evil will come to rest, but sometimes I think that one thing might prevail —those moments when I've felt like running, shouting, because nobody, no one could do it, and it was up to me. I decided that I at least would not remain silent. I questioned residents, went to neighboring Bruay (the two small towns are divided only by somewhat of a ravine) and from a young schoolteacher got Brognart's notebooks: analyses of *Le Cid*, the *Iliad*, in the

1

spindly handwriting of a diligent pupil. That teacher believes to
this day that I was a fraud or a spy because I did nothing with
my strong resolution. If hell is paved with good intentions, then
here the scales tip against me. For, after all, I had not intended
to run around the world with my tongue hanging out, taking
part in the defense of the tortured, especially not in a country
like France where there are enough writers and journalists sensitive in general to the fates of their fellow countrymen. But no
Frenchman had the slightest idea about that which befell Brognart, and no one would have been able to identify with him;
their imagination didn't reach that far. A different training of
the imagination was needed here—mine, from the East of Europe—and I well knew that only I was available.

I made a few attempts, and always found reasons for pushing
Brognart aside. What sort of obstacles were these? First of all,
Brognart was no longer alive. He was part of that numberless
mass, that mass of the beaten, the downtrodden, the maimed,
in the eighth century before Christ or in the twentieth after—
time doesn't matter here. Why him then, him in particular: why
sympathy for him, why objection to his death? Even if I limited
myself to my own lifetime, it was an inadequate reason because
millions like him had perished (and the shirt is closer to the
body than the jacket, goes a Polish saying): I would rather have
chosen someone better known to me than a Frenchman. To tell
you the truth, there was something enigmatic in my sudden
emotional response to the talk in Marles-les-Mines. I suspected
that Brognart interested me so much because he was a substitute, connected by various unnamed strings to this or that person tangible for me. But a good reason was lacking: here were
cars, theaters, flowers, trains stuffed with skiers, that human
vortex which seals its losses up tightly. They didn't want to find
out about things uncomplimentary to themselves, so what did
one Brognart mean? To step onto the forum, to remind them,
only so they could yawn and turn away from the bore or wink
knowingly: another shrewd fellow, even a skillful one, increasing his political assets.

Because Brognart had already become a political matter, not
of his own will—for what can a teenager, with his analyses of
Corneille and Racine, know about politics? As a local issue in
Pas-de-Calais, it was used in an election. Elsewhere it was invading philosophical and literary salons where to mention it
other than with a smirk would have been tactless. And although
I didn't care about tact, this prohibition paralyzed me in one
very specific, indirect way. I was too involved with this story
emotionally. Out of simple respect for the main character I preferred to remain silent, to avoid the suspicion (if only in my
own eyes) that I was using Brognart as one more argument to
justify myself or to defend my own virtue. Of course I saw quite
clearly the outlines of the book I could have put together, even
its scheme and particular chapters. But had it appeared, who
would have needed it? Some would have scoffed at it, citing it
as an example of the "falsified consciousness" of its author;
others would have dismissed it politely or tokenly praised it.
Because what to me was an abyss, the vision of an abyss, to
them was only a weapon in a political game played for reasons
other than some Brognart. But I admit the whole story is fantastic, absurd, atypical, so even those others would have avoided
it, embarrassed.

I won't beat around the bush any longer. Brognart (first name
Gilbert), the son of a foreman, was born in Marles. His father's
family, and his mother's, were native peasant families that had
been digging around in the soil for generations before anyone
suspected that there was coal beneath it. Later their land, and
they didn't diminish it by parceling, gained in value so they quit
farming and took up new work in the coal mines, always
keeping however, this bit of security on the records, so that it
was said in Marles that these families were, well, you know,
well off, and this house was theirs and that one, and this and
that plot of land. But as is usual in France, niggardliness instead
of ostentation, and groans that there wasn't enough for bread
and wine. Gilbert's father left his mother when Gilbert was
little, obtained a divorce, and married for the third time. Gil-

bert saw him rarely because the boy grew up in Marles with his
mother, grandmother, and aunts, while his father lived and
died in Auchel. His mother fretted over her only son maybe
even more than mothers usually fret over their only sons. It was
something of a desperate love, whether for reason of the
divorce or for who knows what dramas in this family that was,
it seems, dying out. One of her sisters, for example, was
deranged—English Tommies raped her when they were stationed there during the first World War and something snapped
in her head.

But it doesn't seem that Gilbert was particularly spoiled or
pampered. He was a completely normal boy, diligent, matter-
of-fact, serious, liked by his friends and good in sports. He
showed no tendencies toward any extravagance or daydreaming beyond the needs of his immediate surroundings. He wasn't
overly ambitious; after the Ecole Primaire, he stayed on at the
same school in the next grades (the Ecole Primaire Supérieure,
according to French nomenclature); afterward, the Collège Mo-
derne. He was preparing himself for mining school, planned on
receiving his engineering diploma there and then returning to
Marles. He was strong in mathematics and physics. From what
his teacher told me about him I've formed, I think, an accurate
picture: a typical peasant from northern France, phlegmatic,
slightly ironic, not exhibiting his emotions, and in addition to
this a strong will, stubbornness, and independence. He never
played a double game; he always said what he thought, this
especially the teacher emphasized. In a group, in the classroom,
or on the playing field, he was dynamic. At first he rode a bike
to school in Bruay; then, when he turned sixteen, his mother
bought him a motorcycle (the only trace of spoiling, though not
much; a bike or motorcycle is a necessity there). A motorcycle
accident gave proof of his composure: his front tire blew, but he
didn't lose his head. When he received pocket money from his
mother, his greatest pleasure was in buying things for others—if
he saw that a friend wanted something, he bought it immediately. Reasonably sociable, he belonged to one organization,
the *Jeunesse Etudiante Chrétienne.*

Brognart's photographs fit the teacher's report: the pleasant face of a stable teenager. Strong chin, delicately shaped lips, a prominent nose somewhat childlike in its pudginess. A direct gaze, alert, somewhat lyrical. It was exactly, I suppose, his eyes and lips that struck me because they reminded me of the eyes and lips of someone close to me in my family. In some of his pictures, it's true, Brognart wore glasses, the kind in a thin metal frame, and there the likeness began to blur.

With all his sobriety he wouldn't have been a kid if he hadn't been drawn by playing around, sniffing the world and roaming. Naturally he was crazy about traveling, about adventure. In Marles he found a companion in this, became friends with the son of a butcher, a Polish family, natives of the city Toruń. It happened that the relatives of the Polish boy invited him to Toruń for summer vacation, and he immediately suggested to Gilbert that they go together. This was an exceptional opportunity. Up to this time Gilbert had never been outside of France, actually not beyond *le Nord*, so he asked his mother to let him go. She probably didn't want to, there is that French mistrust of strange lands, but it was difficult to refuse him—he had just passed his *bachot* exams and was going to enter mining school in the fall. This happened in 1939. Brognart had just turned eighteen, he was born the first of June, 1921. Whether Marles was familiar with international politics, I don't know—Marles isn't Paris. It is likely, however, that his mother had reservations because he didn't get his way immediately, and left for Poland only in the second half of August.

Toruń is a beautiful city, and there in the family of his friend he found a group of boys his age. Everything was new—the architecture, the river, the kayaks—so time passed delightfully and it was in this way that the war took Brognart by surprise in Poland. I say the word *war* but it sounds wooden, inexact. War can mean the Greeks in Troy or big headlines in newspapers read over coffee where it doesn't directly apply to us and simply marks the ups and downs of the stock exchange. Here, however, it wasn't this at all, but a consuming fire from the heavens which buzzed and shook from machines moving across them, and below in the fields the red centers of fires blinked in the smoke as one human society, straining its limits, revealed itself, showing that which is beneath every human society. Those who haven't seen it are lucky. Fleeing the German army and taking bombed roads, Brognart started out on foot for the south with three of his Toruń companions. The three soon turned back because German tanks were everywhere and were already circling Warsaw. He, however, knowing neither language nor country, reached Warsaw after a few days and nights and headed for the French embassy (pangs of conscience, probably, and the thought of his mother).

I said that the story had been developing into a book. In it would have figured not just the experiences of Brognart but the wanderings of his comrades as well: experiences instructive to some and uninteresting to most. Because in Marles I questioned the family of the butcher as well (they answered reluctantly but I did get something out of them), and it occurred to me to ask them about what had later happened to the other three boys. They had returned home to the occupied city. One of them, apparently the most adventurous, didn't stay there long, instead made his way south again, to Warsaw and beyond, into the mountains between Poland and Slovakia. In the first winter of the war, young people stole across there on skis. He got to Hungary and then to France, where he entered the Polish army forming there. He was evacuated to England with his division, underwent schooling to become a pilot, and flew in bombers over Germany: now he was the punishing fire. He died near the end of the war from shock suffered when landing a damaged plane.

For the second boy it went quite differently. He was mobilized and incorporated into the Wehrmacht; the Germans considered Toruń a German town and its citizens Germans. He found a chance to surrender to the Allies in Italy, and then wore a Polish uniform. After the war, when the army was transported from Italy to England, he could have remained there but didn't want to. He returned to Poland, studied, and was already passing his final exams in engineering when he was put in jail. The new powers quite diligently arrested all those who at one time were in the Polish army in the West (not necessarily in the Wehrmacht, of which they were much more tolerant). The third boy—that friend of Brognart's from Marles—got stuck in Toruń, pined for his parents and France, and worked in a factory. The Gestapo arrested him for belonging to an underground organization, and he landed in a concentration camp, Stutthof near Gdańsk. He wasn't there long because he arrived when the German imperium was already reaching its end, but he suffered some internal damage. Later he registered at the university. All was well, he seemed healthy, when one day going up the stairs he fell and died of heart failure.

A digression, the three different fates of one generation in one country. I don't have to make things up, to add anything. But none of the three was struck by such a misfortune as Brognart's. The first of the three had his manly triumphs, his joy; the second, if they did not let him rot too quickly, certainly got out of prison in a few years; and even the third, if he suffered much, did not suffer long.

In Warsaw Brognart found there was no longer any French embassy, that it had been evacuated to the East. How he fended for himself, where he turned, what he ate, where he slept in this alien, unknown city of chaos, of contradictory rumors and panic, along whose dark streets the wind carried the papers of offices and departments which no longer existed, I don't know. He stayed there long and survived the siege (not a bad siege, either: entire streets shot into the air in fountains of brick, on the thoroughfares horse carcasses from which you carved out a steak, and so on). Afterward, in the vanquished capital, the German police picked him up in October, but, keeping him a while, they released him, probably because they did not have time to spend on such trifles as citizens of other countries, already in the bag anyway. Brognart must have reasoned, quite logically, that instead of waiting until they put him into some kind of internment camp he should get himself to a neutral country that harbored his consulates. And of the two countries that divided Poland, one was neutral; it received what it did as payment, as the interest on its neutrality. The border (by virtue of a pact between them) ran not far from Warsaw, and, in November, Brognart crossed this border avoiding the sentries as many then did.

They say that man learns everything, though not right away (his imagination is too confined by his habits). Brognart probably thought that he would find a French consulate immediately, or if not, that he would get on a train and go to Moscow the way one rides from Marles to Paris. When he was told this wasn't allowed he turned quite naturally to the authorities to help him. With the bureaucracy of his own country, the country with the oldest bureaucracy in Europe, he was familiar. He did not know, however, that compared to others this bureaucracy was quite democratic even before the French Revolution. He had never given it any thought. Now he had to find out what happens when no one lifts a finger because the individual has no so-called "natural rights." Furious, he told himself that if this was so, then he would manage without anyone's help. Here and there he gathered bits of information, from which he concluded there were French consulates in neighboring Baltic countries, then still independent. So he simply went. It is even difficult to reproach him with carelessness. The expedition from Warsaw emboldened him though it shouldn't have, it was much easier. In addition even Poles, who it would seem have a calling to know the customs of their neighbors, were naive; they set out in whole groups, like Brognart, only to get out from under the power which had been imposed without asking anyone's opinion. Some made it, some didn't. Perhaps I would have let the whole Brognart matter in Marles-les-Mines go right by me if I had had no concrete images of my own to link me to such border crossings. But I did have them, and strong ones, and I assure you that to experience this is something, after which the years pass and life is ever wondrous, each day like a gift. Well, Brognart got caught on the Latvian border. They kept him in various prisons stuffed with louse-infested masses of humanity: with the young such as himself who wanted to get to the West to the army, with old men and women, and with all nationalities: Poles, Jews, Lithuanians, Byelorussians, who were there for various improprieties but mainly for coming from the wrong social strata.

In such a situation a resourceful and stubborn youth remembers, naturally, that a shipwrecked man ought to pass on news of himself in a bottle entrusted to the sea, and should not lose faith because there is always the chance that someone will fish the bottle out. So Brognart, and here you can see his thoroughness, wrote carefully on the wall of every cell in which he found himself his first name, last, and a request to notify his family. And he didn't err in his calculations. Except that the currents carried his bottle, or not so much the bottle as those who fished it out, a long time—about six years. It was only after the war that letters came to Marles from Polish officers and soldiers of the army which had been in Italy, at one time occupants of the same prisons. Some had read his inscription, others had the Frenchman for a cellmate.

After months in jail, Brognart was read a verdict. Let no one say that rights are not respected there. After all, the rule of law is an attribute of culture and it was invented in the same place as other clever items such as the toothbrush, the steam engine, electricity, and the parliamentary system. To make normal use of the law or elections—well, no, but the fiction even increased the desire for ritual. Brognart probably understood nothing of the ceremony, because in his mind some relation between crime and punishment was supposed to exist; that's what he learned in school, from literature, and from his environment. He didn't, moreover, even understand the language in which he was being spoken to. If they showed him on their fingers how many he got, eight, he didn't get the sense of it right away: that they meant eight years. And if he despaired then here, too, he was wrong. Whether five or eight, it was all the same since the goal was to maintain the same number of working hands in the concentration camps as the weaker prisoners died out. He was transported to one such camp near Archangelsk.

This descendant of generations of thrifty and industrious peasants was resistant. Even for people accustomed to a cold climate from childhood, to live through even four winters there was quite a feat, the average that could be expected from a healthy man. But the seasons came and went, and Brognart wouldn't give in. He continually sent his bottles to sea, believing in rescue. After the war not only did his mother know that he was somewhere in Russia but even the French embassy had received a letter from him (smuggled somehow) in which he gave exactly the what and where. Efforts began, and when his whereabouts were known—at the mouth of the River Pechora —the Russian authorities stopped denying there was such a person. Still it was a long time before they officially admitted that he existed, condemned by legal verdict with an added sentence of ten years "for spreading malicious rumors," and that a review of the trial was impossible. In other words, there in the camps of the north Brognart had not learned docility and just as earlier, in school, always said what he thought.

What his mother lived through I won't attempt to guess. When you mail letters and requests every day, go from one institution to another, go to Thorez[1] too—falling literally at his feet, begging him to save your son—when such attempts last for years, it's possible to break down. Later, when I was in Marles, his mother lived in a psychiatric institution (put there, it's true, at her own request).

Brognart died in 1951. Not a bad accomplishment: eleven years. Families of Russian or Polish prisoners would agree here, too, that few dragged their feet in the camps for such a long time, practically an eternity. The official notice of his death was dispatched to the French embassy with the appropriate delay, about a year later, and then the sensational dailies in France related Brognart's case in the *faits divers* section. Only in Marles

[1]Maurice Thorez, then the Secretary General of the French Communist party.

and in the neighboring districts did the event receive a lot of publicity. There, in *le Nord*, it was mainly the Socialists and Communists who were fighting over votes. The Socialists made an argument of Brognart and this was very uncomfortable for the Communists, because of course it mattered to them to refute all defamation. In Russia, yes, there were corrective camps for political transgressors, for fascists and hitlerites, but who would shed tears over criminals if not an agent of American imperialism? And they had a strong point, because in France didn't *collabos* have to be punished? So everyone, even if they had doubts, kept their mouths shut. Besides, it was so far away, who could check? The countries and the people were faceless. Now unfortunately there was one concrete man, with a face, and that has a stronger impact than an abstract ten million. Brognart? What did he have to do with politics, the kid, why everyone in Marles knew him! That is why they had to find a way. The Communist press dragged out his insane aunt, combined that with the illness of his mother, and had a ready thesis. It was a case of heredity, those alleged reports which Brognart had passed on about himself were the fantasies of a madman. I think the articles were effective; in any case I know that shortly thereafter, when I returned to Paris, talk of Brognart began to die down, until it died out forever.

Now I'll confess my emotional attachment. In the photograph Brognart looked like my cousin, and the moments which I spent in the house of these relatives are important to me even to this day. That cousin, also an only child, is for me quite enigmatic. I sometimes think about what he would have been like, had he grown up. He was sensitive, lyrical, musical, and in addition possessed the very contradictory characteristics of his parents. He was a bit like the heroes in Thomas Mann's early stories. He was fifteen when the Nazis shipped him from Poland to a concentration camp in Germany, and seventeen when he died there. I can't talk about it. If they had only shot him—but that time texture imposed on him, on him in particular.

I want to dwell for a moment on the basic difficulty that

explains why it was better to keep quiet about the various Brog-
narts. Sure, you were allowed to lament the victims of hitlerite
camps, it lowered no one's literary prestige, and if the reader
was bored it was with respect. But nothing could help my
cousin or any other victims of the Nazis, and I felt no desire to
speak of the past. But now masses (enough to populate a
medium-sized European country) like Brognart were still going
out to labor each morning, and the same sun shone upon us. It's
ridiculous, I know, to take upon yourself misfortunes which are
not your own. Am I my brother's keeper? Then why did the
Left Bank cafés feel universal responsibility, why did they jump
from "cause" to "cause" in chronic excitement: in Mississippi
they're torturing Negroes, Madagascar isn't being granted independence, villages are burning in Indochina. Here they weren't
ashamed of sentimentality. So other criteria must have been
used, other springs were tilting the scales unevenly. Before the
mythical East, "aah" with indrawn breath, as before a very
great mountain. There lay progress, the direction of history,
and you should not incur its disfavor but protect your name in
the face of posterity. The causes they would take up were honorable, guaranteed by the future. Just like those others taken up
by Lamennais or Victor Hugo or Zola, who cared about being
warmly mentioned by posterity. Since there is no Heaven, let
there at least be a heaven of good repute. Besides, there were
always plenty of those bustling around Europe who made a profession of anti-Communism to squeeze money out of Americans; they were generally avoided by respectable intellectual
company out of fear of catching leprosy.

Nothing is simple here, French rationalism is a legend, unless
reducing everything to eloquence is taken for rationalism. It is,
rather, a ritual, like ants feeling each other with their antennae.
Although I could have been ironical, I did not treat lightly their
cleverness and sensitivity to conventions which sets fashions for
the enlightened at the eternal supper at Madame Verdurin's,
fashions which later infect Japan or America. The direction of
history which they flaunted was not mere nonsense to me,

though I rather suspected that it did not have in store for them what they had so safely planned. Nevertheless, my pride suffered. If not actually upon Brognart, then I was writing about related matters and ruining my good name. That is, my work was lined with steadily wounded ambition rather than with regular cowardice. I imagined how I looked in their eyes—a maniac, an emigré, in other words a reactionary—and my tone took on desperate hues. Now that all this is behind me, I only know that I would not repeat similar experiences for any price. I molded a mask for myself, a political one that distorted my features, though I have never had strong political interests and never made claims to much political acumen. I wondered instead why amazement at human foolishness was forbidden. Around me they were all swimming in a haze and driveling as if these were not serious matters of life and death that lay deeper than some form of politics. But my surprise really reached its peak a bit later when the ban was lifted, because then one single nasty man was purported to be guilty of all the crimes. Why the breakdowns, why the feigned innocence of two-year-olds? Either you see the state as an institution to which individuals delegate a part of their power and then exercise control, or you believe in a messianic state, and then, in the face of the greatness of the cause, tears shed over the destruction of some number of little human machines are truly crocodile tears. The Mexican priests who offered human sacrifices to keep the sun moving and assure a harvest would likely have been just as depressed had it been proven to them that the sacrifices were unnecessary, having no influence on the movement of the sun. As for me, I simply disliked the monopolistic state, the state-messiah—and this regardless of whether or not it was promised a splendid future—so I was surprised. No, not so much at their breakdowns and disillusionments, but more at the ease with which they immediately mended their shattered faith in the wise movement of history, without drawing any conclusions.

For me these problems were only the surface, and I blamed myself for not reaching deeper and not presenting myself as I really was. I felt guilty of deception. I had to return to myself, to learn how to outline my own hidden convictions, my own real faith, and through this to pay witness. It's a lot of work and I haven't yet learned how to do it. But since I had already begun, Brognart wasn't of much use because he would have steered me toward questions which were too blatant and which would have screened things more difficult for me and more real. Those few people who were against current political fashions and saw me as a valuable ally made dour faces because the world is divided into two blocs, and if you are in one you must beat the hell out of the other, while I was slipping away, withdrawing. What sort of politician was I? Such a mask was not made to fit my face; it was inauthentic, the bondage of circumstance. In human destiny I was looking for sources, and not for the rivers that spilled on downstream.

So I buried Brognart, which does not mean that he didn't haunt me. He haunts me to this day, ever more closely merged with my cousin, so that I can barely tell them apart. It's not really their faces, they show up faintly, it's more their inner state, my imagining of this or that moment behind wire. Peace to their poor souls.

1960

2
Science Fiction and the Coming of the Antichrist

The literary genre called science fiction has been developing for over a hundred years, and its vitality today is surprising. In a narrower sense, a science fiction story is usually a tale of adventure in a world of tomorrow transformed by technology. The classic writer in this vein was Jules Verne. His books show particularly clearly the origin of the genre: the nineteenth century's breakthroughs in science, which created the belief that technological progress would have no limits. Verne's favorite heroes are lonely scientists whose thoughts range further than those of their contemporaries. He often places his action in the present, but that present is visited by the future in the guise of inventions created by minds of genius (Captain Nemo's submarine, television in the *Carpathian Castle*).

Science fiction, however, soon became enriched with new contents. These were images of societies from the day after tomorrow, and in the twentieth century they were mostly pessimistic images. Moreover, no precise borderline could be traced between the technologically oriented imagination and philosophical reflection. An intermediary zone extends from forebodings of "vengeance," in which the creations of the human mind turn against man (for instance, rebelling robots), to sketches of some hypothetical civilizations where the stress is not on technology but on human relationships. We lack a term that would also include such novels as those by H. G. Wells, Aldous Huxley, or George Orwell, so perhaps we are forced to speak of science fiction in a broader sense as well. We would include here any narrative that pretends to be written in the past tense, whereas it should have been written in the *futur accompli*; it should have been, but cannot be, because grammar itself stands in the way. Events that "will have happened" lack sufficient probability, and a hero who "will have done," "will have seen," "will have gone" is not sufficiently real for us. So a prediction (since we are dealing with predictions) is disguised grammatically: a hero living in the year 3000 "did" and "went." But we find the same thing in the Revelation of St. John: that which is predicted is told as something that has already occurred—in a vision on the island of Patmos.

Let us consider that science fiction appears precisely when the dimension of space ceases to stimulate the human imagination and is supplanted in this respect by the dimension of time. From the sixteenth century on, there were a great number of novels about fantastic countries, islands, societies, existing somewhere on the enormous, still unexplored earth. To one such novel California owes its name. Those works underwent a mutation similar to the one we are witnessing today in fantasies about the future—from simple tales of adventures to utopias and philosophical satire. Swift's *Gulliver's Travels* was the fruit of such a mutation. The exploration of the new dimension, time, begins just as the last blank spots on the map disappear and when the last "island paradise," Tahiti, has only one chance to survive—on the canvases of Gauguin. One may object here that science fiction is concerned with space as well, for it often deals with distant planets. Yet those are planets of the future; that is, they are supposed to be reached some day by man who is separated from them less by space than by the time required by his gradually progressing technology.

Though most science fiction is no more than vulgar trash, the genre seems to be increasingly victorious in its competition with the so-called contemporary novel. The collapse of realistic prose is a phenomenon simultaneous with the waning of figurative painting, and the causes are the same. It is a choice between a thing observed by man, a thing possessing its own objective existence, and an observer freely interpreting: impressionist painters opted for the second, and since that time everything has moved quickly. Leaving painting aside, we should simply affirm that narration—whether in the folk tale, the heroic epic, or the novel—has its permanent rules, and one of them is to satisfy the curiosity expressed in the questions, "What happened? What happened next?" In other words, the listener or reader wants to enter a certain reality, forgetting that it is invented. A novel in which reality explodes into fragments, glimpses, signals, and whose reader is zealously reminded that everything is happening only in the narrator's mind, does not conform to the basic rules. The author of a work of science fiction, however, makes no use of tacit references to known surroundings as does an author who places his characters in the 1970s. From the outset he must make his reality consistent and believable. There is something of the chronicler in him—he is preoccupied with facts and the sequence of events—and that compulsion brings his fantasies close to the models of classical narration.

Science fiction is particularly useful for assessing the scope of the human imagination. For that purpose it is enough to take any story from a few decades back—for instance something by H. G. Wells or Aldous Huxley—concerning either new machines or the presumable forms of a future technological civilization, and to compare it with what we know today. It will then be obvious that such works contain astonishingly correct previsions entangled with numerous details bearing the stigma of their own time. It is a kind of dream in which here and there we distinguish the features of our own world, for imagination can only build with the material at its disposal in the here and now. It can reach into the future only to the extent that it is able to grasp potentially promising omens in the present and to separate them from omens that are promising only in appearance but are, in fact, illusory. Jules Verne intuited the hidden potentials of the scientific discoveries of his time, so his heroes travel to the center of the earth or to the moon; but in their thinking, in their manners and dress, they remain the loyal children of the nineteenth century. We also admire the intuition of writers who foresaw the role of drugs as a means of totalitarian control. Yet when reading them now, one exclaims both "How true!" and "How completely untrue!" In philosophical reflections about the future everything becomes quite complex, because moralists and satirists turn their passions toward the society in which they are submerged and toward the catastrophes which threaten it. Thus they meditate upon "what this will lead to." Sometimes, for instance in the works of Stanisław Ignacy Witkiewicz, the dimension of the future is nearly as conventional as the dimension of space in Swift.

The difficulty of judging science fiction is compounded not only by the entangling, the condensation of various elements, but also by the fact that we are confronted with three kinds of time: the time of writing (quite evident in works written several decades ago); the time of the reader; and the time which, in respect to the reader, lies in the future indefinite, somewhere between that which we know from our own experiences and that which may still occur.

Vladimir Solovyov wrote *Three Conversations* at the end of 1899 and at the beginning of 1900 shortly before his death, thus concluding a literary output which was quite abundant though he lived only 47 years.[1] The full title of the book, published in 1900, is *Three Conversations on War, Progress, and the End of World History, Including a Short Tale of the Antichrist and Supplements*. In the introduction, Solovyov defines the aim of his book as polemical and apologetic; it contains a warning and a prophecy. Expressing himself previously only in treatises, lec-

---

[1]Vladimir Solovyov (1853-1900) was a Russian religious philosopher and poet, indebted in some of his ideas to Plato—but also to Dostoevsky. Solovyov influenced the generation of Russian symbolists. Best known among his numerous philosophical works are his *Lectures Concerning God-Manhood* (1877-1884), his long treatise in French written in an ecumenical spirit, *La Russie et L'Église Universelle* (1889), and *The Justification of the Good* (1898).

tures, and poetry, this time Solovyov introduces a few characters. The action of *Three Conversations* takes place both contemporaneously with the author and in the future. A group of Russians meets by chance on the Mediterranean shore, at the foot of the Alps. During the three evenings they spend together, each of them represents a different attitude toward religious and moral problems. Practically all of them display views shared, at least in part, by the author. The characters include the old General, the Politician, Mr. Z., and the Lady. Quite different from these characters is the young Prince. In his reasoning there are signs of a spiritual illness which, according to the author, will contaminate the majority of all people in the future. What that future will be we learn in the third and final conversation, when Mr. Z. reads aloud a manuscript allegedly written by the monk Pansopheus. In it the events of the twentieth and twenty-first centuries are related in the past tense, as in the Revelation of St. John.

We will leave reflections on the life and works of Solovyov, and on the relationship between the *Three Conversations* and his other pronouncements, to more competent people. A number of monographs have been published on Solovyov in various languages. We are interested here in something that, though not necessarily simple, nonetheless concerns us directly. There is no reason to be ashamed of that most normal attraction to curious gossip which, when we chance upon an old prophecy, compels us to ask whether it came true or not. The manuscript of the monk Pansopheus is, formally, nothing but science fiction if we agree to accept the broader sense of that term; it is subject to the same rules, though it derives from a different tradition. Although the laboratories of nineteenth-century scientists spawned a new literary genre, Christian folklore for centuries had been gathering evidence concerning the approach of a crucial event: the Second Coming, preceded by the coming of the Antichrist, the millennium, the end of time. Perhaps the current success of science fiction may be explained precisely by its finding ground already prepared, and thus appealing to old sediments in the subconscious that link it with folklore.

The monk Pansopheus's manuscript is loaded with enough facts for even the most bizarre novel. And we must concede that we recognize in it the contours of our own world, but entangled with notions from the past century and, so to speak, with their proportions shifted. It can be compared to a column of print in which the lines are composed correctly but whose sequence has been jumbled, so that we do not always know what should follow upon what.

It is worthwhile to recall some of Solovyov's basic premises. He detected a hidden logic and a moral meaning in history. For him the point at which all its threads are joined was Christianity, whose division into Catholicism, Orthodoxy, and Protestantism he deplored. Although he ended his life as a faithful believer in the Eastern Orthodox church, he gravitated toward Catholicism, and not only theoretically, as he had once received communion in a Catholic church ("prichastil'sya"). He considered the unification of all Christians and theocracy the only way out for Europe. From the *Three Conversations* one may conclude that this will not be possible, since such an organization of society would mean the end of what we are accustomed to call history.

In Pansopheus's manuscript the twentieth century belongs to Asia. Japan not only takes over technology from Europe but also the ideas known as Pan-Slavism and Pan-Germanism, elaborating its own idea of Pan-Mongolism. Thus armed it undertakes the conquest of China and establishes a Japanese dynasty there, effectively convincing the Chinese that they should modernize themselves and, together with the Japanese, turn against the white race. The Chinese army and navy, trained by Japanese instructors, quickly makes use of the huge human reserves of Manchuria, China, Mongolia, and Tibet. In a couple of decades the French are thrown out of Tonkin and Siam, the English out of Burma, and all of Indo-china falls under the rule of the Chinese empire. Europe, meanwhile, has to cope one last time with the countries of Islam; thus its attention is diverted from the menacing East.

An army of 4 million is concentrated in Chinese Turkestan in order to invade India, or so Chinese diplomacy assures the Russians. The sudden entrance of that army into the Russian part of Asia is accompanied by an uprising of the entire native population, and the pace of the march is so fast that soon the Asiatic troops cross the Ural mountains. The Russian army, hurriedly transferred from the West—from Poland, Lithuania, Finland, the Ukraine—suffers heavy losses in hopeless battles with the Chinese. Another Russian army cut off in Siberia vainly attempts to strike at China from the north. After leaving some of their forces in Russia to fight the guerrillas, the unified Mongols cross over the borders into Germany with their three armies. Here preparations have been made, and one of the three armies is completely routed. But then, in France, a party of revanchists comes to power and a million Frenchmen attack the Germans from the rear (with a typical shifting of circumstances, one can see this as the war of 1914). The Mongols fraternize with their new allies, then massacre them with "Chinese thoroughness."

Revolutionary Paris, in control of workers *sans patrie*, joyously greets the masters from the East. The navy of the conquerors has arrived from the Pacific and is ready to invade England, but the English succeed in buying themselves off with a billion pounds; besides, the Chinese need their navy for actions against America and Australia. In one year, all Europe becomes a vassal of Asia and will now live under occupation for fifty years. A conspiratorial network, carefully woven over a long period of time and aided clandestinely by European governments that manage to fool their Asiatic overlords, finally erupts in a simultaneous uprising in all European countries and the Mongols are expelled.

Europe in the twenty-first century is different from what it was before the invasion. The international solidarity that had been developed in common resistance against the conquerors has now contributed to a weakening of nationalism, and the sovereignty of particular countries has lost its previous importance. Countries are organized more or less democratically into the United States of Europe. Material progress, somewhat hampered over a half a century, again gathers momentum. At the same time a multitude of new discoveries in physiology and psychology shows the insoluble enigmas of life and death, the destinies of the world and of man, in a new light. The materialistic *Weltanschauung* that conceived of the universe as an infinite series of accidental changes now seems naive to man—mankind has grown out of it as a child grows out of clothes. A certain rather high level is observed by both believers and nonbelievers when they discuss religion.

The number of believing Christians is insignificant: on the entire planet they number only 45 million, since they no longer include those who had once considered themselves Christians merely out of social inertia. But what they lost in quantity, the Christians gained in both moral and intellectual quality. They do not limit themselves to naive faith but put into practice the counsel of Paul the Apostle, who advised them not to be children in their understanding. They are still divided into Catholics, Protestants, and Orthodox, but mutual hostility and distrust have disappeared. The non-Christian majority also devotes itself to fervent religious quests. It is an age of syncretism, a blending of beliefs from the West and the East, of neo-Buddhism and Satanic sects.

It is now that the Antichrist appears. In creating this character, Solovyov drew both upon the New Testament and the copious Christian writings stemming from it, as well as upon his own meditations about his contemporaries. The Antichrist is a focus for tendencies already present in the year 1900 which have only to attain their logical conclusion. It should be stressed here that Solovyov is not concerned with philosophical materialism, which he considered a transitory phenomenon. The Prince of the *Three Conversations*, a meek Tolstoyan character who does not claim to be a materialist at all, is an unconscious precursor of the Antichrist.

In his introduction to the *Three Conversations*, Solovyov speaks of a strange sect of "hole worshipers" which, as the newspapers reported, arose in the remote provinces of Russia. Peasants would drill a hole in the wall of their huts and pray to it: "My sacred hole, my sacred hut." But Solovyov also writes of educated "hole worshipers" who are similar to these sectarians and whose teachings spread among the intelligentsia. Their exhortations for universal goodness, justice, and fraternity mean the acceptance of the ethical principles of Christianity along with a rejection of its metaphysical basis. Thus these were no more than exhortations to pray to a hole, a void.

We should remember here that one certainty—death—was central to Solovyov's thought. He did not agree with those who, wishing to assuage the cruelty of biological laws, invoked eternal rebirth in Nature; there is no rebirth in Nature because this particular ant, this particular bird, this particular flower lives only once and gives a new beginning not to itself but to other individuals. Death is sufficient proof of universal corruption, the stigma of the Devil in the universe. Man is confronted with one all-important either/or: either Christ was resurrected and thus victorious over the powers of Hell, or he was not resurrected. Solovyov counsels those who choose the latter to become Buddhists instead of constantly quoting the Gospels.

Why do the people gathered on the shore of the Mediterranean in the *Three Conversations* debate about war and peace? War is a misfortune in which the imperfection of human institutions is most blatantly revealed. A complete renunciation of war on principle, independent of circumstances, would mean that we are able to put the good of our fellow men over our own. The General, one of those modest and pure-hearted soldiers so loved by Russian writers, declares himself in favor of the ideal of the Christian knight and just wars waged in the defense of the oppressed. The Politician maintains that cultural progress makes war more and more loathsome to people, so that in time it will probably disappear. The Prince, however, who is a pacifist-activist, deeply believes that the evangelic love of one's fellow man and nonviolent resistance to injustice will not only put an end to wars but will transform a suffering humanity into a humanity wise and happy. Jesus is, for the Prince, a teacher and lawgiver; he considers Jesus only a man who was defeated by death like everyone else.

The book is a polemic with Tolstoy and indirectly with Rousseau, but it preserves its timeliness because of the importance of its central dilemma. If man is innocent, and depraved and alienated only because of society, then by bettering society it will be possible to restore man's innocence. If, however, "the world dwells in evil" and evil grows out of man's very ego, that lack of innocence should be taken into account in any strivings for social improvement. Otherwise we expose ourselves to the "vengeance" of institutions too ideally conceived. We may here leave the question open as to whether a moderate pessimism can accord with lay humanism or, as Solovyov maintains, only religion can provide a brake upon excessive optimism. To the arguments of the Prince, Mr. Z. (the voice of Solovyov himself) answers by reading the manuscript of the monk Pansopheus. Even though the wars of the twentieth century will belie the Prince's hopes, there will appear in the twenty-first century a wise man of genius, a friend of mankind who—first as the president of the United States of Europe, then as an emperor with his capital in Rome—will accomplish everything for which the Prince longs, securing for the inhabitants of the entire earth peace, justice, and well-being. Unfortunately, he will also be the Antichrist.

Here I will allow myself a personal digression. This essay on Solovyov probably would never have been written were it not for Signorelli's frescoes in the Cathedral of Orvieto, which I saw long ago in my youth. When painting his *Preaching of the Antichrist*, in the beginning of the sixteenth century, Luca Signorelli was most likely inspired by folk woodcuts of a somewhat earlier date. Whether Solovyov had ever been in Orvieto, I cannot say. In any case, the Antichrist of Signorelli proves the persistence of a certain tradition taken over by the Russian philosopher. Signorelli's Antichrist looks exactly like the Christ known from iconography, at least from a distance, yet he listens to what a demon is whispering in his ear.

Solovyov's superman of the twenty-first century combines fantastic intellectual capacities with impeccable ethical standards. He considers his vocation the organizing of society so that the commands of the Gospel are implemented. And, let us stress, he does not know he is the Antichrist. He does not suspect it until the moment when he consciously puts himself above Christ because Christ was no more than his predecessor, who died and was not resurrected, whereas he will accomplish that which was proclaimed by his predecessor. This superman believes he acts out of love for man, but in fact he loves only himself; that is, he performs extraordinary deeds to glorify himself in his own eyes. Here Solovyov is in complete accord with apocalyptic folklore, which saw the cause of evil in the universe as the rebellion of an angel of great wisdom and beauty: that angel preferred himself to God. Solovyov is one of those pessimistic philosophers who hold that every ego repeats the act of the fallen angel; it cannot be otherwise in the order of Nature except through the intervention of divine grace. The more powerful, the more splendid an ego—in men of destiny, leaders, dictators—the more it must pay homage to itself. In a moment of doubt Solovyov's superman attempts to commit suicide but is saved by the Prince of This World, whose voice he hears (this scene is an exact reversal of Jesus' baptism in Jordan). After that critical night he writes his work "The Open Road to Universal Peace and Well-Being"—so intellectually and artistically convincing, so clear, that everybody finds the most obvious truth in it. The book, translated into a multitude of languages, brings him such fame that he is unanimously elected first president of Europe and soon emperor of the nations of the earth.

This man of destiny accomplishes what he promised, and his concern is not only with peace and bread but also with the spiritual needs of mankind. His adviser and friend is a magician, Apollonius—half Asiatic, half European—a Catholic bishop *in partibus infidelium* (later a cardinal) who is as familiar with the most modern methods of Western science as with everything most precious in Oriental mysticism. There are rumors that he is capable of bringing fire down from Heaven. In fact, allying science with magic, Apollonius achieves remarkable results; for instance, just by the concentration of his will, he attracts and uses as he wishes the electricity in the atmosphere. Apollonius is venerated by the neo-Buddhists. The emperor himself, a Freemason and an honorary doctor of theology of the University of Tuebingen, is considered a messiah by the Jews. In the twenty-first century Palestine, with its capital in Jerusalem, is governed and inhabited predominantly by Jews who now number around 30 million. The Emperor moves his residence from Rome to Jerusalem and spreads the news that the aim of his policy is the world dominion of Israel.

In Jerusalem, too, in the fourth year of his reign, the superman is revealed as the Antichrist, after which, in a matter of a few days, follow the events foretold in the Apocalypse. They are the consequence of the emperor's decision to proclaim himself the "Anointed One" and the benefactor of all Christians. He invites Catholics (the papacy, long since expelled from Rome, now has its seat in St. Petersburg), Orthodox, and Protestants to Jerusalem for a huge ecumenical council which declares itself for him, except for a small group led by Pope Peter II, the pious Orthodox monk John, and the German theologian Dr. Pauli. John and Peter II unmask the emperor as the Antichrist, for which they are killed with "fire from Heaven" by Cardinal Apollonius, and their corpses are exposed to public view. The small group of the faithful, with Dr. Pauli at its head, escapes to the desert of Jericho. Elected pope, Apollonius accomplishes the unification of the churches; this should be interpreted as the submission of the spiritual kingdom to secular power, a power offering both terrestrial happiness and scientific-magic miracles.

"The end of the times" and the beginning of the millennium are faintly sketched in the *Three Conversations*. A cycle, short when compared to the entire history of mankind, begins with the birth of a child from the tribe of David and closes in Israel. The revolt of the Jews against the false messiah, the massacre of the Jews and disobedient Christians ordered by the emperor, the resurrection of the monk John and Pope Peter II, the unification of the true churches in the desert, a million-man-strong Jewish army fighting the troops of the Antichrist which advance from Syria, the swallowing up of the emperor and his troops and the pseudo-pope by a fiery crater that opens up near the Dead Sea, Christ descending from Heaven over Jerusalem—all these eschatological images do not precisely fit the polemical goals of the *Three Conversations* and probably for this reason are given rather cursory treatment.

The sketchy nature of the last section of the Pansopheus manuscript may create some doubts as to the concept of the "Anti-Christian good." One may argue here that to feed the hungry, to rescue the oppressed from their degradation, and to secure peace for the nations of the earth is a great deal and it is better to leave metaphysical anxieties to Solovyov and his Christians of the twenty-first century. One may further argue that this very concept is deeply reactionary, because it brands in advance as suspect every striving toward terrestrial happiness. This, however, would be doing an injustice to Solovyov. His superman deserves admiration precisely as a benefactor of man, and if he is the Antichrist it is in spite of that. His rule is based upon a lie that must provoke the worst possible effects; the terror he initiated would probably have been increasingly cruel had he not been swallowed up by the earth. The lie is tantamount to demanding that both what is God's and what Caesar's be rendered unto Caesar—a citizen may be happy, but only at the price of complete obedience in all his thoughts and deeds. The disobedience of the Christians is, for Solovyov, a test thanks to which the ruler of genius reveals who he really is.

Comparing the manuscript of Pansopheus with science fiction allows us to treat the time of writing as a set of possibilities appraised by the writer. Though explosive devices were being rapidly perfected in the nineteenth century, Jules Verne's contemporaries in general did not believe that such devices could land a man on the moon and read novels on that subject as amusing fables. Today, of course, we know that a very long cannon is unnecessary for launching an interplanetary missile because the cannon and the missile are one. Nevertheless, Jules Verne had appraised the possibilities correctly. For the pacifist Prince in the *Three Conversations* the manuscript of Pansopheus is nonsense; and the Prince probably would have died on the spot had anyone been able to convince him that the wars of the twentieth century would, in fact, be fought on such a grand scale. Men in 1900 were not trained in history on a worldwide scale. Though there was much talk about the "yellow peril" (some fifteen years after Solovyov it preoccupied Oswald Spengler), it took quite a leap of the imagination to visualize the conquest of China by Japan and its indirect effects: the victory of the revolutionary army and the military power of China. Solovyov's Japanese dynasty that establishes itself in Peking is, of course, nothing other than Verne's long cannon shooting a vehicle to the moon. Solovyov, however, did not orient himself by scientific probability but by a mysterious order he sensed in the threads and knots of history. Had he oriented himself by probability, he would not have introduced a Jewish state with Jerusalem as its capital and with a Jewish army a million strong when the budding Zionist movement had but a few followers. Imagination when reaching into the future must by necessity extrapolate and extend those lines which in a given moment are considered "lines of development," a procedure that leads to many errors. For instance we cannot be certain that technological progress, after a sudden leap, might not stop or even recede —as has happened more than once in history—and in such a case those who foresee its unlimited continuation will look a trifle naive in the eyes of posterity.

When we read Solovyov we often have the impression that the spiritual makeup of his twenty-first century is quite close to our own. It seems that the Russian intelligentsia of 1900 was able to provide an attentive observer with good premises for making predictions. Because of features peculiar to Russia (for example, the collusion of the Church with the autocracy) the Russian intelligentsia experienced violently the change that, in

Western countries with their complexity of traditional structures and their freedom of thought, proceeded at a slower pace
and was to become only gradually generalized. Acknowledging
their homelessness, the Russian intelligentsia sought compensation in a religion of humanity. Thus arose their unlimited ethical
demands, addressed, however, not to an individual but to a
social milieu responsible for the pollution of an inherently good
human nature.

This motif reappears today in contemporary lay humanism
with its longing for the end of alienation and thus, in fact, for
the fulfillment of time, because that dream cannot be satisfied
by anything less than the advent of a political system that maintains itself without any restraints and institutions. In contrast to
the conditions in 1900, this transformation is occurring both
outside of christianity and within it. We are now witnessing the
gradual mutation of churches into clubs of friends of mankind,
into assemblies of guitar-playing and hand-clapping boy scouts.
And their eagerness to serve all noble causes, from the struggle
against colonialism to the saving of bears in Alaska, is related to
the theology of the death of God even if they themselves are
reluctant to admit this. This trend also has spread to the
Catholic church, which tries at any price to be accessible to the
lay mentality. To be convinced of this, it is sufficient to read
attentively the catechism authorized by the Dutch hierarchy. Its
authors make acrobatic attempts to sidestep certain inconve-
niences: original sin and the existence of the Devil.

For centuries the historic role of Christianity consisted of re-
minding people of the tragic quality of human existence. Man
wants to be good, but he is not good; he wants to be happy, but
he is not happy; he wants to live, but he knows he must die.
This awareness, distinguishing him from all other living creatures, is a sad joke if it cannot save him from the fate of the animals. The conviction that the earth is a "vale of tears" may have
been useful to the strong and the rich, since it contributed to the
resignation of the oppressed. But if Christianity exerted an
assuaging influence upon the barbaric European peoples it was

due primarily to the images of the *Totentanz*, in which the most
lowly and the highest, peasants and kings, are united. Today
we tend too often to forget about that assuaging influence, and
as tourists visiting French Gothic churches we are incredulous
to learn that their builders observed an eight-hour workday and
a five-day week. For many centuries Christ was in no way identified with the philanthropists or revolutionaries: rather he was
a God-man opposed to the order of Nature, breaking that order
with his resurrection—"for the wisdom of the flesh is death," as
St. Paul says. The state of mind of the semi-Christians and post-
Christians of the twentieth century is quite enigmatic since their
disbelief in the God-manhood of Christ seems to force them to
deify Nature and extol the good natural man who is unjustly
repressed by civilization.[2]

I once heard an American activist describe over a dinner his
favorite sport, skin-diving, and what he usually feels when he
swims underwater among the multitude of sea life. It was a fairy
tale in which the customary frolicking elves, friendly to each
other and to mankind, were replaced by fish of various sizes
and colors. It did not enter the heads of his listeners that this
man was simply crazy: his hatred for existing society and his
nostalgia for an ideal society were so strong that he needed to
deceive himself by adorning the naked struggle for survival
among animals and plants with his slogans of universal love
and peace. Since present civilization is bad, Nature *must* be
good; for where else, if not in a hypothetical future return to the
state of nature, could we seek solace and the promise of an
earthly paradise?

Soon after Solovyov's death, mankind entered a cycle of experience so strongly negating all the notions at which the nineteenth century had clutched that imagination, struggling with a
terrifying unnamed reality, turned to the much older archetypes
preserved in folklore. The Devil, seemingly chased off into the

---

[2]Today this is described in language borrowed from Freud, which does not
change the fact that such language is used to mask theological problems and
theological options.

realm of leprechauns and mermaids, suddenly proved to be a personality not in the least funny. The tortures to which the damned are submitted on the canvases of Hieronymus Bosch ceased being the delusions of a sick psyche once men applied the same tortures to millions of other men. Moreover, someone has also noticed that in medieval iconography the Devil is usually represented together with a crematory furnace. How is it then, by what paradox, that Solovyov's twenty-first century, though perhaps not sanguinary enough for our macabre tastes, does not seem entirely alien to us? Of the two Christian traditions concerning the Antichrist, one conceives of him as an incarnation of pure unconcealed evil and the other as a liar feigning meekness, a wolf in sheep's clothing. Solovyov, as Luca Signorelli before him, adopted the second tradition modifying it in his own way; his own idea was the Antichrist who strives for and attains much good, deceiving not only others but himself as well.

We are unable to reduce the present, so full of contradictions, to one common denominator because we live in it and it lives in us. But perhaps its most unexpected trait is a willful blindness, a rejection of historical experience, as if man had learned too much about his own demonic drives and could no longer bear it. Whether the chief cause of this attitude is the sterilization of the tragic elements in religion, the attitude exemplified in the *Three Conversations* by Tolstoy (or, if you prefer, by the Prince), or whether there are other causes present, all those who recommend a return to primeval nakedness and primeval innocence already constitute a great movement of new Adamites in the countries of the West. The emperor of the nations of the earth may remain forever in the sphere of a writer's fantasy. Were such a superman to step forward, however, promising an end to all alienation, and love and peace, we may be certain that millions of mortals, indifferent to truth and untruth, would pay him divine homage.

1971

3
Stanisław Ignacy Witkiewicz: A Writer for Today?

Stanisław Ignacy Witkiewicz fascinated my literary generation in the somber thirties and today, many years after his death, he is no less fascinating to the young in Poland. To write about him is to explore the continuity of certain themes that go back to a more cosmopolitan era of Europe on the eve of World War I.

A few biographical data. He was born in Warsaw in 1885 as the only son of an eminent painter and art critic. His childhood and adolescence were spent in the mountain village of Zakopane in southern Poland, then a newly discovered "primitive area" with its rich folklore and fine specimens of peasant wooden architecture. Already fashionable as a center of mountaineering, Zakopane was a meeting place for intellectuals; young Witkiewicz grew up in a refined milieu. Perhaps the contrast between his physical vigor and the mood obligatory in those circles—that of "decadence," of "fin-de-siècle"—is one of the keys to his development as a thinker and as an artist. A student of fine arts in Kraków in 1904-1905, he traveled to Italy, France, Germany, and in 1914 went to Australia through Ceylon and the Malayan archipelago as a secretary to the anthropologist Bronisław Malinowski. The outbreak of World War I caught him in Australia. As the holder of a Russian passport he had to go back, arrived in St. Petersburg, and without waiting to be drafted, which was unavoidable anyway, volunteered. He fought as an infantry officer in an elite tsarist regiment, was decorated for bravery with the highest Russian distinction (the order of St. Anne) and probably was loved by his soldiers, for at the outbreak of the Revolution they elected him a commissar. We know little, however, of this or of any other wartime incidents. He did not like to talk about them except for a casual remark in a conversation with a friend, for example that counting the minutes before an attack is one of the most dire experiences in the life of man. In 1918 he returned to independent Poland, where he lived mostly in Zakopane and Kraków.

The experience he acquired was of an exceptional scope—in art, in life, in historical situations. His formative years were marked by the ascendancy of the "Young Poland" movement whose great master of ceremonies or witchdoctor was Stanisław Przybyszewski, formerly a student of psychiatry in Berlin and a highly regarded member of the bohemian groups known as "Young Germany" and "Young Scandinavia." Przybyszewski proclaimed a manifesto in 1899 of the absolute supremacy of art over any other human activity and its complete independence from moral, social, or political considerations. Today his formulas sound curiously pre-Freudian: "in the beginning there was lust"; art is an outflow of the "naked soul" uniting man with the unconscious life of the universe. Hence Przybyszewski's preoccupation with satanic forces that revealed the illusory character of "poor, poor consciousness," with medieval witches, sabbaths, hysteria and insanity. But Witkiewicz's plays and essays on drama would be incomprehensible without reference to another leading figure of "Young Poland," Stanislaw Wyspiański, from whom stems the entire modern Polish theater. The staging of his *Wedding* in Kraków in 1901 was a revolutionary event. Wyspiański broke with "imitation of life" on the stage; he conceived of a theatrical spectacle as a unity of color, movement, and sound, and in his dramas fantastic symbolic creatures appeared on an equal footing with lifelike characters. Using today's language we would say he took the spectators on a "trip," for after each of his plays in verse people used to leave the theater reeling. Parenthetically, let us add that contrary to Przybyszewski he advocated a committed art: drama, not unlike Greek tragedy, in his view should be an instrument for exploring all the problems of a national community and a call to energy—but through a peculiar medium of its own having nothing to do with photographic naturalism.

Shaped by the Polish vanguard currents in literature, in painting, and in the theater, Witkiewicz landed in Russia at the very moment of her creative eruption—a period that remains unsurpassed in the excellence of its achievements. The most incredible "isms" were proliferating. The first purely abstract paintings were simultaneously being done in Germany by the Russian Vassily Kandinsky (1910), in Russia by the Pole Kazimierz Malewicz (1913), in Holland by Piet Mondrian (though his canvas of 1911 is still entitled "A Blooming Apple Tree"). Cubism was debated in Moscow and St. Petersburg (a school of poets called themselves "cubofuturists"), and in Moscow Witkiewicz saw the paintings of Picasso, whose exhibition he had already seen in Paris.

Witkiewicz was one of those who by their very behavior give fuel to a personal legend. Perhaps his oddity and humorous eccentricity increased with age, but already as a young man he was puzzling: a huge taciturn beast of prey in an invisible cage, a jester disguising some unavowed potential. He attracted women magnetically. One of them, who remembered him from Zakopane before World War I, related: "He was beautiful like an archangel with those gray-green eyes of his. When he entered a café, my knees shook. And I guess all the women felt the same." In Russia, he shared the peculiar way of life led by elite officers (mostly from aristocratic families), divided into encounters with death and crazy pleasures. It was a time not only of alcohol and of sexual orgies but of a fashion for new drugs. Witkiewicz got acquainted with cocaine and tasted peyote. Later on he experimented with the influence of drugs upon his painting and wrote a book on the subject (many years before Aldous Huxley and Michaux), *Nicotine, Alcohol, Cocaine, Peyote, Morphine, Ether + Appendix* (1932).

The Russian Revolution, as we may guess from his writings, left traumatic traces. Witkiewicz was brought up, let us not forget, on the basic premise of "decadentism"—namely, that Western bourgeois civilization was living out its last decades if not days. The upheaval of the masses in Russia seemed to confirm that view and for Witkiewicz gave it a more tangible shape. He became convinced that universal Comunist revolution was unavoidable. As for himself, he belonged to a world in decline. Revolution would have meant a victory of justice, but he was not primarily interested in "happiness for all," an aim he relegated to the realm of "ethics"; revolution, in his opinion, was but a stage in the general trend toward social conformity and destruction of the individual. This explains his subsequent polemics with Polish Marxists, in which he showed a good knowledge of dialectical materialism.

Upon his return to Poland, Witkiewicz joined a vanguard group of painters and poets in Kraków who called themselves "formists." His book *New Forms in Painting and Resulting Misunderstandings* (1919), as well as his essays on the theater published in magazines from 1920 on and gathered in a book *The Theater* (1923), demonstrated the application of his theory of "pure form" to all the arts. But it is time to ask who, after all, was he—painter, creative writer, or theoretician? He painted, but announced to all and sundry that his "atelier" produced portraits at fixed prices and that he himself did not pretend to the title of artist. It is true, though, that not everybody acceded to the honor of posing as his model. His "psychological portraits," mostly of intellectual friends, resemble by their treatment of line and color what we associate today with psychedelic art. He wrote plays, beginning with *Cockroaches* (when he was eight years old) about cockroaches invading a city; a two-volume edition of his collected plays published in Warsaw in 1962 surpasses in daring "the theater of the absurd." He wrote a few novels, the first in 1910: *622 Downfalls of Bungo or a Demoniac Woman*. Two novels of his are major contributions to Polish literature of the years 1918-1939, yet he excluded the

novel from the domain of "art." For him the novel was a bastard genre, a catchall, a bag, a device to convey the author's
quarrels with his contemporaries. He wrote essays on the
theory of painting and of drama. He had, however, only one
true passion: philosophy. Let me stress this, for his philosophical concepts underlie everything he attempted to do. His first
"metaphysical divagations," as he called them, date from 1904.
For many years, between 1917 and 1932, he worked on a rather
slim concise treatise to which he attached much importance,
Notions and Assertions—Implied by the Notion of Being. A
dilettante—though highly esteemed by university scholars such
as Professor Tadeusz Kotarbiński, the dean of Polish philosophers—Witkiewicz was better equipped than many professionals. He read fluently in Russian, German, French, and
English, not to mention his native tongue.

The state of European and American philosophy, as he
observed it, strengthened his historical pessimism. Philosophers, behaving like the fox who pronounced the grapes sour
because they were too high, were engaged in explaining away
metaphysics as a semantic misunderstanding. Wasn't this a sign
foreboding the end of the search for "unattainable absolute
truth"? To quote from him: "Throughout the entire struggle
with Mystery, veils dropped away one by one and the time has
come when we see a naked, hard body, with nothing more to be
taken off, invincible in the indifference of a dead statue." The
fable of the fox applied not only to the neo-positivists. Witkiewicz raged against Bergson: "intuition" was indeed a meager
substitute for striving toward clear cognition. Pragmatism and
Marxism fared even worse: They exemplified the approaching
era when "ethics will devour metaphysics." Or, to again use his
own words: "Every epoch has the philosophy it deserves. In our
present phase we deserve nothing better than a drug of the most
inferior kind, to lull to sleep the metaphysical anxiety which
hinders our transformation into automatic machines."

Trying to salvage whatever survived from the ambitious
ontological drives of the past, Witkiewicz elaborated a minimal

"system" somewhat akin to Leibniz's monadology. Its analysis does not belong here; I limit myself to a few points. According to Witkiewicz, nothing can be asserted about being except that it predicates "Particular Existences." Every monad embodies what he calls the "Principle of Factual Particular Identity." In man this gives rise to a "Metaphysical Feeling of the Strangeness of Existence," expressed by questions: "Why am I exactly this and not that being? At this point of unlimited space and in this moment of infinite time? In this group of beings, on exactly this planet? Why do I exist, if I could have been without any existence? Why does anything exist at all?"

Mankind looked for answers in religion, then in philosophy. Yet religion was dead and philosophy was dying. Art, which has always been a means of soothing the anxieties provoked by the "Metaphysical Feeling of the Strangeness of Existence," survived. Art in the past functioned, however, in a universe ordered by ontological concepts of religion or of philosophy. Its harmonious forms reflected that serenity which is granted when man has also other means of satisfying his basic craving. Art as the only channel, as a substitute for religion and philosophy, by necessity would change. Its "unity in multiplicity," reflecting the increased sense of identity in its creator, could only be achieved at an increasing cost—namely, a savage intensification of the elements used, lest the harmony become tepid. Here Witkiewicz's formulations are not quite clear. He seemed to believe that modern artists, as opposed to their healthy predecessors, became neurotics because of their inability to quench their metaphysical thirst in any other way than through their art. They were condemned to endow it with their neurosis by choosing as their material more and more ugly, jarring, garish images, sounds, lines, and colors. They were the last representatives of a species marked by a metaphysical "insatiability" and threatened by mass ethics in which the craving that constitutes the very dignity of man was already being twisted. Art was moving toward insanity, and the future was not far off when artists would be imprisoned in insane asylums. Mankind would be "happy," but it would know neither religion, nor a philosophy deserving the name, nor art.

However we judge Witkiewicz's pessimism, one thing is certain: his creative work combines a rare vital energy with a conviction that art should select procedures adapted to its final phase. It should achieve "Pure Form." A painting, for instance, should be no more than a set of "oriented tensions" of line and color (he deviated from his principle when making his "psychological portraits," and that is why he dismissed them as merely an income-bringing craft). In his stress upon "purity" he was, of course, no exception in the Europe of his time: even the French Academy of Literature listened, as early as 1925, to Henri Brémond's lecture on "pure poetry." Yet of great consequence was Witkiewicz's application of the concept to the theater. If modern painting tended toward a refusal to represent anything, could not drama be conceived as "pure action" without any care for reproduction of reality? While posing the problem, he did not want to go so far:

Though we can imagine a painting composed entirely of abstract forms which, unless we indulge in obvious autosuggestion, would not provoke any associations with objects in the external world, no such a theatrical play can even be thought of, because a pure becoming in time is possible only in the sphere of sounds, and the theater without actions of characters, even most strange and improbable characters, is impossible, since the theater is a composite art and not based upon homogenous elements as are the pure arts: music and painting.

But "deformation" (as in cubist art) is not beyond the playwright's reach: "In painting, a new form, pure and abstract, without a direct religious background, was achieved through a deformation of our vision of the external world, and in a similar manner Pure Form in the theater can be achieved at the price of a deformation of psychology and of action." Since he presents his intentions rather clearly, let me continue quoting him: "What matters is the possibility of freely deforming life or an imaginary world in order to create a totality, the sense of which would be determined by a purely internal, purely scenic construction and not by any exigencies of consequent psychology or action, corresponding to the rules of ordinary life." The date when those sentences were written—around 1920—should be kept in mind. It was in Europe a period of radical experimentation. Witkiewicz explains what a play written according to his recipe would be like:

Thus three persons, dressed in red, enter and bow, we do not know to whom. One of them recites a poem (which should make the impression of something necessary exactly at that moment). A gentle old man enters with a cat he leads on a string. Until now everything has been going on against the background of a black curtain. The curtain is drawn apart and an Italian landscape appears. Organ music is heard. The old man talks to the three persons. He says something which corresponds to the created mood. A glass falls from the table. All of them, suddenly on their knees, are weeping. The old man changes into a furious brute and murders a little girl who just crawled out from the left side. At this, a handsome young man runs in and thanks the old man for that murder, while the persons in red sing and dance. The young man then weeps over the corpse of the little girl saying extremely funny things, and the old man changes again into a tender-hearted character chuckling on the sidelines. The sentences he pronounces are sublime and lofty. The costumes may be of any kind, stylized or fantastic—and music may intervene in various parts. So, you would say, this is a lunatic asylum. Or rather the brain of a madman on stage. Perhaps you are right, but we affirm that by applying this method one can write serious plays and if they are staged in a proper way, it would be possible to create things of extraordinary beauty, they may be dramas, tragedies, farces or grotesques, but always in a style not resembling anything that exists. When leaving the theater, one should have the impression of waking up from a strange dream in which the most trite things have an elusive, deep charm, characteristic of dreams, not comparable to anything.

Yet for Witkiewicz programmatic deformation for its own sake, not justified by the real need for formal unity, was to be categorically condemned. He underlined this: "Our aim is not programmatic nonsense, we are trying rather to enlarge the possibilities of composition by abandoning in art any lifelike logic, by introducing a fantastic psychology and fantastic action, in order to win a complete freedom of formal elements."

In spite of those reservations, it is doubtful whether the recipe is conducive to anything but the monotony of a few devices repeated ad infinitum: once all improbabilities are accepted, no increase in dose could ever stir the spectator. Fortunately, Witkiewicz as a theoretician and as a practitioner are two not quite identical persons. In his thirty or so plays written between 1918 and 1934 he gives free vent to his ferocity, a virtue rarely praised by "pure artists." He becomes a high-school prankster who makes us think of Alfred Jarry more than of any other writer. His characters, through their roars and their mad thrashing around, resemble the abominable Father Ubu with his exclamations "merrrrdrre" and his machine for blowing up brains. Witkiewicz delighted in coining names for his characters appropriate to their behavior. Many are untranslatable puns; some, often a cross-breed of several languages, can give an idea of his buffoonery. Thus we are confronted with Doña Scabrosa Macabrescu and her teenage daughter Świntusia (Piggy) Macabrescu, with psychiatrist Mieczysław Valpurg and attorney general Robert Scurvy (meaning in Polish both scurvy and s.o.b.); with Gottfried Reichsgraf von und zu Berchtoldingen, the Great Master of the Teutonic Order; two hassidim, Haberboaz and Rederhagaz; with Princess Alice of Nevermore; Minna Countess de Barnhelm; Maxim Grigorevich Prince Bublikov-Tmutarakanskii, a counteradmiral; with Richard III in person, vicecount Wojciech (Adalbert) de Malensac de Troufières, the naturalist painter Oblivion Grampus. And so on, and so on.

The titles of the plays are often no less promising: *Metaphysics of a Two-headed Calf; Gyubal Wahazar or Along the Cliffs of the Absurd, a Non-Euclidean Drama in Four Acts; Mister Price or Tropical Madness; The Ominous Bastard of Vermiston; The Independence of Triangles.* On his characters two remarks can be made. All of them, men and women, are oversexed; practically all of them are on the verge of bursting asunder, victims of inexpressible yearning. Sex, since it is intimately connected with the "metaphysical feeling of strangeness of existence," was for Witkiewicz akin to art. Yet no discharges are able to calm down his weird puppets. They are under the pressure of a cosmic reality which they feel is "too much." And since they are not supposed to be "probable" as to the language they speak, they deliver tirades mixing slang and terms of modern philosophy whether they are artists, princes, or peasants.

The composition of his plays may be defined as a parody of psychological drama. Instead of middle-class husbands, wives, and mistresses, we find bizarre mathematicians of genius, artist-misfits, unashamedly lurid women, with the author's obvious predilection for the international set, for aristocrats and proletarians, as well as for meetings between figures taken from different epochs; instead of dialogues in a living room, the ravings move into a dimension of *opera-buffa*; instead of murders out of jealousy and suicides, sham murders and sham suicides— plenty of corpses, yes, but they soon resurrect and rejoin the conversation.

Witkiewicz's imagination, nourished by the apocalyptic events of war and revolution in Russia, was ill adapted to what prevailed in the literature of Poland after 1918. The country was independent but provincial, confronted with immediate tasks, and the radical vanguard schools of 1918-1920 soon declined or entrenched themselves in little magazines for the elite. Fortunately for him Poland was a theatrical country, with good repertory theaters directed by people who continued the line of Stanisław Wyspiański. A few plays of Witkiewicz were staged and some reached fifteen, thirty, even forty performances. He obtained the support of intelligent theater critics, and won notoriety as an *enfant terrible* of Polish letters. Yet it is significant that performances of his plays date from the twenties. After this he was more and more isolated, and the majority of his dramas were neither published nor staged in his lifetime. Because of his language—with its humorous-macabre exuberance, puns, parody of styles—he is difficult to render into other languages. But even had he been translated, what chance would he have had abroad if the "theater of the absurd" conquered Paris and London only some thirty years later? At least in Poland the theater was not as commercialized as in Western Europe and directors, if not the public, understood what he was after.

Today, while considerable "freedom of formal elements" has been attained everywhere, Witkiewicz still fails to fit into any accepted category. He started from other premises than *Angst* and alienation; not being-in-an-unbearable-situation, but Being as such, was his primary concern. If we assume that Beckett's *Ah, les beaux jours* is the highest achievement of the theater of the absurd (François Mauriac compared it to Aeschylus) the insectlike, weak buzz of its heroine sinking into the sand (symbolizing time) does not recall anything in the plays of Witkiewicz. Curiously enough, a melancholy perception of transcience is absent from his writings. On the contrary, his characters have to cope with a superabundance of Being as an eternal *now*.

Perhaps more than the insane action, the intellectual contents of his dramas estranged the public. After all, in spite of his theoretical claims, he conveyed his philosophy in them by the very choice of his heroes. A lunatic fringe, the last of a perishing tribe—artists, aristocrats, descendants of rich factory owners—represented an intensification of individuality through delirium and decadence; a kind of "last stand" before universal grayness, historically preordained, swallowed them in. The scene hints more at Russia on the eve of the Revolution than at Poland or any other country, unless one shares (which was not easy at the time) the author's belief in a doomsday awaiting the precarious "normalcy" that was patched together in 1918.

Witkiewicz abandoned writing plays after the twenties, except for one in 1934, the closest to a parable, full of transposed realistic details, a response to the oncoming doomsday which was already announced by the rise of totalitarian dictatorships: *The Shoemakers*. In my view it is not accidental that in departing from "Pure Form" and injecting the work with

"contents" he succeeded so well. As to "contents," to put it
shortly there are the shoemakers (social rebels hungry for good
living and sex galore) who are destined after the revolution to
be playthings of the Super-Worker, a potential bureaucratic
operator; and a primordial male-devouring female, Princess
Irina, personifying the rotten system which is defended by attorney general Robert Scurvy. The attorney makes an alliance
with the "Brave Boys" (a native fascist movement, the last
phase of capitalism) and ends his career on all fours chained as a
dog (smoking a cigarette). Altogether, though it is no less a
lunatic asylum than Witkiewicz's other plays, *The Shoemakers*
follows an anticipated historical logic, which is why it bears the
subtitle: "a scientific play with songs."

The two novels by Witkiewicz, *Farewell to Autumn* (written
1925, published 1927) and *Insatiability* (1931), are populated
with the same kind of personalities as his dramas, often appearing under the same names. They deal with similar problems,
though the author is less bound by his search for "Pure Form."
As I have said already, he excluded the novel from artistic
genres. All of his creative activity, and I hope I am making this
clear, was the result of a tension between his aggressiveness and
his concept of art as unity in multiplicity, indifferent to the
"gut-level" (by which he designated "everyday-life" feelings and
emotions). He was more inclined to attack than to whine, and
"contents" did explode in *The Shoemakers* (which reminds one
the most of his novels). Once he had decided the novel was a
"bag" with freely invented rules, beyond any exigencies of
"art," he could pack it with philosophical treatises, digressions,
and polemics. His novels are powerful, however, for the very
reason that in scorning form he hit upon a specific novelistic
form of his own. In this he was probably helped by his readings
as an adolescent, by the science fiction of Jules Verne, H. G.
Wells, and other authors. Science fiction, before World War I
and immediately after, was undergoing a mutation (not without
some contribution brought by the genre of ironic allegories,
Anatole France's for instance) into a novel of apprehensive anti-

cipation, a novel of antiutopia. Usually the future was visualized as dominated by machines winning their independence and crushing human beings. To give a few examples: in the twenties appeared Karel Čapek's *Krakatit*; in Poland, futurist Bruno Jasieński's *Legs of Isolda Morgan* (1923) and the dialectical stories of Aleksander Wat on the twists and turns of history to come, *Lucifer Unemployed* (1927). Witkiewicz's antiutopias concentrate upon social mechanization, not upon the negative aspects of technology. His vision is close to that of the Russian writer Eugene Zamyatin, whose *We* was published in England in 1924, though whether he read Zamyatin has never been ascertained. His Polish sources are obvious and acknowledged by him: most of all, the wild theosophical imagination of Tadeusz Miciński (killed in 1918 in Russia by a mob which mistook him for a tzarist general) who, shuffling together epochs and countries in his dramas and novels, was in his turn a descendant of Polish romantic historiosophy.

In both novels the action is placed in the future, yet the present—namely the Poland of his day—is easily recognizable as material reshaped, magnified, seasoned with the grotesque; it has been justly said that all the "realistic" fiction of those years could not match Witkiewicz's insights into social and political imbroglios. The names of the characters are construed in his usual prankish way. For instance there is a Polish verb "zipać," to breathe with difficulty; he makes a French verb out of it, "ziper"; concocts a phrase, "je ne zipe qu'à peine"; changes spelling and obtains the name of one of his heroes, Genezyp Kapen. His style is not unlike that of Polish fiction before 1914 with its tendency to the profound and the sublime, especially in love scenes. He pushes the pedal just a bit more, so that the boundary between seriousness and joking is blurred. This serves him particularly well in his erotic passages. As might be expected, for his heroes the sexual act acquires an ontological magnitude comparable only to the act of artistic creation. His women, enamored with their genitalia—spider-females—do not wear ordinary bras and pants: "she took off her metaphysical hyper-panties." Yet because of this overemphasis and ironic grandeur, the brutality of his sexual duels (there is a fundamental hostility between his males and females) is not naturalistic and would not provide excitement for any shy pornographer. Sex for him equals an experience of the overwhelming, orgiastic monstrosity of existence.

Not a brave new world, but the last phase of decay preceding the advent of a brave new world, is the subject of his novels. This renders questionable their classification with the genre that in our century begins with Zamyatin's *We* and embraces Aldous Huxley's already proverbial *Brave New World* (1932) as well as George Orwell's *1984* (1948). A particular society drawn from observation and anticipation lurks behind the artistic and pseudo-artistic milieu on which he focuses. Death of religion (sarcastically treated attempts at "neo-Catholicism"), death of philosophy (whole pages of discussion with logical positivists), art going mad (music being the most tenacious, hence his frequent identification with composers)—such are portents of the approaching change of the social system. In *Farewell to Autumn* it is brought about by two successive revolutions: first bourgeois-democratic (echo of Kerensky in Russia and of the Leninist theory), second of the "Levellers." The last chapters depict a new order in quite Orwellian terms but emphasize universal grayness and shabbiness, not terror. The central figure in the novel, Atanazy Bazakbal—more gifted in sex than in art though he wanted to be an artist—returns home from India at the news of the revolution, is given a small job in one of the state offices, and meditates upon the impotence of the individual to reverse the course of events. While in Zakopane, he decides to escape across the mountains. Witkiewicz was excellent in his descriptions of mountain scenery; the dawn over the summits as seen by Bazakbal, high on cocaine, is treated in a grandiose manner without a bit of mockery. The final pages summarize the author's dilemma throughout his whole career. If what awaits us is an anthill in which it will be forbidden to confess one's metaphysical craving, should not those few who are aware of it launch a warning? Bazakbal, under the influence of cocaine, has a revelation: a warning *must* be launched and it *must* be effective. He retraces his steps but is caught by a border patrol and shot as a spy.

In *Insatiability*, America and most of Europe have participated in counterrevolutionary "crusades" with the result that the "West" is half Communist. Russia has gone in an opposite direction; it has been ruled for a while by White terror. Poland did not join the anti-Bolshevik crusades (echo of 1919-1920 when Piłsudski refused to cooperate with White Russian generals Denikin and Wrangel) and has a native brand of semi-fascism. Europe, however, is threatened by Communist China which has conquered Russia and whose armies are already near the borders of Poland. All hopes turn to the charismatic commander of the army, Kocmoluchowicz (from *kocmoluch*— sooty face). The imminent danger does not disturb Witkiewicz's milieu too much, except as an oppressive atmosphere of futility and paralysis exacerbating their sexual and metaphysical "insatiability." The reader follows the story of a young man, Genezyp Kapen, opening on the night when he is erotically initiated by a homosexual composer, Putrycydes Tenger, and Princess Irina Vsievolodovna de Ticonderoga. A new element is added to Witkiewicz's normal paraphernalia: a magic pill. If the society in this novel, thanks to the author's extrapolation, brings to one's mind more the Western Europe and America of the sixties than that of the twenties, the role ascribed to chemically induced states of "oneness" with the universe sounds little short of prophetic. No more and no less, he writes a report on LSD. The pill is of Eastern provenance; it has been devised by a Malayan-Chinese ideologist, Murti Bing (and Chinese communism is in fact "Murtibingism"), as a means of pacifying the minds. Those who take the pill, provided by mysterious peddlers, become indifferent to such trifles as wars or changes of political systems. Witkiewicz, as it was already mentioned, experimented with drugs and was not a philistine; yet the pill is for him a signal of the end. Both the chemical compound and the philosophical "drugs" of pragmatism, Marxism, "intuition" —and their growing popularity—show that man is ready to renounce what torments him and makes his true stature, a confrontation with the unmitigated nakedness (one is tempted to say "otherness") of Being.

The plot of *Insatiability* leads Genezyp Kapen to the immediate surroundings of General Kocmoluchowicz, a magnificent beast relying only upon instinct and his intuition as a leader, and of his lash-wielding mistress Percy Zvierzontkovskaya (zwierzątko in Polish means a little animal; transcribe it a Russian way, add a Russian ending and the outcome is hilarious to anybody familiar with Slavic languages). The general—no brains, only animal vitality—on the eve of a decisive battle with the Chinese has one of his intuitive strokes of understanding: it is of no use to oppose "historical necessity." He surrenders and with all ceremonies due to his rank is beheaded. In the new order under Chinese rule no harm is done to lunatics such as Genezyp Kapen and his friends. Well paid, they participate in a cultural revolution under the auspices of the Ministry of the Mechanization of Culture and develop a perfect schizophrenia, in the clinical sense, too.

Since both his novels wait until their last chapters to carry the action into a new "happy" society (modeled upon what he knew of postrevolutionary Russia), they do not suffer from that certain leanness of psychological design so typical of science fiction and its social satire mutation. Their density and allusiveness relate them to the psychological novel with a contemporary sociopolitical setting, though the pattern is pushed to a caricature. Some critics maintain that through his handling of plots and characters as mere pretexts for a philosophical debate, with the author's direct commentaries and even footnotes, Witkiewicz merely rejuvenated the eighteenth-century techniques. Probably this is true, provided, however, that we see the genealogy of all "fantasy" fiction as specific, different from that of a "realistic" portrayal of a psyche in its conflicts with externally imposed laws and mores.

Many years separate us from Witkiewicz's death. In September 1939 he left Warsaw, then being surrounded by the Nazi armies, for the Eastern provinces. He committed suicide on September 17, at the news of the Soviet army's advance in fulfillment of the Molotov-Ribbentrop pact. This suicide (he took sleeping pills in a wood, woke up and slashed his wrists with a razor) remains rightly or wrongly blended in the mind of his readers with the tragic ends of both his novels, where the splendor of Polish landscapes in autumn is used as a background.

In postwar Poland, Witkiewicz for a long time was a disquieting case and a taboo. He did not oppose Marxism on political grounds; on the contrary, few Marxist writers or sympathizers could compete with him in his disdainful appraisals of the "free world," and he grasped perhaps even better than they the workings of fascism. Yet Western technology, the mass dementias of the "Brave Boys," and Marxist revolutions were for him the phenomena of an immense twilight, in which he preserved loyalty to a belief in "decadence" shared by European bohemians around 1900. If he was disquieting, it was above all because of his sophistication; a literature able to produce such a writer probably called for more subtle methods of investigation (and direction) than a few vulgarized precepts of "realism." The less one spoke of him, the better. His writings were unhealthy as they prophesied what everybody lived through, especially after 1949: boredom and fear.

The revival of Witkiewicz in Poland after 1956 seems to deny his utter pessimism as to the irreversibility of the historical trend. His plays have never been performed with such a zeal and have never attracted such numerous audiences. They are already a permanent fixture in the repertory of the Polish theater. His theatrical essays are a must for every theater director. One of his novels, *Insatiability*, has appeared in a new edition (not *Farewell to Autumn*, as it is too exact an image of Poland after the revolution of the "Levellers"). His philosophy is avoided but his admirers managed to give it attention, profiting from a temporary relaxation of censorship, in a symposium

Stanislaw Witkiewicz, Man and Creator (Warsaw, 1957). He is an acting force in Polish letters, thus his "hope against hope" is at least in part vindicated. His significance, however, transcends the limits traced by one historical moment and one language. It depends upon the judgment we make about the theme of decadence, so persistent in the history of European civilization since the second half of the nineteenth century. Desperate Jules Laforgue, Spengler, T. S. Eliot in search of "live water" in the wasteland, as well as those playwrights and film makers of today who popularized what they stole from poets—all are relatives of characters in Witkiewicz's plays and novels. As the transformation of social organisms into abstract Molochs gathers momentum, we observe a parallel rebellion against society as a machine nobody can control, with the resulting proliferation of bohemian attitudes of withdrawal.

It is possible Witkiewicz was not dialectical enough and underestimated the resourcefulness of our species, its sly, waterlike flowing around obstacles which are but a solidified, frozen vestige of our creative powers. In all probability we are going through another crisis of the Renaissance man when "the world was out of joint." Yet Witkiewicz was hardly wrong, it seems to me, in his realization that something strange had happened to religion, philosophy, and art, even though their radical mutation did not equal their disappearance.[1]

1967

---

[1]Witkiewicz's plays have now been translated into several languages, and some have been staged with success in the United States as well. Two collections of his plays appeared in English: *The Madman and the Nun and Other Plays*, trans. and ed. Daniel C. Gerould and C. S. Durer with a foreword by Jan Kott (Seattle: University of Washington Press, 1966) and *Tropical Madness*, four plays trans. Daniel and Eleanor Gerould with introd. by Martin Esslin (New York: Winter House Ltd., 1972). The novel *Insatiability*, translated by Louis Iribarne, is scheduled to appear forthwith.

4

Krasiński's Retreat[1]

As the historians of literature have written a great deal about
Krasiński, it is doubtful whether there is anything to add to
their conscientious investigations. But every writer and every
work acquire new meanings as our field of vision expands, as
we experience the increasing elasticity of our minds shaped, as
they are, by history. A mountain village seen from an altitude
of three thousand feet is something different from that same village seen from an altitude of six thousand feet—that is to say its
ties with the surrounding landscape, at first imperceptible, have
now become apparent. This comparison is, however, too static
and therefore only approximately accurate, inasmuch as the relationship between any past work and ourselves is not merely
one of contemplation. The work was read by our forefathers
and entered into the formation of our cultural heritage; it is
therefore in us although at the same time it is outside us. The
image of the mountain may suggest morally evaluative judgments that are improper in this case. In our minds the "highest"
is associated with the "best." The grasp and flexibility of human
knowledge about the world, however, has neither boundaries
nor summit; and when an ideal standard of measurement is
lacking we cannot know whether we are nearer the truth than
our predecessors. Nevertheless, it is our duty to try to look with

[1]Zygmunt Krasiński (1812-1855) belonged to the triad of Polish Romantic
poets. The two others were Adam Mickiewicz and Juliusz Słowacki. His tragedy, *The Undivine Comedy*, was written in 1833.

our own eyes from the point at which we stand, remembering that one day we shall in our turn "be seen." This is perhaps, in short, the basis for every revision made in the history of literature. A thoroughgoing study of Krasiński would be outside my competence; I shall therefore limit myself to posing a few questions that it might be proper to answer in such a hypothetical study.

Zygmunt Krasiński at the age of twenty-one wrote a work of genius, the *Undivine Comedy*; yet in all the rest of his works he was a second-rate writer. Such an occurrence is rare enough, but it is even more rare for an author to be enshrined in the national pantheon because of one little book, with the help of the exaggerated merits of his other works, as though from a feeling of shame that he had deceived the hopes placed in him. Mickiewicz, in devoting a series of lectures at the Collège de France to the *Undivine Comedy* but passing over *Iridion* in silence, gave proof thereby of great discernment.

I base the term "genius" on the impression left by two readings: one while I was still in school, the other recently. The words "beauty" and "perfection" cannot be used by way of explanation, because this work is certainly far from perfection. But there is in it an awesome power, and because I read it when I was very young it made an indelible impression. A different kind of impression than Antoni Malczewski's *Maria* or Juliusz Słowacki's "Godzina myśli" ("The Hour of Thought") but nonetheless a similar one, just because of its bitterness and despair restrained by the dictates of style. After many years have passed, after many phases of history have been concluded, the *Undivine Comedy* has lost none of its agonizing tone.

Krasiński's poems are not regarded as important in the development of Polish poetry; opinion is in general agreement on this point. Yet an attempt was made, using the whole apparatus of research, to build up the prestige of *Iridion*. However, the empirical conclusions based on the reactions of the contemporary reader—which disregard the respect prescribed by all the scholarly commentaries—show the fruitlessness of such attempts. The conception is gigantesque but the style remains, in relation to that conception, something external. Despite some beautiful fragments, no fusion occurs which in the *Undivine Comedy* changed a romantic singsong into a speech of real tragedy more durable than the fashions of the moment. *Iridion* is a drama the language of which has miscarried; it must share the fate of similar poems of the romantic era which, when detached from the surroundings of their times, lose their colors like a deep-sea fish brought to the surface of the sea. A comparison with Byron comes to mind here. His *Manfred*, when read today, elicits a smirk and reminds one of the elaborations of student graphomaniacs who customarily set down on paper whatever they remember from their reading and think the consequent facility of writing is a mark of inspiration. Of course *Manfred* is not one of Byron's best works. Who knows, however, whether Byron's influence on the Continent, which has always exceeded his influence in England, is not to be explained by the poor acquaintance of his readers with English poetry.

How is it that Krasiński had it in him to perform such an unusual creative act as a young man and never thereafter? He did not have sufficient talent, he was finished. Inspiration failed him. But why? If we regard talent as something wafted down to us from on high or taken away from us, as if it were a supplement to the person, we are evading the issue with the aid of tautology. Sometimes, in the case of a poet "by the grace of God," we must content ourselves with such truisms because we are unable to find anything with which to fill the noticeable gap between their individuality and their work. It is also permissible, occasionally, to have recourse to the "ebb and flow of vital energy." But Krasiński had a keen mind, and the *Undivine Comedy* is not a lyric in honor of Corinne or Justine, or even the self-destroying eruption of a volcano such as the verse of Rimbaud. It is a fixed position of conscience, a sterner one than that taken by anyone in Europe at that time. Besides, the term "sudden silence" is not applicable here as it is to Rimbaud—or to Mickiewicz after *Pan Tadeusz*—where the magic quality is violently broken off and instead of poetry, another activity invades the scene. In Krasiński's case, seemingly, the continuity of thought is preserved and the poet undergoes a further evolution while continuing to write. However, while before the *Undivine Comedy* he was no more than a too-well-educated, too-susceptible young man, he became afterwards merely a romantic aristocrat, just one of many writers, a dilettante in philosophy who derived moral advantage from his reputation as a bard.

If there is an explanation, it is to be found in the use he made of his knowledge. Let us venture the following thesis. He succeeded once in making a great leap, and in so doing stepped over the threshold beyond which his personal hell began. Then he immediately retreated and for the rest of his life engaged in a camouflage directed against himself, seeking intellectual pretexts to keep from looking into his hell. The *Undivine Comedy* is a contradiction, a personal and historical contradiction, presented without consolation or illusions. Already there appears the idealistic Hegelian triad but it is still sensual, still palpable, perceived with the flesh. Later on philosophy serves as a layer of varnish, sealing the doors leading to the forbidden cave. Because Krasiński's intelligence was extraordinary, he had to seek methods that were commensurate with it; that is, he had to falsify his knowledge so every disturbing signal from behind the terrible door would take on a meaning that he could accept. There is nothing wrong in this if it is indulged in occasionally by a man of action or even by a journalist, but a writer is always punished for it. The journey into the dark region of one's own fate is necessary even when exploration can yield only modest results, for without it there is no art.

If we accept such a thesis then Delfina Potocka, philosophy, and—above all—Krasiński's epistolary mania can be conjoined and viewed as an incessant silencing of his knowledge, a knowledge so malicious that one cannot allow the demons to show even the tips of their noses. Hence the unreality, the incorporeal quality of his thinking and his style. The jeers that posterity permitted itself over the poem *Dawn* probably originated from a feeling of that basic falsity.

The reasons for such flights are impossible to discover, and we are reduced to conjecture. The contradictions inherent in Krasinski's very psycho-physical constitution, in his private life and in his social situation, emerged only once; later, instead of trying to find a solution, Krasiński tried to veil them. Among these contradictions the easiest to grasp are perhaps the social determinants, although of course they do not explain everything, Krasiński had to organize himself inwardly so a disdain for aristocracy would not hinder him from being an aristocrat, something he could achieve only by believing that he was an incorporeal spirit, that he had only accidentally been endowed with a count's title and money. Mickiewicz the teacher, but even more so Słowacki the son of a professor, or Norwid the draftsman and sculptor, already belonged to the new stratum, but more significantly to a certain literary-political milieu; in their youth they could pass through a more or less lengthy period of friendships with their equals. But Krasiński, abused by his fellow students for his loyalty to his father, was symbolically forced back into his own class, and his wealth protected him later from the company of literati with threadbare elbows, of conspiring émigrés, and of raving pilgrims from the Parisian pavements. As a dispassionate observer, and such was his fate, he gained very much: his judgments were at times penetrating. But he also lost much, for he had never been in the midst of events. It is no accident that his castle of the Holy Trinity rises high above the valley which seethes with suffering and insane humanity. Circumstances worked against Krasiński; in order to overcome them he would have needed animal vitality, malice, and a sanguine temperament. But he had none of these traits and was incapable of humor.

The *Undivine Comedy* is indebted for all its qualities to a fear neurosis equal to Kafka's. It is the product of two tragedies, one private and the other historical (as if a correlate of the self-sustaining stories in Mickiewicz's *Forefathers' Eve*—the story of

Gustav and the story of Konrad), but the link between these two tragedies would have been artificial if the neurosis were not the same in each case. The romantic accessories and the "problem" of the first part of the drama may easily obscure the truth of the experiences which made use of those tools. Those who enjoy investigating literary influences have not failed to depict this mask. For the problem of the artist, of art bought at the price of personal corruption, is not a rarity in the literature of the nineteenth century. It is interesting to consider a particularly poignant variant. Poetry appears in the person of a marvelous Maiden who destroys domestic happiness, charms the poet to the brink of the precipice (a real precipice, on the seacoast), and then reveals her true nature: ghastly decay. The diabolic character of art, to which one must pledge one's soul and thus detach oneself from the stable society of average citizens, has not in general been questioned by the groups bearing the name "bohemians." In this Krasiński is one of the precursors, since Lautréamont, the patron of the surrealists, mentions in his works the "*Comédie Infernale* d'un Polonais." Let us leave chronology aside, however. The Maiden has been incarnated variously in the "fatal woman," in the "false paradises" of hashish and opium, in absinthe, homosexuality, all the way up to Esmeralda the goddess of syphilis in Thomas Mann's *Doctor Faustus*. The kiss of the Maiden-skeleton was a sign of condemnation of, and separation from, a society which lives by buying and selling.

But something else is involved here. The fear neurosis in the *Undivine Comedy* is connected with an aversion to one's own degeneration, of which talent is a characteristic feature. Let us be brutally frank and say that the personal essence of this work is determined by the dread of procreating and perpetuating the line. Little Orcio is the nightmarish dream of a man so wounded by the world that he would consider it the greatest sin to bequeath his own helplessness to the unborn. If Orcio, almost an oleograph, is one of the three principal heroes (Count Henry, Orcio, Pancras), and if he is so touching it is because he is the

creation of an obsession. Furthermore, it is not unlikely that
this child affected by blindness has been endowed by the author
with more than one significance. Orcio seems to be a dream
about both Krasiński's own child and Krasiński himself, while
the husband, Count Henry, imperceptibly becomes the author's
father, General Wincenty Krasiński. Let us note above all else
that the child is pushed one step further into degeneration (his
infirmity) and that he is the last of his line. This same fear of the
world is expressed in the second part of the drama with the aid
of symbols: the elevation above the valley (that is, above the
whole earth) of the towers of the Holy Trinity, the isolation
from mankind by thick walls. But within those walls there is no
salvation, because there begins the descent into the underground of conscience where abides sin, Orcio himself. Kafka's
neurosis was somewhat similar: the feeling of inferiority toward
his father, the conviction that he was not permitted to have a
child, the premonition that a European cataclysm was
approaching. It is not difficult to find in literature other examples of the use of towers on mountains as a defensive gesture by
misanthropes; it suffices to mention Jules Verne's *Castle in the
Carpathians.*

So many secrets, so many enigmas, yet literary investigators
have argued mainly about the "ideas of Krasiński." Literary investigations should rather bear on the ways in which he deceived himself and others with ideas after that one opening of
the door. What was there in him to cause such an aversion
toward himself, his conviction that he was physically condemned, debased? And was not Revolution, which was sweep-
ing away his class, already the initial translation—into a language more suited to the expression of abstractions—of the personal terror of the people? And did not two dirty country boys
on his father's estate, when the young master felt awkward and
guilty in their presence, at times have more importance than a
close reading of the Parisian revolutionary dailies? And finally,
why was he immediately seized by the fear of his own phobia?
He set down his equation faultlessly—art versus happiness, art
versus action—and this equation was that of one suited neither

for happiness nor for action. And art is a lie, because every emotion, at the moment it is being experienced, is changed into an aesthetic and hence a reflective value: "You are composing a drama?" Such an antinomy might provide the work of a lifetime, as William Butler Yeats proved many years later, but only by constantly attacking, by maintaining tension between the two extremes of the contradiction. Krasiński chose a compromise, ideas, and used them in a most effective manner to immure his secrets. By comparison with Krasiński, Frederick Chopin is almost a jovial Pantagruel with his feet on very ordinary ground. It would be fitting, therefore, to establish what the *Undivine Comedy* truly reveals in order to appraise the extent of the later decline.

The *Undivine Comedy* is a rarity in world literature by virtue of its dialectical conception of *The* Revolution (not just any revolution). It is difficult today to believe that the *Comedy* was written when Karl Marx was scarcely a stripling, more than eighty years before 1917 in Russia. Although the pattern was taken from the French Revolution—the "masses" versus the aristocracy—the author's transforming vision is so extensive that the image grew beyond anything that took place in France. It is not a triumphal procession of lawyers, journalists, merchants, and the "people." One will, one brain, is actively directing: the professional revolutionary Pancras, who uses his general staff as an instrument, as a conveyor for transmitting his energy to the masses. The pattern is therefore a totalitarian one. Coming from a country where there was no middle-class upheaval and where the third estate counted for almost nothing, Krasiński achieved the prophetic blending of two revolutions into one. Future events showed that in economically backward countries such as Russia, a middle-class democratic revolution can be transformed into an anticapitalistic revolution; the defeat of the Mensheviks reduced the transitional phase to a few months.

Pancras possesses all the qualities of a leader called to direct both the battle and the coming new humanity. His intellect dominates followers and opponents alike; he considers neither

cost nor morality; he sacrifices himself and others in his striving
toward the great goal. But above all else he reads in the book of
history and knows what is inevitable and predetermined, hence
his certainty of victory. Krasiński thus introduces the concept
of historical necessity. Pancras' world outlook is very clearly
that of historical materialism, though neither the concept nor
the term existed at the time Krasiński created his hero. This
shows how much Marx later took from the very atmosphere of
his time, from that which was already in the air, imparting new
colorings to Hegel's writings. Pancras is—even in physical appearance—an advance portrait of Lenin.

Krasiński's dialectical approach is that only the amalgama-
tion of Pancras and Count Henry would produce a complete
Man. And Pancras is wise enough to know this; hence his weakness for Henry, as a suppressed part of his own person. But such
a union can exist only in dreams. Reality demands that these
two powers struggle with each other, that one of them be
crushed, and that only after the victory certain characteristics
of the vanquished be taken over by the victor. The nature of
these characteristics depends on historical conditions; but these
conceal irony. Sometimes we have the cult of tradition actu-
alized in Alexander Nevsky, Peter the Great, and imperial
policy; sometimes the cult of Kochanowski, Kościuszko, or
Mickiewicz. The very conclusion of the *Undivine Comedy*
seems artistically undigested and might suggest the thought that
"Galilaee vicisti" provides the vanquished with a posthumous
revenge on Pancras, that their cause was morally right. It is
doubtful whether such was Krasiński's intention. If the triad is
to be correct, then the final triumph of Christianity cannot signify that one of the sides was right; nor can it imply a sum of the
virtues of both sides for which, despite his self-deception, Pancras thirsts deep down in his heart. The triumph of Christianity
can only mean something that cannot be imagined, something
absolutely superior to both adversaries, for synthesis is always
a chemical combination rather than the sum of the thesis and
the antithesis. It is of no importance whether Krasiński was
aware of all the implications or was simply guided by the need

to place a stress, since had Pancras stood victoriously on the stage there would have been a lack of tragedy inasmuch as Henry has been for the most part discredited by the author and has ended by committing suicide, something not permissible for a Christian: that is to say Henry has unmasked his religious attachment as a mere class convention and phraseology. Whatever the considerations that guided the author, the Cross is revealed to Pancras rather than to Henry. The Revolution must be accomplished so that by destroying Christianity, it can restore it to a higher turn of the spiral of history. This concept reappears only in the twentieth century, particularly in Russia.

The Revolution must be a totalitarian one because combat imposes the dictatorship principle. Krasiński establishes three levels of hierarchy: one, the leader, a fanatic endowed with a cold awareness; two, his staff, fanatical but with little understanding and inspired to battle by rhetoric; three, the masses, moved by class hatred but used as a tool. The young aristocrat thereby gave proof that he understood the mechanism of revolution considerably better than did the revolutionaries of the nineteenth century, who derived their concept of revolution from their immediate environment, first from the storming of the Bastille and subsequently from the Paris Commune. They were strongly attracted by the idea of an elemental popular explosion; the edict of history was to be incarnated in the masses, the masses themselves were to overthrow the weakened order, while submitting to military discipline neither before the battle nor after it. Marx never went beyond this concept. Only Lenin constructed, theoretically and practically, the apparatus of professionals through which the passions of the masses might be turned into the desired channel.

It would be too much to say that Krasiński understood. He only guessed, but he guessed right, thanks to his neurosis. Only an impressionability comparable to the sensitivity of bare flesh is capable of separating some elements confused with others, distilling them, and presenting them in a pure state. Something similar occurred with George Orwell in his *1984*, a neurotic book written by a consumptive who hastened before his death to address to the world a warning against totalitarianism. The sensitivity of Orwell was also an aristocratic one, obsessed with the smell of sauerkraut, with colorlessness and misery; this, as well as his solidarity with the "proles," is clear from his other books, especially his descriptions of how, starving to death, he washed dishes in the basements of Parisian restaurants and slept in shelters for tramps. Krasiński feared revolution; Orwell feared a regime in which colorlessness and the smell of sauerkraut would receive state sanction and could thus no longer be fought against as unjust.

Why, in the *Comedy*, is Pancras' staff composed of "citizen converts"? This, again, is a contribution from Eastern Europe. When the Jews were emancipated in Western Europe, they were fused into a powerful and wealthy middle class; on the other hand, in Poland (and also, through the partition of the territory of the former commonwealth, in Russia) they stood out—or rather were to stand out, because Krasiński continually projects himself into the future—as the intellectually most active and most energetic, if not the only, urban ferment. The threat from their side was twofold: they were a battering ram that struck a blow at the patriarchal edifice in which everyone was obliged to "know his place"; furthermore, in breaking away from Judaism these people were committing the offense of suggesting by their very example that man can live without tradition. It is useful to observe that in spite of, or perhaps because of their zeal and revolutionary enthusiasm, they are no more than assistants to the leader Pancras. Their zeal, and at the same time their dislike of Russian imperial tradition, destined them to be the leaven for all manner of heresies in Russia after 1917, within some ten years of which date the "Old Bolsheviks," predominantly of Jewish origin, had been liquidated. In Orwell the "quarter-hour for hate" prescribed by the authorities has as its target the face of the diabolical Goldstein on the television screen.

The complete novelty of the *Undivine Comedy* reflects at the same time the complete novelty of the inventions of the nine-teenth century in the annals of the human species, primarily through the introduction of the idea of the "current" of history with which the hero swims or against which he struggles. Henceforth one need only appeal to this current for help, to be sure of victory and see the enemy's weapon fall from his hand as if by the action of a magic spell. Count Henry like all his class is sentenced by Krasiński to extermination, and this end of aristocracy is synonymous not with the birth of a democratic-mercantile society but with total revolution; that is to say, the French Revolution merely initiated a series. The question must be posed: how far does Krasiński go in his criticism of Count Henry and his class? And is this not also a criticism, *avant la lettre*, of everything with which he later consoled himself? In the *Undivine Comedy*, Krasiński is the only Bolshevik among the Polish writers of his century, just because he posed the dilemma of two alternative extremes. According to this logic the Polish Democratic Society, the Grudziąż circle,[2] and the socialistic vacillations of Mickiewicz must have appeared only as tiny ripples made by blind men on the surface of one single upheaval. Such a cold awareness is possible only as a flash, but it shares all the vices of the attitude of the initiate who encompasses time in abbreviation and who, like a bird on the wing, disregards the granular structure of time, its delicate texture. During the eighty years from the date of publication of the *Undivine Comedy* to the fulfillment of its prophecy, many powerful phenomena were produced that are now bearing—and will bear—fruit in the crisis of the twentieth century, but Krasiński's historical vision provided no one with stimulus and proved sterile. Did he, then, suffer punishment for a forbidden flash of awareness, and was the poet's defeat rendered inevitable because he wrote the *Undivine Comedy*? Perhaps, for as none of his contemporaries he drew from history a great generalization. And thereupon, in his retreat from the world of the senses, he dematerialized reality in its movement and sought refuge in the world of ideas.

1959

[2] A group of Polish radical democrats in Portsmouth, most of whose members were former prisoners in the fortress of Grudziąż after the 1830 Polish uprising, and who had separated themselves from the Polish Democratic Society.

5

On Pasternak Soberly

For those who were familiar with the poetry of Boris Pasternak long before he acquired international fame, the Nobel Prize given to him in 1958 had something ironic in it. A poet whose equal in Russia was only Akhmatova, and a congenial translator of Shakespeare, had to write a big novel and that novel had to become a sensation and a best seller before poets of the Slavic countries were honored for the first time in his person by the jury of Stockholm. Had the prize been awarded to Pasternak a few years earlier, no misgivings would have been possible. As it was, the honor had a bitter taste and could hardly be considered as proof of genuine interest in Eastern European literatures on the part of the Western reading public—this quite apart from the good intentions of the Swedish academy.

After *Doctor Zhivago* Pasternak found himself entangled in the kind of ambiguity that would be a nightmare for any author. While he always stressed the unity of his work, that unity was broken by circumstances. Abuse was heaped on him in Russia for a novel nobody had ever read. Praise was lavished on him in the West for a novel isolated from his lifelong labors: his poetry is nearly untranslatable. No man wishes to be changed into a symbol, whether the symbolic features lent him are those of a valiant knight or of a bugaboo: in such cases he is not judged by what he cherishes as his achievement but becomes a focal point of forces largely external to his will. In the last years of his life Pasternak lost, so to speak, the right to his personality, and his name served to designate a cause. I am far from intending to reduce that cause to momentary political games. Pasternak stood for the individual against whom the huge state apparatus turns in hatred with all its police, armies, and rockets. The emotional response to such a predicament was rooted in deep-seated fears, so justified in our time. The ignominious behavior of Pasternak's Russian colleagues, writers who took the side of power against a man armed only with his pen, created a Shakespearian situation; no wonder if in the West sympathies went to Hamlet and not to the courtiers of Elsinore.

The attention the critics centered on *Doctor Zhivago* delayed, however, an assessment of Pasternak's work as a whole. We are possibly now witnessing only the first gropings in that direction. My attempt here is not so much to make a nearly balanced appraisal as to stress a few aspects of his writings.

I became acquainted with his poetry in the thirties, when he was highly regarded in Polish literary circles. This was the Pasternak of *The Second Birth* (1932); the rhythm of certain "ballads" printed in that volume has been haunting me ever since. Yet Pasternak did not appear to his Polish readers as an exotic animal; it was precisely what was familiar in his poems that created some obstacles to unqualified approval. In spite of the considerable differences between Polish and Russian poetry, those poets who had been shaped by "modernistic" trends victorious at the beginning of the century showed striking similarities due to their cosmopolitan formation. Pasternak, through his very treatment of verse, could be placed within a spiritual family somewhere between Bolesław Leśmian, who achieved maturity when Pasternak was an adolescent, and Jarosław Iwaszkiewicz or Julian Tuwim, Pasternak's juniors by a few years. Now the fact is that in the thirties the poetics represented by those eminent figures was breaking down. The young poets who claimed the name of "avant-garde" paid lip service to the recognized brilliance of their elders but looked at them with suspicion and often attacked them openly. In spite of all the loose talk proper to so-called literary movements some serious matters were at stake, though veiled by disputes over metaphor and syntax. Those quarrels proved to be fruitful and later gave a new perspective on the writers then in combat. But Pasternak, to the extent that he was used as an argument by the traditionalists, partisans of the "sonorous" verse inherited from symbolism, had to share the fate of his allies, venerated and mistrusted at the same time by the young.

I say all this in order to show that my approach to Pasternak is colored by developments within Polish poetry of the last decades. My approach is also different, for other reasons, both from that of an American knowing Russian and from that of a Russian. My Slavic ear is sensitive to pulsations of Russian verse, yet I remain on my guard and submit myself with reluctance to the rhythmical spell inherent in the language, which reluctance can be explained by the more subdued accentuation of Western-Slavic tongues like Polish or Czech. Perhaps I lose a good deal that way, but it makes me more resistant to the gestures of a mesmerizer. Of Pasternak's eminence I have never had any doubts. In an article written in 1954 (before *Doctor Zhivago*) I predicted that a statue of Pasternak would stand one day in Moscow.

THE IMAGE OF THE POET

Half a century separates us from the Russian Revolution. When we consider that the Revolution was expected to bring about the end of the alienation of the writer and of the artist, and consequently to inaugurate new poetry of a kind never known before, the place Pasternak occupies today in Russian poetry is astounding. After all, his formative years preceded World War I and his craft retained some habits of that era. Like many of his contemporaries in various countries, he drew upon the heritage of French *poètes maudits*. In every avant-garde movement, the native traditions expressed through the exploration of linguistic possibilities are perhaps more important than any foreign influences. I am not concerned, however, with literary genealogy but with an image which determines the poet's tactics—an image of himself and of his role. A peculiar image was created by French poets of the nineteenth century, not without help from the minor German romantics and Edgar Allan Poe; this image soon became common property of the international avant-garde. The poet saw himself as a man estranged from a society serving false values, an inhabitant of *la cité infernale*, or, if you prefer, of the wasteland and passionately opposed to it. He was the only man in quest of true values, aware of surrounding falsity, and had to suffer because of his awareness. Whether he chose rebellion or contemplative art for art's sake, his revolutionary technique of writing served a double purpose: to destroy the automatism of opinions and beliefs transmitted through a frozen, inherited style; and to mark his distance from the idiom of those who lived false lives. Speculative thought, monopolized by optimistic philistines, was proclaimed taboo: the poet moved in another realm, nearer to the heart of things. Theories of two languages were elaborated: *le langage lyrique* was presented as autonomous, not translatable into any logical terms proper to *le langage scientifique*. Yet the poet had to pay the price: there are limits beyond which he could not go and maintain communication with his readers. Few are connoisseurs. Sophistication, or as Tolstoy called it *utoncheniïe*, is self-perpetuating like drug addiction.

This dilemma of the poet is still with us; that is why we tend to project it into the past. Yet great poets of other periods did not know it at all. We saw how in our century poets of the Communist obedience, disgusted by the increasingly narrow scope of modern poetry, turned to the camp of speculative thought endowed as it was with a new prestige since it dealt in historical optimism (but no longer of the bourgeois variety). And speculative thought, whether incarnated in the police or simply installed in poets' minds, destroyed their art and often also their persons. As for the West, sophistication or *uton-*

cheniie has been destroying poets so successfully that a poem on the page of a magazine is avoided by every self-respecting reader.

The image of the poet that we find in the early poems of Pasternak corresponds to the pattern dear to literary schools at the turn of the century: the poet is a mysterious, elusive creature living in accordance with his own laws which are not the laws of ordinary mortals. To quote Pasternak: "When a poet is in love, a displaced god falls in love and chaos crawls out into the world again as in the time of fossils." A man born with an ultra-perceptive sensory apparatus gradually discovers that personal destiny which estranges him from the world and transforms a familiar reality into phantasmagoria: "Thus the seas, sudden as a sigh, open up flowing over the fences, to where houses should have stood; thus the iambs start." The weird, incongruous core of things unveils itself to the poet. He is overpowered by elemental forces speaking through him, his words are magical incantation—he is a shaman, a witch doctor.

Here I can refer to my experience. What my generation reproached Polish contemporaries of Pasternak for was less a certain literary technique than a certain philosophy underlying the rocking singsong of their verse. For instance Julian Tuwim, who shows hallucinating similarities to Pasternak, was shaped by a programmatic scorn for all the programs, by a cult of "life," of an élan vital, by the cultural atmosphere permeated with the direct or indirect influence of Henri Bergson. He evolved from the enthusiastic vitality of his youth toward the horrified screams of a Cassandra tortured by Apollo, but had always been a shaman in trance. Intellectual helplessness, a "sacred naïveté" jealously defended, were typical of him no less than of nearly all his Polish colleagues who started to write about 1912 or 1913. They seemed to elude the dilemma which for my generation was insoluble but oppressive: for us a lyrical stream, a poetic idiom liberated from the chores of discourse was not enough, the poet should also be a *thinking* creature; yet in our efforts to build a poem as an "act of mind" we encountered an obstacle: speculative thought is vile, cunning, it eats up the internal resources of a poet from inside. In any case, if modern poetry had been moving away from traditional meter and rhyme, it was not because of fads and fashions but in the hope of elaborating a new style which would restore an equilibrium between emotional and intellectual elements.

Pasternak achieved perfection within the framework of traditional meter; one can also say that the wisdom of his maturity grew slowly and organically out of the image of the poet he shared in his youth with many poets. His poetry is written in rhymed stanzas, mostly quatrains. His experimentation consisted in inventing incredible assonances and in weighting every line to the breaking point with metaphors. Such a superabundance should have inclined him, it seems, to search for a principle of construction other than that of pure musicality. Perhaps Pasternak was afraid that his world of flickering bits of colors, of lights and of shadows, would disintegrate if deprived of a unifying singsong. He is often a prestidigitator in a corset, which he wears as if to enhance his skill in the reader's eyes. It so happened that in this attachment to meter he fulfilled, at least outwardly, the official requirements. Strangely enough, in Russia meter and rhyme acceded to political dignity through the rulers' decision to freeze art and literature in their "healthy" stages of the past. Here an analogy between poetry and painting imposes itself. Certain popular notions of the distinctive marks proper to the poet and to the painter have been carefully preserved: the poet is a man who writes columns of rhymed lines, the painter is a man who puts people and landscapes on his canvas "as if they were alive." Those who depart from that rule lack the necessary artistic qualities.

Pasternak's poetry is antispeculative, anti-intellectual. It is poetry of sensory perception. His worship of life meant a fascination with what can be called nature's moods—air, rain, clouds, snow in the streets, a detail changing thanks to the time of the day or night, to the season. Yet this is a very *linguistic* nature. In the Slavic languages words denoting planets, plants, and animals preserve their ancient power, they are loaded with the prestige of their feminity or masculinity. Hence the obsessive desire to identify the word with the object. Julian Tuwim, for instance, wrote a long poem consisting of variations on the word "green." "Greenery," in its double meaning of a quality and of vegetation—together with its retinue of names, adjectives, and verbs stemming from the same root—was for him a sort of vegetable goddess of the dictionary.

Pasternak gradually modified for his peculiar use his image of the poet as an exceptional being in direct contact with the forces of universal life. More and more he stressed passive receptivity as the poet's greatest virtue. The following pronouncement (from 1922) is characteristic:

Contemporary trends conceived art as a fountain though it is a sponge. They decided it should spring forth, though it should absorb and become saturated. In their estimation it can be decomposed into inventive procedures, though it is made of the organs of reception. Art should always be among the spectators and should look in a purer, more receptive, truer way than any spectator does; yet in our days art got acquainted with powder and the dressing room; it showed itself upon the stage as if there were in the world two arts, and one of them, since the other was always in reserve, could afford the luxury of self-distortion, equal to a suicide. It shows itself off, though it should hide itself up in the gallery, in anonymity.

Did Pasternak when writing these words think of himself in contrast with Vladimir Mayakovsky? Perhaps. Mayakovsky wanted to smash to pieces the image of the poet as a man who withdraws. He wanted to be a Walt Whitman—as the Europeans imagined Walt Whitman. We are not concerned here with his illusions and his tragedy. Let us note only that the instinctive sympathy many of us feel when reading those words of Pasternak can be misleading. We have been trained to identify a poet's purity with his withdrawal up into the gallery seat of a theater, where in addition he wears a mask. Already some hundred years ago poetry had been assigned a kind of reservation for a perishing tribe; having conditioned reflexes we, of course, admire "pure lyricism."

Not all Pasternak's poems are personal notes from his private diary or, to put it differently, "Les jardins sous la pluie" of Claude Debussy. As befitted a poet in the Soviet Union, in the twenties he took to vast historical panoramas foretelling *Doctor Zhivago*. He enlivened a textbook cliché (I do not pretend to judge that cliché, it can be quite close to reality and be sublime) with all the treasures of detail registered by the eye of an adolescent witness; Pasternak was fifteen when the revolutionary events occurred that are described in the long poems "The Year 1905" and "Lieutenant Schmidt." Compared with his short poems, they seem to me failures; the technique of patches and glimpses does not fit the subject. There is no overall commitment, the intellect is recognized as inferior to the five senses and is refused access to the material. As a result, we have the theme and the embroidery; the theme, however, returns to the quality of a cliché.

Thus I tend to accuse Pasternak, as I accused his contemporaries in Poland, of a programmatic helplessness in the face of the world, of a carefully cultivated irrational attitude. Yet it was exactly this attitude that saved Pasternak's art and perhaps his life in the sad Stalinist era. Pasternak's more intellectually inclined colleagues answered argument by argument, and in consequence they were either liquidated or they accepted the supreme wisdom of the official doctrine. Pasternak eluded all categories; the "meaning" of his poems was that of lizards or butterflies, and who could pin down such phenomena using Hegelian terms? He did not pluck fruits from the tree of reason, the tree of life was enough for him. Confronted by argument, he replied with his sacred dance.

We can agree that in the given conditions that was the only victory possible. Yet if we assume that those periods when poetry is amputated, forbidden thought, reduced to imagery and musicality, are not the most healthy, then Pasternak's was a Pyrrhic victory. When a poet can preserve his freedom only if he is deemed a harmless fool, a *yurodivy* holy because bereft of reason, his society is sick. Pasternak noticed that he had been maneuvered into Hamlet's position. As a weird being, he was protected from the ruler's anger and had to play the card of his weirdness. But what could he do with his moral indignation at the sight of the crime perpetrated upon millions of people, what could he do with his love for suffering Russia? That was the question.

His mature poetry underwent a serious evolution. He was right, I feel, when at the end of his life he confessed that he did not like his style prior to 1940:

My hearing was spoiled then by the general freakishness and the breakage of everything customary—procedures which ruled then around me. Anything said in a normal way shocked me. I used to forget that words can contain something and mean something in themselves, apart from the trinkets with which they are adorned.... I searched everywhere not for essence but for extraneous pungency.

We can read into that judgment more than a farewell to a technique. He never lost his belief in the redeeming power of art understood as a moral discipline, but his late poems can be called Tolstoyan in their nakedness. He strives to give in them explicitly a certain vision of the human condition.

I did not find in Pasternak's work any hint of his philosophical opposition to the official Soviet doctrine, unless his reluctance to deal with abstractions—so that the terms "abstract" and "false" were for him synonymous—is a proof of his resistance. The life of Soviet citizens was his life, and in his patriotic poems he was not paying mere lip service. He was no more rebellious than any average Russian. *Doctor Zhivago* is a Christian book, yet there is no trace in it of that polemic with the anti-Christian concept of man which makes the strength of Dostoevsky. Pasternak's Christianity is atheological. It is very difficult to analyze a Weltanschauung which pretends not to be a Weltanschauung at all, but simply "closeness to life," while in fact it blends contradictory ideas borrowed from extensive readings. Perhaps we should not analyze. Pasternak was a man spellbound by reality, which was for him miraculous. He accepted suffering because the very essence of life is suffering,

death, and rebirth. And he treated art as a gift of the Holy
Spirit.

We would not know, however, of his hidden faith without
Doctor Zhivago. His poetry—even if we put aside the question
of censorship—was too fragile an instrument to express, after
all, ideas. To do his Hamlet deed Pasternak had to write a big
novel. By that deed he created a new myth of the writer, and we
may conjecture that it will endure in Russian literature like
other already mythical events: Pushkin's duel, Gogol's struggles
with the Devil, Tolstoy's escape from Yasnaya Poliana.

A NOVEL OF ADVENTURES,
RECOGNITIONS, HORRORS, AND SECRETS

The success of *Doctor Zhivago* in the West cannot be explained by the scandal accompanying its publication or by political thrills. Western novel readers have been reduced in our
times to quite lean fare; the novel, beset by its enemy, psychology, has been moving toward the programmatic leanness of the
antinovel. *Doctor Zhivago* satisfied a legitimate yearning for a
narrative full of extraordinary happenings, narrow escapes,
crisscrossing plots and, contrary to the microscopic analyses of
Western novelists, open to huge vistas of space and historical
time. The novel reader is a glutton, and he knows immediately
whether a writer is one also. In his desire to embrace the unex-
pectedness and wonderful fluidity of life, Pasternak showed a
gluttony equal to that of his nineteenth-century predecessors.

Critics have not been able to agree as to how *Doctor Zhivago*
should be classified. The most obvious thing was to speak of a
revival of great Russin prose and to invoke the name of Tolstoy. But then the improbable encounters and nearly miraculous interventions Pasternak is so fond of had to be dismissed as
mistakes and offenses against realism. Other critics, like
Edmund Wilson, treated the novel as a web of symbols, going
so far sometimes in this direction that Pasternak in his letters

had to deny he ever meant all that. Still others, such as Professor Gleb Struve, tried to mitigate this tendency yet conceded that *Doctor Zhivago* was related to Russian symbolist prose of the beginning of the century. The suggestion I am going to make has been advanced by no one, as far as I know.

It is appropriate, I feel, to start with a simple fact: Pasternak was a Soviet writer. One may add, to displease his enemies and some of his friends, that he was not an *internal émigré* but shared the joys and sorrows of the writers' community in Moscow. If his community turned against him in a decisive moment, it proves only that every literary confraternity is a nest of vipers and that servile vipers can be particularly nasty. Unavoidably he followed the interminable discussions in the literary press and at meetings—discussions lasting over the years and arising from the zigzags of the political line. He must also have read many theoretical books, and theory of literature in the Soviet Union is not an innocent lotus-eaters' pastime but more like acrobatics on a tightrope with a precipice below. Since of all the literary genres fiction has the widest appeal and can best be used as an ideological weapon, many of these studies were dedicated to prose.

According to the official doctrine, in a class society vigorous literature could be produced only by a vigorous ascending class. The novel, as a new literary genre, swept eighteenth-century England. Thanks to its buoyant realism it was a weapon of the ascending bourgeoisie and served to debunk the receding aristocratic order. Since the proletariat is a victorious class it should have an appropriate literature, namely, a literature as vigorous as the bourgeoisie had in its upsurge. This is the era of Socialist Realism, and Soviet writers should learn from "healthy" novelists of the past centuries while avoiding neurotic writings produced in the West by the bourgeoisie in its decline. This reasoning, which I oversimplify for the sake of clarity, but not too much, explains the enormous prestige of the English eighteenth-century novel in the Soviet Union.

Pasternak did not have to share the official opinions as to the economic causes and literary effects in order to feel pleasure in reading English "classics," as they are called in Russia. A professional translator for many years, mostly from English, he probably had them all in his own library in the original. While the idea of his major work was slowly maturing in his mind he must often have thought of the disquieting trends in modern Western fiction. In the West fiction lived by denying more and more its nature, or even by behaving like the magician whose last trick is to unveil how his tricks were done. Yet in Russia Socialist Realism was an artistic flop and of course nobody heeded the repeated advice to learn from the "classics": an invitation to joyous movement addressed to people in straitjackets is nothing more than a crude joke. And what if somebody, in the spirit of spite, tried to learn?

Doctor Zhivago, a book of hide-and-seek with fate, reminds me irresistibly of one English novel: Fielding's *Tom Jones*. True, we may have to make some effort to connect the horses and inns of a countryside England with the railroads and woods of Russia, yet we are forced to do so by the travel through enigmas in both novels. Were the devices applied mechanically by Pasternak, the parallel with Fielding would be of no consequence. But in *Doctor Zhivago* they become signs which convey his affirmation of the universe, of life, to use his preferred word. They hint at his sly denial of the trim, rationalized, ordered reality of the Marxist philosophers and reclaim another richer subterranean reality. Moreover, the devices correspond perfectly to the experience of Pasternak himself and of all the Russians. Anyone who has lived through wars and revolutions knows that in a human anthill on fire the number of extraordinary meetings, unbelievable coincidences, multiplies tremendously in comparison with periods of peace and everyday routine. One survives because one was five minutes late at a given address where everybody got arrested, or because one did not catch a train that was soon to be blown to pieces. Was that an accident, fate, or providence?

If we assume that Pasternak consciously borrowed his devices from the eighteenth-century novel, his supposed sins against realism will not seem so disquieting. He had his own views on realism. Also we shall be less tempted to hunt for symbols in *Doctor Zhivago* as for raisins in a cake. Pasternak perceived the very texture of life as symbolic, so its description did not call for those protruding and all too obvious allegories. Situations and characters sufficed; to those who do not feel the eighteenth-century flavor in the novel, I can point to the interventions of the enigmatic Yevgraf, the half-Asiatic natural brother of Yuri Zhivago, who emerges from the crowd every time the hero is in extreme danger and, after accomplishing what he has to, returns to anonymity. He is a benevolent lord protector of Yuri; instead of an aristocratic title, he has connections at the top of the Communist party. Here again the situation is realistic: to secure an ally at the top of the hierarchy is the first rule of behavior in such countries as the Soviet Union.

THE POET AS A HERO

Yuri Zhivago is a poet, a successor to the Western European bohemian, torn asunder by two contradictory urges: withdrawal into himself, the only receptable or creator of value; movement toward society, which has to be saved. He is also a successor to the Russian "superfluous man." As for virtues, he cannot be said to possess much initiative and manliness. Nevertheless the reader is in deep sympathy with Yuri since he, the author affirms, is a bearer of charisma, a defender of vegetal "inner freedom." A passive witness of bloodshed, of lies and debasement, Yuri must do something to deny the utter insignificance of the individual. Two ways are offered to him: either the way of Eastern Christianity or the way of Hamlet.

Pity and respect for the *yurodivy*—a half-wit in tatters, a being at the very bottom of the social scale—has ancient roots in Russia. The *yurodivy*, protected by his madness, spoke truth in the teeth of the powerful and wealthy. He was outside society and denounced it in the name of God's ideal order. Possibly in many cases his madness was only a mask. In some respects he recalls Shakespeare's fool; in fact Pushkin merges the two figures in his *Boris Godunov*, where the half-wit Nikolka is the only man bold enough to shout the ruler's crimes in the streets.

Yuri Zhivago in the years following the civil war makes a plunge to the bottom of the social pyramid. He forgets his medical diploma and leads a shady existence as the husband of the daughter of his former janitor, doing menial jobs, provided with what in the political slang of Eastern Europe are called "madman's papers." His refusal to become a member of the "new intelligentsia" implies that withdrawal from the world is the only way to preserve integrity in a city ruled by falsehood. Yet in Yuri Zhivago there is another trait. He writes poems on Hamlet and sees himself as Hamlet. Yes, but Hamlet is basically a man with a goal, and action is inseparable from understanding the game. Yuri has an intuitive grasp of good and evil, but is no more able to understand what is going on in Russia than a bee can analyze chemically the glass of a windowpane against which it is beating. Thus the only act left to Yuri is a poetic act, equated with the defense of the language menaced by the totalitarian double-talk or, in other words, with the defense of authenticity. The circle closes; a poet who rushed out of his tower is back in his tower.

Yuri's difficulty is that of Pasternak and of his Soviet contemporaries. Pasternak solved it a little better than his hero by writing not poems but a novel, his Hamletic act; the difficulty persists, though, throughout the book. It is engendered by the acceptance of a view of history so widespread in the Soviet Union that it is a part of the air one breathes. According to this view history proceeds along preordained tracks, it moves forward by "jumps," and the Russian Revolution (together with what followed) was such a jump of cosmic dimension. To be for or against an explosion of historical forces is as ridiculous as to be for or against a tempest or the rotation of the seasons. The human will does not count in such a cataclysm, since even the

leaders are but tools of mighty "processes." As many pages of
his work testify, Pasternak did not question that view. Did he
not say in one of his poems that everything by which this century will live is in Moscow? He seemed to be interpreting Marxism in a religious way. And is not Marxism a secularized biblical faith in the final accomplishment, implying a providential
plan? No wonder Pasternak, as he says in his letter to Jacqueline
de Proyart, liked the writings of Teilhard de Chardin so much.
The French Jesuit also believed in the Christological character of
lay history, and curiously combined Christianity with the Berg-
sonian "creative evolution" as well as with the Hegelian ascending movement.

Let us note that Pasternak was probably the first to read Teilhard de Chardin in Russia. One may be justly puzzled by the
influence of that poet-anthropologist, growing in the last
decade both in the West and in the countries of the Soviet bloc.
Perhaps man in our century is longing for solace at any price,
even at the price of sheer romanticism in theology. Teilhard de
Chardin has predecessors, to mention only Alexander Blok's
"music of history" or some pages of Berdiaev. The latent "Teil-
hardism" of *Doctor Zhivago* makes it a Soviet novel in the sense
that one might read into it an esoteric interpretation of the
Revolution as opposed to the exoteric interpretation offered by
official pronouncements. The historical tragedy is endowed
with all the trappings of necessity working toward the ultimate
good. Perhaps the novel is a tale about the individual versus
Caesar, but with a difference: the new Caesar's might has its
source not only in his legions.

What could poor Yuri Zhivago do in the face of a system
blessed by history and yet repugnant to his notions of good and
evil? Intellectually, he was paralyzed. He could only rely on his
subliminal self, descend deeper than state-monopolized thought.
Being a poet, he clutches at his belief in communion with ever
reborn life. Life will take care of itself. Persephone always
comes back from the underground, winter's ice is dissolved,
dark eras are necessary as stages of preparations, life and his-

tory have a hidden Christian meaning. And suffering purifies.

Pasternak overcame his isolation by listening to the silent
complaint of the Russian people; we respond strongly to the
atmosphere of hope pervading *Doctor Zhivago*. Not without
some doubts, however. Life rarely takes care of itself unless
human beings decide to take care of themselves. Sufferings can
either purify or corrupt, and too great a suffering too often cor-
rupts. Of course hope itself, if it is shared by all the nation, may
be a powerful factor for change. Yet, when at the end of the
novel, friends of the long-dead Yuri Zhivago console themselves with timid expectations, they are counting upon an
indefinite something (death of the tyrant?) and their political
thinking is not far from the grim Soviet joke about the best constitution in the world being one that grants to every citizen the
right to a postmortem rehabilitation.

But Pasternak's weaknesses are dialectically bound up with
his great discovery. He conceded so much to his adversary,
speculative thought, that what remained was to make a jump
into a completely different dimension. *Doctor Zhivago* is not a
novel of social criticism, it does not advocate a return to Lenin
or to the young Marx. It is profoundly arevisionist. Its message
summarizes the experience of Pasternak the poet: whoever engages in a polemic with the thought embodied in the state will
destroy himself for he will become a hollow man. It is impossible to talk to the new Caesar, for then you choose the
encounter on his ground. What is needed is a new beginning,
new in the present conditions but not new in Russia marked as it
is by centuries of Christianity. The literature of Socialist Realism should be shelved and forgotten; the new dimension is that
of every man's mysterious destiny, of compassion and faith. In
this Pasternak revived the best tradition of Russian literature,
and he will have successors. He already has one in Solzhenitsyn.

The paradox of Pasternak lies in his narcissistic art leading
him beyond the confines of his ego. Also in his reedlike pliabil-
ity, so that he often absorbed *les idées reçues* without examining
them thoroughly as ideas but without being crushed by them

either. Probably no reader of Russian poets resists a temptation to juxtapose the two fates: Pasternak's and Mandelstam's. The survival of the first and the death in a concentration camp of the second may be ascribed to various factors, to good luck and bad luck. And yet there is something in Mandelstam's poetry, intellectually structured, that doomed him in advance. From what I have said about my generation's quarrel with worshipers of "Life," it should be obvious that Mandelstam, not Pasternak, is for me the ideal of a modern classical poet. But he had too few weaknesses, was crystalline, resistant, and therefore fragile. Pasternak—more exuberant, less exacting, uneven—was called to write a novel that, in spite and because of its contradictions, is a great book.

1963

6

On Modern Russian Literature and the West

It was said long ago that amazement is the mother of philosophy, and this is undoubtedly true. Yet in our approach to literature we often tend to be ashamed of our most naïve reactions. The few words that follow are an attempt to be as uninhibited and simple as possible.

One thing is absolutely incomprehensible to me in all the success of such Russian writers as Pasternak or Solzhenitsyn with the Western public, especially Western literary critics. If we assume that critics and reviewers who praise these writers so highly are sincere, a question arises which it is perhaps tactless to ask—but in matters of human spirit tact is an ally of hypocrisy. I wonder if these critics and readers are aware that they are maintaining double standards.

It is obvious that a literary critic who writes on those Russian authors is compelled, by the very nature of his profession, to look at them in conjunction with their contemporaries in other countries—their rivals for fame. He must compare, juxtapose, draw parallels, establish contrasts. And any normal human being who reads these Russian writers in America, for instance, must have one dominant feeling—that of shame. Not because he himself is privileged, lives in an affluent society, and is not endangered by the whims of those in power, while the Russian writers tell of suffering imposed upon millions of their fellow-men, but because freedom of choice is being misused today by Western writers for the purpose of creating dehumanized literature perhaps, it is true, under the pretext of rebelling against a dehumanized world. But are the Western writers themselves conscious of the difference between genuine concern and what is just subservience to fashion or a marketing device?

To put it briefly, Pasternak's and Solzhenitsyn's works, in a sense, "judge" all contemporary literature by reintroducing a hierarchy of values, the renunciation of which threatens mankind with madness. Or to put it another way, they reestablish a clear distinction between what is serious in human life and what is considered serious by people who *s zhiru besyatsya*.[1]

Let me note a formidable paradox: in the countries where Christian churches thrive there are practically no genuinely Christian novels. Truly Christian writing has had to come from Russia, where Christians have been persecuted for several decades. Then how can a critic, if he is a hot-blooded creature and not a frog, placidly bypass such a challenge and not shout on the rooftops his protest against the use made of freedom by Western literati?

I have my reservations as to Pasternak's poetics and Solzhenitsyn's novelistic technique. Yet poetics and techniques should be appraised not as abstract notions but according to the function they perform in given circumstances. Pasternak's high regard for the poet as a passive receptacle, as a shaman in touch with the ineffable forces of life, stems from a premise common to the all-European artistic movement prior to World War I, namely that art is the highest ritual, replacing religion. A peculiar logic of development led then in the West to a gradual estrangement of the poet from ordinary mortals, and to a break in communication. An analogous transformation, behind which there is a desire to make art completely autonomous, may be observed in painting: after all, modern painting may be considered the result of the destruction of the human figure, which was accomplished by cubists prior to World War I. But Pasternak's belief in the supreme poetic wisdom, achieved by the poet through passivity, proved to be his best defense. It pro-

[1] Are driven out of their minds by good living.

tected him from ratiocinations. Under circumstances where anyone who engaged in discourse was lost, he succeeded in safeguarding his integrity and dignity. Moreover, that which in the West favored a priestly hauteur of the poet, and thus contributed to his isolation, became for Pasternak an encouragement to listen and to convey innumerable voices of human despair, with love and compassion. As for Solzhenitsyn, he is often weighed down by a technique which bears a strong imprint of Socialist Realism. Yet in his effort to convert Socialist Realism into realism he achieves a directness which has been lost by the post-Joycean novel.

I am preparing for print the memoirs of my late friend, the Polish poet Aleksander Wat. Since many chapters deal with his odyssey through Soviet prisons including Lubyanka, and are in fact a gallery of portraits from various strata of Soviet society, I live very much in the Russia depicted by Pasternak and Solzhenitsyn. Instead of hammering upon the contrast between the meaning of the written word in Russia and in the West, I take the liberty of translating two fragments of those memoirs, as they tell more than I would be able to say.

Wat found himself in October of 1940 in a transfer prison (*peresylnaya tyurma*) in Kiev, and he relates his readings of graffiti in the prison toilet:

Inscriptions by Russians: if not written for underworld communications (*blatnyie*) and not for practical purposes, they are philosophic. Many poems, *chastushkas*. Mostly obscene, but not without a wild energy, by members of the authentic underworld, the pseudo-underworld, and the intelligentsia. Some words linger in my memory:

> Ot Vorkuty idut katorzhanie,
> Vory, blyadi, millionaya rat'.
> [From Vorkuta prisoners are walking,
> Thieves, whores, an army million-strong.]

—a lyrical poem, the work of a true poet, poignant.

I was most impressed by the meditative sentences I was to find later on, the same in every provincial prison.

> Bud' proklyat kto vydumal nazvaniïe
> Ispravitelno-trudovye lagerya.
> [Be cursed whoever invented the name:
> Corrective labor camps]:

—this is the beginning of a poem.
  The most beautiful was an age-old maxim:

> Ot sumy i tyurmy ne otkazyvaïsya.
> Vxodyashchy ne sumis,
> Vyxodyashchy ne raduysya.
> [Do not refuse the beggar's bag and prison.
> Entering, be not disturbed,
> Leaving, do not rejoice.]

—like the antiphon of a chorus, in the ancient tragedy of the Russian people. In this old maxim of runaway serfs and pilgrims the fate of all the nation expressed itself now, most fully, most truthfully, and with the greatest dignity. I was spellbound by the solemn tone of that sentence, by its severe truth. But I, a newcomer from another world, defended myself against such spells: "The terror of the bolsheviks could not maintain itself without a national acquiescence to the beggar's bag and to prison; *les idées-forces*—conceived in the West by a monstrous tangle of oppression and rebellion—found in Russia their land of election," I thought scornfully. But when I returned to my plankbed and, among the quarrels of my miserable co-prisoners so Occidental a short time ago, I repeated those words in their solemn anapestic cadence, I knew: here was a sacred thing. I closed my eyes and I tried to visualize the face of an unknown prisoner who on the dirty wall of a prison toilet, instead of crying "Help, help!" wrote those solemnly humble words. A man from the people? One of millions? In senselessness and in aimlessness, in the spontaneous accidental nature of his own agony, he found the meaning for the fate of his nation. After twenty-five years, when I read *One Day in the Life of Ivan Denisovich* and "Matryona's Home," those words return and with them the face, as I imagined it, of the Christian and, at the same time, stoic sage of the Russia of concentration camps.

Here is another fragment—Wat's reflections upon the behavior of his cellmate at Lubyanka, a young sailor, and upon Soviet youth in general:

I observed innumerable times, later, already out of prison, that in the young people's minds there was an iron barrier between large and small prohibitions. The big prohibitions were taboos and were surrounded by an appropriate halo as in a primeval era. But by breaking small prohibitions one proved one's toughness and defied good manners which in, one's opinion, had been condemned by history; it was a compensation for obeying taboos. In 1944, in Ili (Kazakhstan), a convalescent soldier of my acquaintance raved about the riches and distractions to be found in small Bulgarian towns, where he had been during the campaign. "Would you like to stay there for good?" I asked. "Never in the world! No freedom there." I established without difficulty that he had in mind freedom, for instance, to get dead drunk in a public place, to spit and blow his nose on the floor, to push old men and women in a streetcar, to curse without inhibition, etc. Other freedoms not only were of no use to him but encumbered him like Nessos' net, and, what is worse, would enforce upon him free decisions as to his fate, while he had been taught to abandon them forever. In this sense, Stalin's terroristic paternalism reduced a few Soviet generations to the level of the Guarani Indians in the eighteenth-century Jesuit communistic republic. The barrier in the minds I am speaking of, was, however, movable: that brought an element of diversity into the routine of the Stalinist era. For instance, the word *zhid* was in 1942 under the rigors of a taboo, but already two years later, in Ili, the deported Polish Jews were showered with a hail of that insult as well as occasional stones by children and teenagers from the local high school. Today, in 1965, those pioneers from Ili are young engineers, literary critics, apparatchiks. Whoever in the West does not realize that there is such an "iron barrier" in their minds and is unable to understand the answer of the soldier, will not comprehend very much of psycho-ideology and of the young people's rebellion in the USSR.

In order to liberate themselves from Stalin's heritage in *their souls*, they must first "detach themselves from the enemy"; as a snake sheds its skin in the springtime, they must throw off not only any concern with Stalinism, Communism, revisionism, but those ugly words as well. In this sense, the free men are not Andrey Voznesensky, Yevtushenko, or Tarsis, but such people as the poet Iosif Brodsky, the Solzhenitsyn of "Matryona's Home," Tertz-Sinyavsky in his last (apolitical!) works. For political thinking has become so distorted and so depraved during the long, long half-century, that one has to begin with tearing it out, along with its roots, from one's soul, so that the ground can be prepared for a political thing, healthy, humane, which makes for the *virtú* of a free citizen. Anticommunists in the West do not understand this. Of course, acts of political rebellion and, even more, a political rebellion of the mind, are useful, for they squeeze concessions from the rulers, but in the Russian Empire they will remain—for many years to come—abortive, powerless to touch off a movement of the masses. Personally I see the hope of Russia not in rebellion but in life itself, in existing (*Sein*) in an utterly different spiritual space.

With what delight the adolescent Brodsky discovered John Donne and how beautifully his discovery bore fruit! How effectively Sinyavsky (in his aphorisms), liberated himself from the nightmares of anti-Stalinist neurosis and renewed himself at the sources of ancient Russian folk religion! What great internal beauty emanates from the folkish-Christian *caritas* of Solzhenitsyn! How movingly Pasternak identified himself with the misfortune of the whole, immense *mnogostradalny* Russian people! With what depth of suffering Akhmatova set herself and the world aflame, when standing at her son's prison. No other such values have been created by Russian literature since Blok's "The Twelve," in nearly fifty years. Thinking young Soviet men and women know incomparably more about the miseries and monstrosities of Communism than do Western Sovietologists; every word of authentic religion, of idealistic thought and of disinterested beauty in poetry and in ethics falls there upon fertile ground. Could I but repeat here my recent conversations with representatives of that thinking youth! Beckett, Gombrowicz, Genet, Sartre, various stripteases (though personally, I esteem them) can only blight young seedlings there.

This is what Wat said. I, too, have a considerable amount of esteem for literary "stripteases." Yet I think of them with sadness. Perhaps in the crazy, careening rush of artistic revolutions succeeding each other in Western literature and art there is a sort of inevitability. But we live in one world. If thinking Russians are ready to pay dearly with their careers, their lives, for their attempts to restore moral and artistic values, while their Western colleagues engage in sheer destruction for destruction's sake, what can we expect from a true, and not official, meeting of the East and the West? And how can literary critics writing on Pasternak or Solzhenitsyn so easily shirk their duty, which calls them to point out this ominous disparity?

1971

7

The Importance of Simone Weil

France offered a rare gift to the contemporary world in the person of Simone Weil. The appearance of such a writer in the twentieth century was against all the rules of probability, yet improbable things do happen.

The life of Simone Weil was short. Born in 1909 in Paris, she died in England in 1943 at the age of thirty-four. None of her books appeared during her own lifetime. Since the end of the war her scattered articles and her manuscripts—diaries, essays —have been published and translated into many languages. Her work has found admirers all over the world, yet because of its austerity it attracts only a limited number of readers in every country. I hope my presentation will be useful to those who have never heard of her.

Perhaps we live in an age that is atheological only in appearance. Millions were killed during the First World War, millions killed or tortured to death in Russia during and after the revolution; and countless victims of Nazism and the Second World War. All this had to have a strong impact upon European thinking. And it seems to me that European thinking has been circling around one problem so old that many people are ashamed to name it. It happens sometimes that old enigmas of mankind are kept dormant or veiled for several generations, then recover their vitality and are formulated in a new language. And the problem is: who can justify the suffering of the innocent? Albert Camus, in *The Plague*, took up the subject already treated in the Book of Job. Should we return our ticket like Ivan Kara-mazov because the tear of a child is enough to tip the scale? Should we rebel? Against whom? Can God exist if he is respon-sible, if he allows what our values condemn as a monstrosity? Camus said no. We are alone in the universe; our human fate is to hurl an eternal defiance at blind inhuman forces, without the comfort of having an ally somewhere, without any metaphysi-cal foundation.

But perhaps if not God, there is a goddess who walks through battlefields and concentration camps, penetrates prisons, gathers every drop of blood, every curse? She knows that those who complain simply do not understand. Everything is counted, everything is an unavoidable part of the pangs of birth and will be recompensed. Man will become a God for man. On the road toward that accomplishment he has to pass through Calvary. The goddess' name is pronounced with trembling in our age: she is History.

Leszek Kołakowski, a Marxist professor of philosophy in Warsaw,[1] states bluntly that all the structures of modern philo-sophy, including Marxist philosophy, have been elaborated in the Middle Ages by theologians and that an attentive observer can distinguish old quarrels under new formulations. He points out that History, for instance, is being discussed by Marxists in the terms of theodicy—justification of God.[2]

Irony would be out of place here. The question of Provi-dence, or of lack of Providence, can also be presented in another way. Is there any immanent force located in *le devenir*, in what is in the state of becoming, a force that pulls mankind up toward perfection? Is there any *cooperation* between man and a universe that is subject to constant change? So worded, the question is related to the quite recent discovery of the his-torical dimension, unknown to the rather immobile societies of the past. Curiously enough, Christian theologians are helpless

---

[1] At the time of this writing.
[2] His essay "The Priest and the Jester," English translation in *Towards a Marxist Humanism.*

when confronted with those issues. They are ashamed of the providentialist philosophy propagated by Bossuet and other preachers, according to whom God, a super-king, helped good rulers and punished the bad. If it were true, and certainly it is not, the enigma of every individual's commitment would still remain unsolved. At least one French theologian, Father Féssard, affirms that this is the basic intellectual weakness of modern Christians. As soon as they touch historical problems, they succumb to habits of philosophy alien to them; they become, consciously or unconsciously, Hegelians or Marxists. Their weakness reflects a gap in Thomist doctrine. In Saint Thomas Aquinas, affirms Father Féssard, there are no traces of pronouncements on the historical dimension. He was interested only in the *order of reason* and in the *order of nature.* "If the historical," says Father Féssard, "plays a capital role in Hegel, in Marx, and in many philosophers of existence, in the opinion of good judges it is, or rather it seems to be, completely absent from the Thomist doctrine." So a Christian dialectician has to invent his very conceptual tools.

Here I end my introduction. It leads toward some vital points in Simone Weil's thought.

Simone Weil was born into a family of intellectuals of Jewish origin. Her father's family was from Alsace, her mother's family had migrated to France from Russia. She grew up among people who respected learning above all, and all her life she preserved a lively interest in modern physics and mathematics. She mastered foreign languages early: besides Latin and Greek as taught in French schools (and her excellent knowledge of Greek proved decisive for her future evolution), German and English. She was not brought up in any religious denomination, and throughout her youth was not concerned with religious problems.

After having completed her university studies at the École Normale Supérieure (where one of her colleagues was Simone de Beauvoir, then a Catholic), Simone Weil started her brief career as a teacher of Greek and of philosophy. A brilliant professor, she was often in trouble with the authorities because of her eccentricity. She was politely ironic toward her bourgeois surroundings and sided with people looked at by the French middle class with horror: the militants of the labor unions and the unemployed workers. Those were the years of the economic crisis. She refused herself the right to earn money if others were starving and kept only a small part of her salary, giving the rest away to union funds and workers' periodicals. Politically she was on the left, but she never had anything to do with the French Communist party. She was closest to a small group, "La Révolution Prolétarienne," which followed the traditions of French syndicalism. Her numerous political articles on the chances of the workers' struggle in France, on economic policy, on the causes of Nazism in Germany, as well as her studies on the mechanism of society and on the history of Europe, have been recently collected in a few volumes. Only some of them had been published in her lifetime, in little known magazines.

The desire to share the fate of the oppressed led her to a momentous decision. In spite of bad health, she worked for a year (1934-35) as a simple worker in Paris metallurgical factories; she thus acquired a firsthand knowledge of manual labor. Her essays on that subject (a volume entitled *La Condition Ouvrière*) are a terrible indictment of brutality, callousness, physical and spiritual misery. As she confesses, that year in the factories destroyed her youth and forever left the indelible stigma of a slave upon her ("like those stigmas branded on the foreheads of slaves by the ancient Romans").

When the Spanish civil war broke out, Simone Weil left for Barcelona (in 1936), where she enlisted as a soldier in the "Colonna Durutti," an anarchist brigade. I stress anarchist—she chose it because the ideal of the anarchists was utopian. But owing to an accident and resulting illness, her stay in Spain was very short.

In 1938 Simone Weil, to use her words, was "captured by Christ." Nobody has the right to present her biography as a pious story of conversion. We know the pattern: the more violent the turn, the more complete the negation, the better for educational purposes. In her case, one should not use the term "conversion." She says she had never believed before that such a thing, a personal contact with God, was possible. But she says also that through all her conscious life her attitude had been Christian. I quote: "One can be obedient to God only if one receives orders. How did it happen that I received orders in my early youth when I professed atheism?" I quote again: "Religion, in so far as it is a source of consolation, is a hindrance to true faith: in this sense atheism is a purification. I have to be atheistic with the part of myself which is not for God. Among those men in whom the supernatural part has not been awakened, the atheists are right and the believers wrong."

The unique place of Simone Weil in the modern world is due to the perfect continuity of her thought. Unlike those who have to reject their past when they become Christians, she developed her ideas from before 1938 even further, introducing more order into them, thanks to the new light. Those ideas concerned society, history, Marxism, science.

Simone Weil was convinced that the Roman Catholic Church is the only legitimate guardian of the truth revealed by God incarnate. She strongly believed in the presence, real and not symbolic, of Christ in the Eucharist. She considered belonging to the Church a great happiness. Yet she refused herself that happiness. In her decision not to be baptized and to remain faithful to Christ but outside of His Church, we should distinguish two motives. First, her feeling of personal vocation, of obedience to God who wanted her to stay "at the gate" all her life together with all the neo-pagans. Second, her opposition to the punitive power of the Church directed against the heretics.

After the defeat of France she lived in Marseilles for a while, and in 1942 took a boat to Casablanca and from there to New York in the hope of joining the Committee of Free Frenchmen in London. Her intention was to serve the cause of France with arms in hand if possible. She arrived in London after a few months spent in New York. In 1943 she died in the sanitarium at

Ashford, apparently from malnutrition, as she limited her food to the level of rations allotted by the Germans to the French population.

Such was the life of Simone Weil. A life of deliberate *foolishness*. In one of her last letters to her family, commenting upon the role of fools in Shakespeare's plays, she says: "In this world only human beings reduced to the lowest degree of humiliation, much lower than mendicancy, not only without any social position but considered by everybody as deprived of elementary human dignity, of reason—only such beings have the possibility of telling the truth. All others lie." And on herself: "Ravings about my intelligence have for their aim the avoidance of the question: Does she tell the truth or not? My position of 'intelligent one' is like being labeled 'foolish,' as are fools. How much more I would prefer their label!"

Tactless in her writings and completely indifferent to fashions, she was able to go straight to the heart of the matter which preoccupies so many people today. I quote: "A man whose whole family died under tortue, and who had himself been tortured for a long time in a concentration camp. Or a sixteenth-century Indian, the sole survivor after the total extermination of his people. Such men if they had previously believed in the mercy of God would either believe it no more, or else they would conceive of it quite differently than before." Conceive of it how? the solution proposed by Simone Weil is not to the taste of those who worship the goddess of History; it may be heretical from the Thomist point of view as well.

A few words should be said about Simone Weil's road to Christianity. She was imbued with Greek philosophy. Her beloved master was Plato, read and reread in the original. One can notice a paradox of similarity between our times and the times of decadent Rome, when for many people Plato—that "Greek Moses," as he was sometimes called—served as a guide to the promised land of Christendom. Such was the love of Simone Weil for Greece that she looked at all Greek philosophy as eminently Christian—with one exception: Aristotle, in her

words "a bad tree which bore bad fruit." She rejected practically all Judaic tradition. She was never acquainted with Judaism and did not want to be, as she was unable to pardon the
ancient Hebrews their cruelties, for instance the ruthless extermination of all the inhabitants of Canaan. A strange leftist, she
categorically opposed any notion of progress in morality, that
widely spread view according to which crimes committed three
thousand years ago can be justified to a certain extent because
men at that time were "less developed." And she was making
early Christianity responsible for introducing, through the idea
of "divine pedagogy," a "poison," namely, the notion of historical progress in morality. She says: "The great mistake of the
Marxists and of the whole of the nineteenth century was to
think that by walking straight ahead one would rise into the
air." In her opinion, crimes of the remote past had to be judged
as severely as those committed today. That is why she had a
true horror of ancient Rome, a totalitarian state not much better
than the Hitlerian. She felt early Christians were right when
they gave Rome the name of the Apocalyptic Beast. Rome completely destroyed the old civilizations of Europe, probably
superior to the civilization of the Romans who were nothing but
barbarians, so skillful in slandering their victims that they falsified for centuries our image of pre-Roman Europe. Rome also
contaminated Christianity in its early formative stage. The principle, *anathema sit*, is of Roman origin. The only true Christian
civilization was emerging in the eleventh and twelfth centuries
in the countries of the Langue d'Oc, between the Mediterranean
and the Loire. After it was destroyed by the Frenchmen who
invaded that territory from the north and massacred the heretics
—the Albigensians—there has not been any Christian civilization anywhere.

Violent in her judgments and uncompromising, Simone Weil
was, at least by temperament, an Albigensian, a Cathar; this is
the key to her thought. She drew extreme conclusions from the
Platonic current in Christianity. Here we touch perhaps upon
hidden ties between her and Albert Camus. The first work by

Camus was his university dissertation on Saint Augustine. Camus, in my opinion, was also a Cathar, a pure one, and if he rejected God it was out of love for God because he was not able to justify Him. The last novel written by Camus, *The Fall*, is nothing else but a treatise on Grace—absent grace—though it is also a satire: the talkative hero, Jean-Baptiste Clamence, who reverses the words of Jesus and instead of "Judge not and ye shall not be judged" gives the advice "Judge, and ye shall not be judged," could be, I have reasons to suspect, Jean Paul Sartre.

The Albigensians were rooted in the old Manichaean tradition and, through it, akin to some sects of the Eastern Church of Bulgaria and of Russia. In their eyes God the monarch worshiped by the believers, could not be justified as he was a false God, a cruel Jehovah, an inferior demiurge, identical with the Prince of Darkness. Following the Manichaean tradition, Simone Weil used to say that when we pronounce the words of the Lord's Prayer: "Thy kingdom come" we pray for the end of the world as only then the power of the Prince of Darkness will be abolished. Yet she immediately added that "Thy will be done on earth" means our agreement to the existence of the world. All her philosophy is placed between these two poles.

There is a contradiction between our longing for the good, and the cold universe absolutely indifferent to any values, subject to the iron necessity of causes and effects. That contradiction has been solved by the rationalists and progressives of various kinds who placed the good in this world, in matter, and usually in the future. The philosophy of Hegel and of his followers crowned those attempts by inventing the idea of the good in movement, walking toward fuller and fuller accomplishment in history. Simone Weil, a staunch determinist (in this respect she was not unlike Spinoza), combatted such solutions as illegitimate. Her efforts were directed toward making the contradiction as acute as possible. Whoever tries to escape an inevitable contradiction by patching it up, is, she affirms, a coward. That is why she had been accused of having been too rigid and of having lacked a dialectical touch. Yet one can ask whether she was not more dialectical than many who practice the dialectical art by changing it into an art of compromises and who buy the unity of the opposites too cheaply.

Certainly her vision is not comforting. In the center we find the idea of the willful abdication of God, of the withdrawal of God from the universe. I quote: "God committed all phenomena without exception to the mechanism of the world." "The distance between the necessary and the good is the selfsame distance as that between the creature and the Creator." "Necessity is God's veil." "We must let the rational in the Cartesian sense, that is to say mechanical rule or necessity in its humanly demonstrable form, reside wherever we are able to imagine it, so that we might bring to light that which lies outside its range." "The absence of God is the most marvelous testimony of perfect love, and that is why pure necessity, necessity which is manifestly different from the good, is so beautiful." She allows neither the Providence of the traditional Christian preachers, nor the historical Providence of the progressive preachers. Does it mean that we are completely in the power of *la pesanteur*, gravity, that the cry of our heart is never answered? No. There is one exception from the universal determinism and that is Grace. "Contradiction" says Simone Weil, "is a lever of transcendence." "Impossibility is the door of the supernatural. We can only knock at it. Someone else opens it." God absent, God hidden, *Deus absconditus*, acts in the world through persuasion, through grace which pulls us out of *la pesanteur*, gravity, if we do not reject his gift. Those who believe that the contradiction between necessity and the good can be solved on any level other than that of mystery delude themselves. "We have to be in a desert. For he whom we must love is absent." "To love God through and across the destruction of Troy and Carthage, and without consolation. Love is not consolation, it is light."

For Simone Weil society is as subject to the rule of necessity as all the phenomena of the world. Yet if Nature is nothing but necessity and therefore innocent, below the level of good and evil, society is a domain where beings endowed with consciousness suffer under the heel of an ally and tenant of necessity, the Prince of Darkness. She says: "The Devil is collective (this is the God of Durkheim)." Her stand in politics is summed up in a metaphor she used often, taken from Plato. Plato compares society to a Great Beast. Every citizen has a relationship with that Beast, with the result that asked what is the good, everyone gives an answer in accordance with his function: for one the good consists in combing the hair of the Beast, for another in scratching its skin, for the third in cleaning its nails. In that way men lose the possibility of knowing the true good. In this Simone Weil saw the source of all absurdities and injustices. Man in the clutches of social determinism is no more than an unconscious worshiper of the Great Beast. She was against idealistic moral philosophy as it is a reflection of imperceptible pressures exerted upon individuals by a given social body. According to her, Protestantism also leads inevitably to conventional ethics reflecting national or class interests. As for Karl Marx, he was a seeker of pure truth; he wanted to liberate man from the visible and invisible pressures of group ethics by denouncing them and by showing how they operate. Because of that initial intention of Marx, Marxism is much more precious for the Christians than any idealistic philosophy. Yet Marx, in his desire for truth and justice, while trying to avoid one error fell into another which, argues Simone Weil, always happens if one rejects transcendence, the only foundation of the good accessible to man. Marx opposed class-dominated ethics with the new ethics of professional revolutionaries, also group ethics, and thus paved the way for a new form of domination by the Great Beast. This short aphorism sums up her views: "The whole of Marxism, in so far as it is true, is contained in that page of Plato on the Great Beast; and its refutation is there, too."

But Simone Weil did not turn her back on history and was a partisan of personal commitment. She denied that there is any "Marxist doctrine" and denounced dialectical materialism as a philosophical misunderstanding. In her view dialectical materialism simply does not exist, as the dialectical element and the materialist element, put together, burst the term asunder. By such a criticism she revealed the unpleasant secret known only to the inner circles of the Communist parties. On the contrary, class struggle, filling thousands of years of history, was for her the most palpable reality. Meditations on social determinism led her to certain conclusions as to the main problem of technical civilization. That problem looks as follows. Primitive man was oppressed by the hostile forces of Nature. Gradually he won his freedom in constant struggle against it, he harnessed the powers of water, of fire, of electricity and put them to his use. Yet he could not accomplish that without introducing a division of labor and an organization of production. Very primitive societies are egalitarian, they live in the state of "primitive communism." Members of such communities are not oppressed by other members, fear is located outside as the community is menaced by wild animals, natural cataclysms, and sometimes other human groups. As soon as the efforts of man in his struggle with his surroundings become more productive, the community differentiates into those who order and those who obey. Oppression of man by man grows proportionally to the increase of his realm of action; it seems to be its necessary price. Facing Nature, the member of a technical civilization holds the position of a god, but he is a slave of society. The ultimate sanction of any domination of man by man is the punishment of death—either by the sword, the gun, or from starvation. Collective humanity emancipated itself. "But this collective humanity has itself taken on with respect to the individual the oppressive function formerly exercised by Nature."

Today Simone Weil could have backed her social analyses with many new examples; it is often being said that underdeveloped countries can industrialize themselves only at the price of accepting totalitarian systems. China, for instance, would have provided her with much material for reflection.

The basic social and political issue of the twentieth century is: "Can this emancipation, won by society, be transferred to the individual?" Simone Weil was pessimistic. The end of the struggle between those who obey and those who give orders is not in sight, she argued. The dominating groups do not relinquish their privileges unless forced to. Yet in spite of the upheavals of the masses, the very organization of production soon engenders new masters and the struggle continues under new banners and new names. Heraclitus was right: struggle is the mother of gods and men.

This does not mean we can dismiss history, seeing it as eternal recurrence, and shrug at its spectacle. Willing or not, we are committed. We should throw our act into the balance by siding with the oppressed and by diminishing as much as possible the oppressive power of those who give orders. Without expecting too much: *hubris*, lack of measure, is punished by Fate, inherent in the laws of iron necessity.

The importance of Simone Weil should be, I feel, assessed in the perspective of our common shortcomings. We do not like to think to the bitter end. We escape consequences in advance. Through the rigor exemplified by her life and her writing (classical, dry, concise), she is able to provoke a salutary shame. Why does she fascinate so many intellectuals today? Such is my hypothesis: If this is a theological age, it has a marked bias for Manichaeism. Modern literature testifies to a sort of rage directed against the world which no longer seems the work of a wise clockmaker. The humor of that literature (and think of Beckett, Ionesco, Genet), if it is humor at all, is a sneer, a *ricanement*, thrown in the face of the universe. Professor Michael Polany has recently advanced the thesis that the most characteristic feature of the last decades has been not a moral laxity but a moral frenzy exploding in the literature of the absurd as well as in revolutionary movements. Political assassination has been practiced in the name of man's victory over the brutal order of Nature. Yet the belief in the magic blessings of History is being undermined by the very outcome of that belief: industrialization. It is more and more obvious (in the countries of Eastern Europe as well) that refrigerators and television sets, or even rockets sent to the moon, do not change man into God. Old conflicts between human groups have been abolished but are replaced by new ones, perhaps more acute.

I translated the selected works of Simone Weil into Polish in 1958 not because I pretended to be a "Weilian." I wrote frankly in the preface that I consider myself a Caliban, too fleshy, too heavy, to take on the feathers of an Ariel. Simone Weil was an Ariel. My aim was utilitarian, in accordance, I am sure, with her wishes as to the disposition of her works. A few years ago I spent many afternoons in her family's apartment overlooking the Luxembourg Gardens—at her table covered with ink stains from her pen—talking to her mother, a wonderful woman in her eighties. Albert Camus took refuge in that apartment the day he received the Nobel prize and was hunted by photographers and journalists. My aim, as I say, was utilitarian. I resented the division of Poland into two camps: the clerical and the anticlerical, nationalistic Catholic and Marxist—I exclude of course the *aparatchiki*, bureaucrats just catching every wind from Moscow. I suspect unorthodox Marxists (I use that word for lack of a better one) and nonnationalistic Catholics have very much in common, at least common interests. Simone Weil attacked the type of religion that is only a social or national conformism. She also attacked the shallowness of the so-called progressives. Perhaps my intention, when preparing a Polish selection of her works, was malicious. But if a theological fight is going on—as it is in Poland, especially in high schools and universities—then every weapon is good to make adversaries goggle-eyed and to show that the choice between Christianity as represented by a national religion and the official Marxist ideology is not the only choice left to us today.

In the present world torn asunder by a much more serious religious crisis than appearances would permit us to guess, Catholic writers are often rejected by people who are aware of their own misery as seekers and who have a reflex of defense when they meet proud possessors of the truth. The works of Simone Weil are read by Catholics and Protestants, atheists and agnostics. She has instilled a new leaven into the life of believers and unbelievers by proving that one should not be deluded by existing divergences of opinion and that many a Christian is a pagan, many a pagan a Christian in his heart. Perhaps she lived exactly for that. Her intelligence, the precision of her style were nothing but a very high degree of attention given to the sufferings of mankind. And, as she says, "Absolutely unmixed attention is prayer."

1960

8

Shestov,
or the Purity of Despair

There was once a young woman by the name of Sorana Gurian. She emigrated to Paris in the 1950s from her native Rumania after adventures about which, she felt, the less said the better. In Paris her life of poverty as a refugee did not particularly disturb her. In fact of the group of students, young writers, and artists among whom she lived she was the first to make her way; a good publisher, Juillard, accepted her first and second novels. Then, all of a sudden (how could it have happened if not all of a sudden?), she discovered that she had breast cancer. An operation followed, then another. Although cases of recovery are rare, they do occur; after the second operation, her doctors were optimistic. Whether Sorana had complete confidence in them I do not know. In any case, one battle was won. Being a writer she had to write about what concerned her most, and she wrote a book about her illness—a battle report on her fight against despair. That book, *Le Récit d'un combat*, was published by Juillard in 1956. Her respite, however, lasted only a year or two.

I met Sorana shortly before her death; through mutual friends she had expressed a wish to meet me. When I visited her in her small student hotel on the Left Bank, she was spending most of the day in bed with a fever. We talked about many things, including writers. She showed me the books on her night table; they were books by Shestov in French translation. She spoke of them with that reticent ardor we reserve for what is most precious to us. "Read Shestov, Miłosz, read Shestov."

The name of Sorana Gurian will not be preserved in the chronicles of humanity. If I tell about her, it is because I cannot imagine a more proper introduction to a few reflections on Shestov.

Lev Shestov (pen name of Lev Isaakovich Schwarzman) was born in Kiev in 1866. Thus by the turn of the century he was already a mature man, the author of a doctoral dissertation in law, which failed to bring him the degree because it was considered too influenced by revolutionary Marxism, and of a book of literary criticism (on Shakespeare and his critic Brandes). His book *Dobro v uchenii grafa Tolstogo i Nitsshe— filosofia i propoved'* (*The Good in the Teaching of Count Tolstoy and Nietzshe: Philosophy and Preaching*) was published in 1900. In the same year he formed a lifelong friendship with Nikolai Berdyaev, one that was warm in spite of basic disagreements that often ended in their shouting angrily at one another. His friendship with Berdyaev and Sergei Bulgakov places Shestov in the ranks of those Russian thinkers who, about 1900, came to discover a metaphysical enigma behind the social problems which had preoccupied them in their early youth. Shestov's philosophy took shape in several books of essays and notes written before 1917. His collected works (1911) can be found in the larger American libraries. The fate of his writings in Russia after the revolution, and whether their meaning has been lost for new generations, is hard to assess. In any case Shestov expressed himself most fully, it seems to me, in his books published abroad after he left Russia in 1919 and settled in Paris, where he lived till his death in 1938. These are *Vlast' klyuchei: Potestas Clavium* (*The Power of the Keys*), 1923 and *Na vesakh Iova* (*In Job's Balances*), 1929; those volumes which first appeared in translation, *Kierkegaard et la philosophie existentielle*, 1938 (Russian edition, 1939), and *Athènes et Jérusalem: un essai de philosophie religieuse*, 1938 (Russian edition, 1951); lastly those posthumously published in book form, *Tol'ko veroi: Sola Fide* (*By Faith Alone*), 1966, and *Umozreniïe*

*i otkroveniïe: religioznaya filosofia Vladimira Solovyova i
drugïie stat'i (Speculation and Revelation: The Religious Philosophy of Vladimir Solovyov and Other Essays),* 1964.[1]

Shestov has been translated into many languages. Yet in his
lifetime he never attained the fame surrounding the name of his
friend Berdyaev. He remained a writer for the few, and if by disciples we mean those who "sit at the feet of the master," he had
only one, the French poet Benjamine Fondane, a Rumanian Jew
later killed by the Nazis. But Shestov was an active force in
European letters, and his influence reached deeper than one
might surmise from the number of copies of his works sold.
Though the quarrel about existentialism that raged in Paris after
1945 seems to us today somewhat stale, it had serious consequences. In *The Myth of Sisyphus*—a youthful and not very
good book, but most typical of that period—Albert Camus considers Kierkegaard, Shestov, Heidegger, Jaspers, and Husserl to
be the philosophers most important to the new "man of the
absurd." For the moment it is enough to say that though Shestov has often been compared with Kierkegaard he discovered
the Danish author only late in his life, and that his close personal friendship with Husserl consisted of philosophical opposition—which did not prevent him from calling Husserl his second master after Dostoevsky.

I am not going to pretend that I have "read through" Shestov.
If one is asked whether one has read Pascal, the answer should
always be in the negative, no matter how many times one has
looked at his pages. In the case of Shestov, however, there are

[1]The English-language reader has at his disposal *A Shestov Anthology*,
edited with an introduction by Bernard Martin (Ohio University Press, 1970).
Also available are the following translations of books by Shestov: *The Good
in the Teaching of Tolstoy and Nietzsche: Philosophy and Preaching*; Part I of
Dostoevsky, Tolstoy, and Nietzsche, trans. Bernard Martin (1969); *Dostoevsky and Nietzsche: The Philosophy of Tragedy*, Part II of *Dostoevsky, Tolstoy, and Nietzsche*, trans. Spencer Roberts (1969); *Potestas Clavium*, trans.
Bernard Martin (1968); *Kierkegaard and Existential Philosophy*, trans. Eleanor Hewitt (1970); *Athens and Jerusalem*, trans. Bernard Martin (1966). All
these were published by Ohio University Press. *Chekhov and Other Essays*
(1966), was published by the University of Michigan Press.

obstacles other than density. His *oeuvre* is, as Camus defined it, of "admirable monotony." Shestov hammers at one theme again and again, and after a while we learn that it will emerge inevitably in every essay; we also know that when the theme emerges, his voice will change in tone and sustain with its usual sarcasm the inevitable conclusion. His voice when he enters an argument is that of a priest angry at the sight of holy vessels being desecrated. Convinced that he will not be applauded because his message seems bizarre to his contemporaries, he does nothing to diminish our resistance, which is provoked most of all by what Lévy-Brühl, in a polemic with him, called "hogging the covers." Shestov was often reproached for finding in Shakespeare, in Dostoevsky, and in Nietzsche much that is not there at all, and for too freely interpreting the opinions of his antagonists (numerous, for these included practically all the philosophers of the past three thousand years). He dismissed the reproach with a laugh: he was not such a genius, he would say, that he could create so many geniuses anew. Yet the reproach is not without validity.

He knew he was not understood; probably he did not want to be overly clear. But the difficulty in assimilating him is not caused by any deviousness on his part or by any levels of ironic meaning or aphoristic conciseness. He always develops a logical argument in well-balanced sentences which, especially in their original Russian, captivate the reader with their scornful vigor. Shestov is probably one of the most readable philosophic essayists of the century. The trouble lies in his opposition to those who separate the propositions of a given man from his personal tragedy—to those who, for instance, refuse to speak of Kierkegaard's sexual impotence or of Nietzsche's incurable disease. My guess is that Shestov, too, had his own drama, that of lacking the talent to become a poet, to approach the mystery of existence more directly than through mere concepts. And although he does not mix genres, or write "poetic prose," one feels that at a given moment he falls silent and leaves much unsaid because the border of the communicable has been crossed. That is why in self-defense he sometimes quotes Pascal: *"Qu'on ne nous reproche donc plus le manque de clarté, puisque nous en faisons profession"*—"Then let people not blame us any more for our lack of clarity, since we practice this deliberately."

To associate Shestov with a transitory phase of existentialism would be to diminish his stature. Few writers of any time could match his daring, even insolence, in raising the naughty child's questions which have always had the power to throw philosophers into a panic. For that reason such questions have been wrapped in highly professional technical terms and, once placed in a syntactic cocoon, neutralized. The social function of language is, after all, both to protect and to reveal. Perhaps Shestov exemplifies the advantages of Russia's "cultural time lag": no centuries of scholastic theology and philosophy in the past, no university philosophy to speak of—but on the other hand a lot of people philosophizing, and passionately at that, on their own. Shestov was a well-educated man, but he lacked the polite indoctrination one received at Western European universities; he simply did not care whether what he was saying about Plato or Spinoza was against the rules of the game—that is, indecent. It was precisely because of this freedom that his thought was a gift to people who found themselves in desperate situations and knew that syntactic cocoons were of no use any more. Sorana Gurian after all was an agnostic, largely beyond the pale of religious tradition, and not a philosopher in the technical sense of the word. Whom could she read? Thomas Aquinas? Hegel? Treatises in mathematical logic? Or, better still, should she have tried solving crossword puzzles?

What does a creature that calls itself "I" want for itself? It wants to be. Quite a demand! Early in life it begins to discover, however, that its demand is perhaps excessive. Objects behave in their own impassive manner and show a lack of concern for the central importance of "I." A wall is hard and hurts you if you bump against it, fire burns your fingers; if you drop a glass on the floor, it breaks into pieces. This is the preamble to a long education the gist of which is a respect for the durability of "the

outside" as contrasted with the frailty of the "I." Moreover,
what is "inside" gradually loses its unique character. Its urges,
desires, passions appear to be no different from those of other
members of the species. Without exaggeration we may say that
the "I" also loses its body: in a mirror it sees a being that is born,
grows up, is subject to the destructive action of time, and must
die. If a doctor tells you that you are dying of a certain disease,
then you are just another case; that is, chance is a statistical
regularity. It is just your bad luck that you are among such-and-
such a number of cases occurring every year.

The "I" has to recognize that it is confronted with a world
that follows its own laws, a world whose name is Necessity.
This, according to Shestov, is precisely what lies at the foundations of traditional philosophy—first Greek, then every philosophy faithful to the Greeks. Only the necessary, the general,
and the always valid will merit investigation and reflection. The
contingent, the particular, and the momentary are spoilers of
unity—a teaching that dates back to Anaximander. Later Greek
thinkers exalted the all-embracing Oneness and represented
individual existence as a crack in the perfectly smooth surface of
the One, a flaw for which the individual had to pay with his
death. From a Shestovian perspective, Greek science and
morality both follow the same path. The sum of the angles in a
triangle equals two right angles; the general, eternal truth reigns
high above breeding and dying mortals just as eternal good does
not change whether or not there is a living man to aspire to it.

The "I" is invaded by Necessity from the inside as well, but
always feels it as an alien force. Nevertheless the "I" must accept
the inevitable order of the world. The wisdom of centuries consists precisely in advising acquiescence and resignation. In
simple language, "Grin and bear it"; in more sophisticated language, *"Fata volentem ducunt, nolentem trahunt"*—"The Fates
lead the willing man, they drag the unwilling." Stoicism, whose
very essence is to curb the shameful pretense of transitory
individual existence in the name of universal order (or, if you
prefer, Nature), was the final word of Graeco-Roman civiliza-

tion. But, says Shestov, stoicism has survived under many disguises and is still with us.

Shestov simply refuses to play this game of chess, however, and overturns the table with a kick. For why should the "I" accept "wisdom," which obviously violates its most intense desire? Why respect "the immutable laws"? Whence comes the certainty that what is presumably impossible is really impossible? And is a philosophy preoccupied with *ho anthropos*, with man in general, of any use to *tis anthropos*, a certain man who lives only once in space and time? Isn't there something horrible in Spinoza's advice to philosophers? *"Non ridere, non lugere, neque detestari, sed intelligere"*—"Not to laugh, not to weep, not to hate, but to understand"? On the contrary, says Shestov, a man should shout, scream, laugh, jeer, protest. In the Bible, Job wailed and screamed to the indignation of his wise friends.

Shestov (and he was not the first, for Rozanov had already made the same suggestion) believed that Dostoevsky's most significant work was *Notes from Underground*, and considered the major novels that followed as commentaries and attempts to solve the riddle set forth in the *Notes*. He expressed this opinion in an essay written in 1921 for the hundredth anniversary of Dostoevsky's birth. Shestov believed that the true critique of pure reason was not Kant's achievement but Dostoevsky's, and in the *Notes* specifically. He admired Dostoevsky's philosophical genius without reservation—and accepted as true the disparaging rumors about his personal life, rumors spread mostly by Strakhov. It also suited his purpose to see such characters as the Underground Man, Svidrigailov, Ippolit in *The Idiot*, Stavrogin, and Ivan Karamazov as Dostoevsky's true spokesmen, and even to a large extent autobiographical portraits; and to dismiss Father Zosima and Alyosha as *lubok* (cheap block prints). To Shestov peace of mind was suspect, for the earth we live on does not predispose us to it. He loved only those who, like Pascal, *"cherchent en gémissant"*—who "seek while moaning." This approach to Dostoevsky should appeal to those critics who believe the *Notes* reveal much that this conservative publicist and orthodox Christian tried to stifle in himself. There is, however, one basic difference between Shestov and those who think of Dostoevsky as a humanist, often mentioning the vision of earthly paradise (modeled on Claude Lorrain's painting "Acis and Galatea" in the Dresden gallery) in his later writings. The vision, they believe, is proof that a young Fourieriest was still alive in the conservative author of *The Diary of a Writer*. Shestov does not agree with this "humanistic" interpretation.

The narrator of Dostoevsky's *Dream of a Ridiculous Man* visits in his sleep, in a state of anamnesis perhaps, a humanity living in the Golden Age before the loss of innocence and happiness. Now for Shestov the story of the Garden of Eden, because of its unfathomable depth and complexity, spoke for the superhuman origin of the whole Scripture. Explanations of the Fall advanced by both theologians and the popular imagination seemed childish to him when compared with chapters 2 and 3 of Genesis. Dostoevsky's intuition enabled him, Shestov felt, to guess at a *metaphysical state* of man before the Fall, not just to visualize a happy Rousseauistic society: "their knowledge was higher and deeper than the knowledge we derive from our science; for our science seeks to explain what life is and strives to understand it in order to *teach others how to live* [the italics are mine], while they knew how to live without science. I understood that, but I couldn't understand their knowledge. They pointed out the trees to me, and I could not understand the intense love with which they looked on them; it was as though they were talking with beings like themselves. And, you know, I don't think I am exaggerating in saying that they talked with them!" (David Magarshack's translation). Shestov doesn't hesitate to speak of man before he tasted from the tree of knowledge of good and evil as possessing omniscience and absolute freedom. What, then, was the Fall? A choice of an inferior faculty with its passion for a *distinguo* and for general ideas, with pairs of opposites: good, evil; true, untrue; possible, impossible. Man renounced faith in order to gain knowledge. Shestov names his enemy: Reason. He even says the fruits of the forbidden tree could just as well be called synthetic judgments a priori. And if Dostoevsky's *Notes from Underground* occupies a central place for Shestov, it is because the hero screams "No!" to "two and two make four" and wants "something else."

According to Shestov, Hellenistic civilization could accept neither the God of the Old Testament nor Christ of the New Testament. It had to adapt the scandalous particularity of a personal God to its general ideas, shaped as they were through speculation. "The good is God," "Love is God"—to such equations the Hellenized citizens of the Roman Empire could give assent. But the equations are nonsensicial, says Shestov, for here the abstract is put before the living. He reminds us with relish that Saint Augustine hated the Stoics as much as Dostoevsky hated the liberals; both the Stoics and the liberals recommended a morality of self-sufficing Reason.

The gnosis, when it absorbed Christian elements, was nothing more than an attempt to trim the Scriptures of their "capriciousness," of their antigenerality equated with untruth. The heresy of Marcion in the beginning of the second century, inspired by the gnosis, altogether rejects the Jehovah of the Old Testament as an evil demiurge because his *incomprehensible* behavior seems offensive to an enlightened mind. But similar Hellenization of the Scriptures continued throughout the Middle Ages. Where the Scholastics affirmed that God created the universe by making use of some preexisting laws of Nature (two and two make four, the principle of contradiction, and so on, as eternal principles) they in fact put Necessity (universal laws) above the God of Genesis. They paved the way for the modern attitude that calls religion before the tribunal of Reason. The modern mind, Shestov affirms, is completely under the spell of formulas found in their most perfect form in two representative thinkers: Spinoza and Hegel. The latter said: "In philosophy religion receives its justification. Thinking is the absolute judge before whom the content of religion must justify and explain itself." And the reader who does not share Shestov's belief in the Garden of Eden should be aware of the basic issue; by voicing his disbelief he takes the side of knowledge against faith.

Shestov opposed Jerusalem to Athens in a most radical, uncompromising manner. Those names stood for faith versus reason, revelation versus speculation, the particular versus the general, a cry *de profundis* versus the ethics of, as Ivan Karamazov said, "accursed good and evil." Shestov liked to quote Tertullian: *"Crucifixus est Dei filius; non pudet, quia pudendum est. Et mortuus est Dei filius; prorsus credibile est, quia ineptum est. Et sepultus resurrexit; certum est quia impossibile est"*—"The Son of God was crucified; this does not bring shame, because it is shameful. And the Son of God died; again this is believable because it is absurd. And having been buried, he rose from the dead; this is certain because it is impossible." Contemporaries of Tertullian, perhaps no less than their remote descendants of the twentieth century, disliked everything in the New Testament which was in their eyes *"pudendum," "ineptum," "impossibile."* Shestov's men were Pascal because he had faith in the God of Abraham, Isaac, and Jacob, and not in the God of philosophers; Martin Luther because he relied on "faith alone" and because he used to say that blasphemy is sometimes dearer to God than praise; Nietzsche because he saw through the speculative nature of ethics devised to supplant the killed God; and, finally, Kierkegaard.

Shestov's articles attacking Edmund Husserl in *La Revue Philosophique* had an unexpected effect: a meeting of the two men, at the philosophical congress in Amsterdam in 1928, which developed into a friendship. They respected each other, always stressing that they stood at opposite poles in their concept of philosophy. It was Husserl who literally forced Shestov to read a thinker with whom he himself disagreed—Kierkegaard. Shestov thus found out that he was less a maverick than he had thought. It must have been quite a surprise for him to learn that Kierkegaard saw the source of philosophy not in amazement, as did the ancients, but in despair, and that he too opposed Job to Plato and Hegel. Those were Shestov's own most cherished thoughts. A remark by Kierkegaard testifying to his stake in the Absurd, "Human cowardice cannot bear what insanity and death have to tell us," could have been made by Shestov as well. From Kierkegaard he took the name applicable *ex post* to his own meditation, "existential philosophy" as distinguished from speculative philosophy.

No wonder Camus in *The Myth of Sisyphus,* when invoking the protagonists of paradox and the Absurd, mentioned Kierkegaard and Shestov first of all. The similarities, however, between the Parisian existentialism of the 1940s and 1950s on the one hand, and Kierkegaard and Shestov on the other, are superficial. Camus, it is true, was perhaps no less fascinated than was Shestov with Dostoevsky's *Notes from Underground,* even to the extent that his last book, *The Fall,* is essentially the *Notes* rewritten. Yet Shestov, convinced as he was that the Underground Man deserved salvation because of his longing after "something else," would not leave him a victim of his desperate, crazy, solitary ego. Certainly he was skeptical of the alternatives proposed by Dostoevsky—the peasant pilgrim Makar Dolgoruky, Father Zosima, Alyosha. Nevertheless, he was a man of the Scriptures. He would probably have gladly accepted the epithet Plato often hurled at his opponents in a dispute— *Misologos,* a hater of reason—but only to stress the absurd of the human condition, which is masked by Reason. There was a way out: "The good is not God. We must seek that which is higher than the good. We must seek God." Which means that the despair that seizes us when we are faced with the Absurd leads us beyond good and evil to an act of faith. There is nothing impossible for God and for those who truly believe in him. An absurd affirmation, for who ever saw a mountain moved by prayer? But do we have a choice? The fruits of the tree of knowledge bring only death. It should be noted that Shestov was not a preacher; he tried only to present a dilemma in all its acuteness. Most definitely he was neither a moralist nor a theologian.

For Camus, despair was not a point of departure but a perma-

nent state of existence not excluding happiness. He wanted us to
believe that even Sisyphus could be happy. He was drawn thus
by the French moralistic tradition toward some sort of accom-
modation with a world deprived of meaning. Perhaps it sounds
strange, but his atheist existentialism is less radical than Shestov's precisely because of that moralistic (Greek, after all) bent.
To Camus Shestov's God seemed capricious, wicked, immoral,
and as such was rejected. "His [God's] proof is in his inhuman-
ity." For the humanist this was unacceptable. In *The Myth of
Sisyphus* Camus defines the difference between his Parisian
contemporaries' position and that of Shestov: "For Shestov reason is useless, but there is something beyond reason. For the
absurd mind, reason is useless and there is nothing beyond
reason." Camus preserved that complete bereavement till the
end. In *The Fall*, his last book, the narrator and hero settles
down in a bar near the port of Amsterdam in an underground
private hell where there is no aspiration and no promise.

Either/or. Shestov's categorical opposition between faith and
reason reminds one of the theory of two parallel truths, elaborated in the thirteenth century; but, in fact, he rejects the truth
of reason completely;[2] the world of the "laws of Nature" is, as
he says, a nightmare from which we should waken. His criticism
is directed primarily against those who eschew the fundamental
"either/or" and who, even though they pronounce themselves
for faith, imperceptibly move to the side of their adversary.
Thus the case of all devisers of theodicy: since the world created
by God is not a very happy place, something should be done to
lift from God the responsibility for evil—and thence the
attempts at a "justification of God" accomplished by means of
human reason. This aspect of Shestov's struggle is well represented by his essays on Vladimir Solovyov and Nikolai Berdyaev in his posthumous volume *Umozreniie i otkroveniie*. Let
us concede that his severe, unornamented style makes Solovyov
sound by contrast verbose if not wooly, and Berdyaev, fre-

[2]In the Eastern Church this radical antirationalism goes back to St. Maxi-
mus the Confessor (580-662).

quently rhetorical. But Shestov also argues well. Without detracting from Solovyov's imposing stature, he accuses him of nothing less than an unintentional falsity. He "placed on his banner a philosophy of Revelation, but practiced, like Hegel, a dialectical philosophy." "The idea of a 'philosophy of Revelation' seduced Solovyov as if it were itself the Revelation and, without his noticing it, took the place of the Revelation, just as for Hegel the rational took the place of the real." What happened to Solovyov had happened before; when a mind introduces rational order into the Revelation which defies order ("For the wisdom of this world is foolishness with God," I Corinthians 3:19) it ends by taking refuge in an ethical system, in a moral ideal, to be realized of course in some future kingdom of God on earth. Solovyov, contends Shestov, came gradually to conclusions quite similar to the moralistic and antimetaphysical teachings of Tolstoy—then woke up and took fright. Solovyov's last book, *Three Conversations* (1900), is a complete reversal. It is directed at Tolstoy, but perhaps the author really settles accounts with himself. After all, its focus is the story of the Antichrist who comes disguised as a lover of mankind. Such a change in Solovyov's orientation was to Shestov's liking. The pivotal points in his interpretation of the Scriptures were the Fall and the renewal of man by his partaking from the tree of life as promised in the Apocalypse. The last event was to occur, however, in a metaphysical rather than purely historical dimension. We cannot be more specific, because we simply do not know what Shestov meant in his references to the Revelation of St. John; we have to respect his silence. In any case, Solovyov was guilty in Shestov's opinion of an inadmissable attachment to ethics at the expense of the sacred and of bowing before the tribunal of reason, as had Spinoza and the German idealistic philosophy.

The essay on Berdyaev is most revealing. The exaltation of human freedom gave to Berdyaev's writings their tone of unbridled optimism; mankind called to collaborate with God would attain "Godmanhood" ("Bogochelovechestvo"); in this respect he may be counted among many of Teilhard de Chardin's predecessors. But for Berdyaev, the belief that free action can transform the face of the earth had its roots in the eschatological and apocalyptic orientation of the Russian nineteenth-century mind, continuing the line of Slavic messianism. When in the last pages of *The Russian Idea* Berdyaev praises the Polish messianic philosopher August Cieszkowski and his voluminous work *Our Father*, he confirms this estimation. It is precisely this lofty notion of human freedom and man's unlimited possibilities in the pursuit of good that Shestov attacks. He suspects that for his friend freedom is an expedient means of explaining away the horror of existence. Evil in the world results from man's freedom, man could only have been created free, thus Berdyaev does not go beyond the Christian doctrine. Yes, but his teachers are German mystics—Meister Eckhart, Jakob Boehme, Angelus Silesius—who affirm that a sort of dialectical movement *preceded* the creation of the universe. The ideas of these mystics were to inspire the whole of German idealistic philosophy which Shestov belabors now in the person of its precursors. According to the German mystics man's freedom—meaning the possibility of evil, which has existed since before the beginning of time—is due to the dark force of the preexisting Naught that limits the power of God. Indeed, above God the mystics put *Deitas*, an eternal law. But this is the gnosis!, exlaims Shestov. In striving to equate the good with God, Berdyaev made God depend on man in his struggle against a dark preexisting nothingness to such an extent that man, absolutely necessary to God, began to play the central role. Why should "Godmanhood" succeed where God fails? Why not transform "Godmanhood" into "Mangodhood"? And that, Shestov feels, is what Berdyaev does in fact. His philosophy of freedom, presumably an existential philosophy, deals with the illusory, exaggerated freedom of the Pelagians and is not existential; the latter is a philosophy *de profundis* recognizable by its refusal to explain away suffering and death, no matter which "dynamic process" is supposed to achieve the victory of the good. When Ivan

Karamazov says that the tear of a child outweighs all the possible harmony of the universe, he cannot and should not be answered with historical dynamism.

Perhaps Shestov in his polemic with Berdyaev "pulls the blanket to his side" a little. Yet if we compare his essay on Berdyaev with his essay on Husserl (his last, written in 1938 to honor the memory of his friend who had just died) we must conclude that, contrary to appearances, Shestov probably had more in common with Husserl than with Berdyaev, even though in the Great "either/or" Husserl opted for science. Husserl thus intended Reason to be an instrument for discovering absolute and eternal truths untouched by relativism, truths valid for gods, angels, and men, on earth and in the universe. By "more in common" I mean the sternness proper to both men. Shestov admired Husserl precisely because he was a man ready to accept a verdict of reason even if it provided him with no comfort at all. If he himself chose the Scriptures, it was not because they brought him comfort but because he believed them to contain the truth.

Future studies of Shestov, it seems to me, should not devote more than a very limited space to the French intellectual scene, even though Shestov lived in Paris for nearly two decades. There is one exception, however. The *oeuvre* of Simone Weil throws some of his propositions into relief, and conversely Shestov enables us to see her basic premises better. Not that they knew each other. Perhaps Shestov used to pass her in the Latin Quarter when she was a student at the Ecole Normale Supérieure. Her colleague there was Simone de Beauvoir, and the fate of these two women provides us with an awe-inspiring lesson. Simone de Beauvoir was responsive to the intellectual and literary fashions of the day and became a famous but not first-rate writer, one of those who make a lot of splash in a lifetime but are soon forgotten. Simone Weil—antimodern, aloof, quixotic, a searcher for the ultimate truth—died in London in 1943 at the age of thirty-four completely unknown, but her notes and maxims published posthumously secured her a permanent place in the history of religious ideas. My mention here of Simone de Beauvoir is not totally arbitrary. Immediately after World War II she, with Sartre and Camus, was promoting the "existentialist movement." Yet the very problems that concerned Shestov remained outside her sphere of interest. To apply any epithet to Weil's philosophy would be futile; that she, as it seems, read some Shestov is not material either. What matters is a similarity of temperament in the two thinkers, expressing itself in their classicism and nakedness of style, and in general in the same attitude toward time. Shestov wrangled not only with Spinoza as if he were his contemporary, but also with Plato, and saw the last three thousand years practically as one short moment. Simone Weil's notebooks are full of quotations in the original Greek, of mathematical equations, and of references to Hinduism, Zen, and Taoism—which did not hinder her in her passionate twentieth-century commitments. But there is something else that authorizes us to speak of Shestov and Simone Weil in one breath. It is the central theme of their thought, the phenomenon of suffering and death. These are her words: "A Discourse of Ivan in the Karamazovs. Even if that immense factory brings the most extraordinary marvels and costs only a single tear of a single child, I refuse. I adhere completely to that feeling. No matter which motive people might offer me, nothing could compensate for the tear of a child and nothing will make me accept that tear. Nothing, absolutely nothing conceivable by intelligence. One thing only, intelligible only to supernatural love: God willed it thus. And for that reason I would also accept a world of pure evil, the consequences of which would be as bad as one tear of a child."[3] Shestov could have written these lines, but they would have had a different meaning to him.

Although Simone Weil was Jewish, she was raised in an areligious family and was unacquainted with Judaism. In Kiev Shestov absorbed Jewish religious literature, including legends and folklore, at an early age. Simone Weil's sacred book was Homer's *Iliad;* her thought was inspired by Plato, later by the

[3]*Cahiers,* III, 31-21.

New Testament. She was as thoroughly Hellenized as it was possible for pupils of the French *lycées* in the early decades of our century to be. And, had Shestov lived to read her work, he would have quoted her as an example confirming his thesis about the irreconcilable feud between Athens and Jerusalem. With the exception of the Book of Job, Simone Weil did not venerate the Old Testament and spoke harshly of the God of the Old Testament and of the Jews, reproaching them for cruelty and superstition. She was totally on the side of Athens; besides, she believed Greek and Hindu metaphysics to be identical in essential points. Her God was Greek. She even hinted at the possibility of Dionysus having been an incarnation of God, before Christ. And the gnostic penchants typical of early Hellenized Christians can be easily detected in her work. For instance, in her historical essays the indignation with which she describes the French crusade against the Albigensians and the conquest of the land speaking Oc, meaning Occitan (now the south of France), is due not only to her sympathy for the massacred and the oppressed but in large part to her identification with Albigensian Christianity related through Manichaeism to the gnosis of Marcion.

Future investigation—and I do not doubt that there will be one—should be centered in the first place on Shestov's and Weil's concept of Necessity as well as on different treatments of the relationship between Oneness and the particular. For Shestov, universal Necessity was a scandal. He felt that its horror was best described by Dostoevsky in *The Idiot* where there is talk of Holbein's painting of the *Deposition from the Cross*: "Looking at that picture, you get the impression of Nature as some enormous, implacable, and dumb beast, or, to put it more correctly, much more correctly, though it might seem strange, as some huge engine of the latest design which has senselessly seized, cut to pieces, and swallowed up—impassively and unfeelingly—a great and priceless Being, a Being worth the whole of Nature and all its laws, worth the entire earth, which was perhaps created solely for the coming of that Being! The picture seems to give expression to the idea of a cold, insolent, and senselessly eternal power to which everything is subordinated." Shestov wanted man to oppose that beast with an unflinching "No."

Simone Weil's attitude, on the other hand, was similar to the wonder a mathematician feels when confronted with the complexities of numbers. A few quotations will suffice to show this: "Necessity is a veil of God"; "God entrusted all phenomena without exception to the mechanism of the world"; "In God not only is there an analogy of all human virtues, but also an analogy of obedience. In this world he gives necessity free play"; "The distance between necessity and the good is the very distance between the Creation and the Creator"; "The distance between necessity and the good. To contemplate it without end. A great discovery made by the Greeks. Undoubtedly the fall of Troy taught them this"; "God can be present in Creation only in the form of absence"; "God is not omnipotent because he is the Creator. Creation is an abdication. But he is omnipotent in the sense that his abdication is voluntary; he knows its effects and wants them."[4]

For Simone Weil the "terrifying beauty" of the world was mysteriously linked to mathematical Necessity. Yet she would not disagree with Shestov when he denounced "the beast," since she believed that the determinism of Nature is the domain of the Prince of this World acting on God's authority. But as a philosopher (also a college professor of philosophy) whose intellectual antecedents were essentially Greek, she would not turn against Reason. Applying ideas of reduction, she conceded as much as possible to the immutable structure of the world. The power of God to act through Grace is, by his own will, infinitely small but sufficient to save man. It is the mustard seed of the Gospel (or the silence of Christ in the "Legend of the Grand Inquisitor"). It makes it possible for us to accept an existence which, when looked at rationally and soberly, is unbearable. Shestov fumed against Greek wisdom which led to stoical resig-

[4]All quotations are from *La Pesanteur et la grâce.*

nation. He even reproached Nietzsche, whom he esteemed, with *amor fati*, a final blessing given to fate. Simone Weil interpreted "Thy Kingdom come" as a prayer asking for the end of evil, for the end of the world, and "Thy will be done" as an assent to the existence of a world bound by the laws of Necessity. Moreover, that heroic assent was in her view the very core of Christianity: "Just as a child hides from his mother, laughing, behind an armchair, so God plays at separating himself from himself through the act of Creation. We are God's joke"; "To believe that reality is love, seeing it for what it is. To love what is impossible to bear. To embrace iron, to press one's body against the cold of hard metal. That is not a variety of masochism. Masochists are excited by fake cruelty. For they do not know what cruelty is. One must embrace, not cruelty, but blind indifference and blind brutality. Only in such a manner does love become impersonal."[5]

Why should love become impersonal? Here again Shestov would not agree. In the Jansenist *"Le moi est haïssable"*—"the I is hateful"—of Pascal, with whom he otherwise agreed, he suspected a glimmer of the old Greek nostalgia for the immutable, eternal, general Oneness in which the particular disappears. Why should we hate "I"? Was it not the "I" of Job that complained and wailed? Was not the God who would demand such an impossible detachment from us a God of philosophers rather than a God of prophets? Simone Weil's response to these questions points to her latent Platonism and to the Platonic myth of the world as a prison of souls longing after their native land, the empyrean of pure ideas. Many of her maxims amount to a confession of guilt, the basic guilt of existing, and to a desire for self-annihilation. "My existence diminishes God's glory. God gave it to me so that I may wish to lose it."[6] She was aware that a self-imposed renunciation of the "I" was nearly impossible, and yet she rated the very aspiration to achieve renunciation as a high spiritual attainment. She referred more than once to two

[5]*La Connaissance surnaturelle.*
[6]Ibid.

lines in Racine's *Phèdre* (again we are in a Jansenist climate):

> *Et la mort à mes yeux ravissant la clarté*
> *Rend au jour qu'ils souillaient toute sa pureté.*
> [And death, ravishing the light from my eyes,
> Gives all purity back to the day they defiled.]

This is, however, an essay on Shestov, not on Simone Weil. Their judgments often converge, yet in general these two move in realms that bear only a tangential relationship to each other. Not only was she passionately interested in social problems (she worked as a laborer in the Renault factory and participated in the Spanish civil war) but her religious, even mystical, experience was drawing her to Roman Catholicism and to a discussion of religion as an institution. For very personal reasons she decided not to receive the sacrament of baptism. Nevertheless, Catholic theology and the history of the Roman Catholic church occupy a prominent position in her writings. Shestov was dominated by a violent scorn for speculative philosophy because he believed that although it pretends to bring solace, in truth its consolations are illusory. Paradoxically he waged his war as an antirationalist using rational argument as his weapon. We know nothing about his confessional options and not much about the intensity of his personal faith.

What could Sorana Gurian, a young woman dying of cancer, get from her reading of Shestov? Not the promise of a miraculous cure. He did not maintain that you can knock down the wall of Necessity by beating your head against it. To the sober-minded who criticized the Absurd of Kierkegaard and his faith in the impossible, he used to reply that Kierkegaard knew perfectly well the weight of reality: Regina Olsen would not be restored to him. Yet there is a great difference between our looking at ourselves as ciphers on a statistical sheet and our grasping our destiny as something that is personal and unique. Simone Weil, though she advocated the voluntary renunciation of the "I," also considered the destruction of the "I" by an external force as a sign of utter misfortune: prisoners and prostitutes are compelled by *others* to visualize themselves as *objects*, statistical ciphers, interchangeable units. Shestov did not fight science. Yet in his rebellion against philosophy we may sense an implied rejection of the terror exerted by a whole purely quantitative, scientific *Weltanschauung*. Such a scientific code of self-perception, imposed by education and the mass media, eats up our individual substance from the inside, so to speak.

To Sorana the God of the Scriptures defended by the stern priest Shestov would probably not have meant an afterlife and a palm tree in Heaven. He must have appeared to her as he did to the Russian author, as pure anti-Necessity. The question was not the existence of Heaven and Hell, not even the "existence" of God himself. Above any notions, but revealed by his voice in the Scriptures, he is able to create anything, even a personal heaven and earth for Sorana Gurian. Or for each one of us.

1973

9

Dostoevsky and Swedenborg

Very few books and studies on Dostoevsky appeared in the first
two decades after his death. The year 1900 may be chosen as the
turning point; after that date the number of publications, first in
Russian and then in other languages, increased steadily. By the
middle of our century the canon of Dostoevsky scholarship was
well established, so that hardly any new departures seemed to
be possible. Today, whether our attention is focused upon Dostoevsky's opinions or upon the stylistic devices and structures
of his novels, we note that practically every method of approach has already been tried by at least one of our predecessors. Thus Dostoevsky, not unlike Nietzsche, was discovered
and appropriated by the first half of the twentieth century. It
was then that he grew to the stature he now possesses, and it
was then that he was recognized as a forerunner of new trends
in European literature and philosophy.

Seen from the present, as the past recedes in time, it is quite
normal for the perspective to change and for some habits of
thought once accepted as universal to reveal their conventional
character. These habits explain certain blind spots or unintentional omissions, while new questions arise concerning Dostoevsky's significance as a historical phenomenon. This essay
toys with some interpretations of Dostoevsky which may be
applied in the future, when the present transitional stage is
over. It introduces the name of Emanuel Swedenborg as a useful
catalyst.

Swedenborg may be linked with Dostoevsky in two ways. First, Russia's cultural lag left the Russian intelligentsia open to a sudden onslaught of Western scientific thinking, with centuries compressed into a few decades. That is why Dostoevsky the religious thinker is similar in many respects to religious thinkers in the West who earlier resisted the corroding impact of scientific innovations. Not infrequently he resembles and even sounds like Pascal. In the seventeenth century Pascal was, after all, the most representative of those writers engaged in the defense of the faith against the skeptics. Also the Age of Reason, as personified by Voltaire, oppressed Dostoevsky, as did nineteenth-century science, personified for him by Claude Bernard ("Bernardy" in *The Brothers Karamazov*). As a theologian confronted with the rationalistic science of the day Swedenborg had recourse to an aggressive exegesis of Christianity, and an analogous tendency can be distinguished in Dostoevsky.

A second link is provided by Dostoevsky's borrowings from Swedenborg. To affirm that they exist is not farfetched, for even the books in Dostoevsky's library supply a sort of material proof. The catalog of Dostoevsky's library, published in 1922 by Leonid Grossman,[1] lists three such books. These are, all in Russian, the following: A. N. Aksakov, *The Gospel according to Swedenborg. Five chapters of the Gospel of John with an exposition and a discussion of their spiritual meaning according to the teaching on correspondences* (Leipzig, 1864); A. N. Aksakov, *On Heaven, the world of spirits and on Hell, as they were seen and heard by Swedenborg*, translation from the Latin (Leipzig, 1863); A. N. Aksakov, *The Rationalism of Swedenborg. A critical analysis of his teaching on the Holy Writ* (Leipzig, 1870). A. N. Aksakov was in Russia a chief proponent of spiritism or, as we would say today, parapsychology—an interest which was treated unkindly by Dostoevsky in *The Diary of a Writer*. He became acquainted with Swedenborg, however,

---

[1]L. P. Grossman, *Seminarii po Dostoevskomu* (Gosudarstvennoe Izdatel'stvo, 1922; reprint Great Britain: Prideaux Press, 1972).

thanks to Aksakov's essays and translations and he took from these books what suited his purpose.

SWEDENBORG IN THE FIRST HALF
OF THE TWENTIETH CENTURY

During the first half of our century much attention was paid to so-called symbolism in poetry. It seems strange that, in spite of this preoccupation, Swedenborg was little known. After all, Baudelaire's sonnet "Les Correspondences"—a poem crucial to symbolist poetics—took its title and its contents from Swedenborg. Curiosity alone should have directed critics to explore the original concept, not just its derivatives. The truth is that every epoch has dusty storage rooms of its own where disreputable relics of the past are preserved. Swedenborg was left there together with the quacks, miracle workers, and clairvoyants so typical of the not-so-reasonable Age of Reason—people like Count Cagliostro, the legendary Count Saint-Germain, and an initiator of the "mystical lodges" in France, Martinez Pasqualis. The risk of taking Swedenborg seriously was too great; besides, nobody seemed to know what to think of him.

Neither his contemporaries nor posterity ought to be blamed too much for this neglect. Swedenborg's destiny was extraordinary. A scientist of wide reputation who pursued researches in various disciplines from geology to anatomy, a member of the Royal Mining Commission in Sweden, he had a sudden moment of illumination, abandoned his scientific pursuits, and produced a voluminous *oeuvre* in which he described his travels through Heaven and Hell and his conversations with spirits. He continued to frequent the high society to which he belonged as a royal counselor, and even though he claimed to move simultaneously in the other world, his congeniality and humor disarmed those who would have been ready to call him a madman. After his death in 1772 his works, translated into English, made several converts who organized themselves into the Swedenborgian Church of New Jerusalem. Romanticism in its turn made use of Swedenborg, adapting him to its own needs. For its adherents an ethereal, spiritual world opposed to the world of matter was most alluring: it was this they saw, albeit not quite correctly, in Swedenborg's teachings. Balzac's *Seraphita* is typical of such a Romantic misinterpretation.

Swedenborg's legend was still alive at the time of Balzac and Baudelaire, but gradually it waned during subsequent decades. In the period which interest us, namely the first half of the twentieth century, Swedenborg was at best an enigma attracting explorers of mental abnormality. It will suffice here to mention two major names which exemplify an attitude of uncertainty, if not of actual helplessness.

The first name is that of Karl Jaspers, who published a study of schizophrenia in 1922; he chose Strindberg, Van Gogh, Swedenborg, and Hölderin as cases of famous schizophrenics. The second name is that of Paul Valéry, whose 1936 essay on Swedenborg is quite curious. Valéry was once at the center of the symbolist movement; moreover, as a brilliant essayist he dominated the French literary scene for several decades. He confesses that Swedenborg has always been for him no more than a literary myth and leaves one wondering whether he has ever read the author with whom he is dealing. Valéry's essay was written as an introduction to the French translation of a book on Swedenborg by the Swedish scholar Martin Lamm. The book does not provide any answer to the question which preoccupies Valéry, namely: "How is a Swedenborg possible?" so he looks for a solution of his own, rejecting the most common hypotheses, those of charlatanism and of insanity. But his own, psychological, explanation sounds even less convincing than Jaspers' diagnosis of mental illness and betrays Valéry's positivistic bias. His rather weak essay on Swedenborg offers us an insight into the positivistic background of French symbolism, into its basic duality. Swedenborg's visions were, according to Valéry, a kind of daydreaming—they occurred in a state between sleep and wakefulness. Perhaps we would not be guilty of insolence if we read into that statement, precisely because it lacks Valéry's usual sharpness, an avowal of his skepticism regarding creations of the human mind. He is very tactful and voices his respect for the "real" reality of Nature and of human society; another reality, that of the artist, of the visionary, is autonomous, a separate area where veracity and delusion are on an equal footing.

Swedenborg was not the only writer who was something of a nuisance then. Another was William Blake. The question of Blake's mental illness was debated quite seriously at the beginning of our century, and though his admirers rejected it as nonsense, their studies published in the thirties and in the forties were known to relatively few people. The fact that Blake today has become a major figure of English literature is one of the signs indicating a serious change in attitude. And of course an acquaintance with Blake must awaken interest in Swedenborg, not only because Blake was influenced by him but also because Swedenborg can best be understood when approached using Blake's own criteria.

Let us pose a simplistic question: did Swedenborg really travel through Heaven and Hell and did his conversations with spirits really take place? The most obvious answer is: no, not really. He only believed that he had access to the other world at any time, for instance when attending a party or walking in his garden. Everything happened only in his mind. This amounts to conceding that Jaspers was right when he pronounced his verdict: schizophrenia. We should note that Romanticism had already treated Swedenborg in a way no different from the way positivistic psychiatry did later on, namely, a split into the material (that is, real) and the spiritual (that is, illusory) had been accepted, but with a plus sign, not a minus, added to the phantoms of our mind. If, however, William Blake's help is enlisted in reading Swedenborg, the picture changes radically. The question asked and the answer given would be rejected by Blake as absurd. Blake read Swedenborg exactly as he read Dante: these were for him works of the supreme human faculty, Imagination, thanks to which all men will one day be united in Divine Humanity. Through Imagination spiritual truths are transformed into visible forms. While opposing Swedenborg on certain crucial matters, Blake felt much closer to his system than to the system of Dante, whom he accused of atheism. Blake's *Marriage of Heaven and Hell* is modeled upon Swedenborg, and he would have been amused by an inquiry into whether he had "really" seen the devils and angels which he describes. The crux of the problem—and a serious challenge to the mind—is Blake's respect both for the imagination of Dante, who was a poet, and the imagination of Swedenborg, whose works are written in quite pedestrian Latin prose. Dante was regarded by his contemporaries as a man who had visited the other world. Yet Jaspers would not have called him a schizophrenic, because the right of the poet to invent—that is, to lie—was recognized in Jaspers' lifetime as something obvious. It is not easy to grasp the consequences of the aesthetic theories which have emerged as the flotsam and jetsam of the scientific and technological revolution. The pressure of habit still forces us to exlaim: "Well, then, Swedenborg wrote fiction and he was aware it was no more than fiction!" But, tempting as it is, the statement would be false. Neither Swedenborg nor Blake were aestheticians; they did not enclose the spiritual within the domain of art and poetry and oppose it to the material. At the risk of simplifying the issue by using a definition, let us say rather that they both were primarily concerned with the *energy* which reveals itself in a constant interaction of Imagination with the things perceived by our five senses.

SWEDENBORGIAN ELEMENTS IN *CRIME AND PUNISHMENT*

The doctrine of correspondences is treated at length in Swedenborg's *Heaven and Hell*, which Dostoevsky may have purchased or read in Aksakov's translation during his stay in

Germany in 1865. Let us note the place of publication, Leipzig, and the date, 1863. *Crime and Punishment* was begun in Wiesbaden in 1865. That Baudelaire in his *Flowers of Evil* was indebted to Swedenborg is well known, but there are in my opinion strong traces of Swedenborg's influence in *Crime and Punishment* also. A big phantasmagoric city, whether it be Paris, literally called by Baudelaire *la cité infernale*, or St. Petersburg, where Raskolnikov is beset by nightmares, already seems to be the modern form of a Dantesque hell; a description of it may refer implicitly to the doctrine of correspondences. To sound convincing, one ought to quote numerous passages from Swedenborg. However, this is beyond the scope of a brief essay and I shall limit myself to a few sentences.

"What a correspondence is, is not known at the present day" —says Swedenborg—"for several reasons, the chief of which is that man has withdrawn himsel from heaven by the love of self and love of the world."[2] That lost vision embraced Creation as a unity, because "the whole natural world corresponds to the spiritual world, and not merely the natural world in general, but also every particular of it; and as a consequence everything in the natural world that springs from the spiritual is called correspondent."[3] Man by virtue of his mind is part of the spiritual world and therefore "whatever effects are produced in the body, whether in the face, in speech, or in bodily movements, are called correspondences."[4] Perhaps the gist of Swedenborg's teaching resides in his carrying the anthropocentric vision implied by Christianity to an extreme. The maxim: "as above, so below" has always been invoked by hermetic Christian movements with their system of mirrors, for according to them the macrocosm was reflected in the microcosm and thus correspondences are to be found in the whole tradition of alchemy and in Jakob Boehme. But Swedenborg went one step further: for him the whole universe in its only valid essence, celestial

[2] *Heaven and Hell*, p. 87.
[3] Ibid., p. 89.
[4] Ibid., p. 91.

and spiritual or infernal, had a human shape: "It has been shown that the entire heaven reflects a single man, and that it is in image a man and is therefore called the Greatest Man."[5] As a consequence everything human acquires an extraordinary importance, for this entire world to which we apply physics and chemistry exists so as to provide *human* imagination with archetypes and human language with signs.[6] Any man may live in a constant relationship with the Greatest, Cosmic, Man—in other words, live in Heaven—but he may also avoid it and keep company with the Cosmic Evil Man—in other words live in Hell. When he dies he finds himself in one of the innumerable heavens or hells which are nothing other than societies composed of people of the same inclination. Every heaven or hell is a precise reproduction of the states of mind a given man experienced when on earth and it appears accordingly—as beautiful gardens, groves, or the slums of a big city. Thus everything on earth perceived by the five senses will accompany a man as a source of joy or of suffering much as the alphabet, once learned, may be composed into comforting or depressing books. In the eigh-

[5] Ibid., p. 94.
[6] In this respect an English metaphysical poet, Thomas Traherne, is Swedenborg's predecessor, as for instance in the following stanza:

> This made me present evermore
> With whatsoere I saw.
> An object, if it were before
> My Ey, was by Dame Natures Law,
> Within my Soul. Her Store
> Was all at once within me; all her Treasures
> Were my imediat and Internal Pleasures,
> Substantial Joys, which did inform my Mind.
> With all she wraught,
> My Soul was fraught,
> And evry Object in my Heart a Thought
> Begot, or was; I could not tell,
> Whether the Things did there
> Themselves appear,
> Which in my Spirit truly seemd to dwell;
> Or whether my conforming Mind
> Were not even all that therin shind.

"My Spirit" in *The Poetical Works of Thomas Traherne* (New York, 1965).

teenth century Swedenborg was not alone in discovering this strange dimension: the dimension of human inwardness. Others as well searched for a counterbalance to the world of scientists, which was conceived as a mechanism seen *from the outside.* Different as they are from each other, in many ways several thinkers have in common this search for *the inside:* Berkeley with his *esse est percipi*—to be is to be perceived—Kant with his categories of the mind, and of course Blake. Swedenborg's choice of states of mind and images as the foundation of his system was to appeal to romantic and symbolist poets for obvious reasons. Yet by shifting the emphasis they obtained the opposite of the original idea. Correspondences are not symbols to be arbitrarily chosen by a poet or a novelist. If the word symbol applies here, they are "objective symbols," preordained by God and determined by the very structure of Nature and of human imagination. A visionary, a prophet unveils them and Swedenborg, who assigned himself a prophetic role, deciphered with their help the hidden spiritual meaning of the Bible. All this had little to do with literature, at least as far as he was concerned. It was not destined to become a basis for legitimizing uncontrolled subjectivity or for establishing a democratic equality of subjective symbols and metaphors. It is true, some poets have noticed that not all symbols are of equal power and they have valued the most those which have their roots in archetypes. But this is a separate issue, alien to Dostoevsky, at least on a conscious level.

In *Crime and Punishment* the streets of St. Petersburg, the dust, the water of the canals, the stairs of tenement houses are described as seen by Raskolnikov; thus they acquire the quality of his feverish states. His dreams, his coffinlike room, and the city itself are woven into the rich symbolic texture of the novel. All this is not unfamiliar to a reader of the early Dostoevsky, and seems only to intensify the devices already used in *The Double* or in *The Landlady.* There is, however, one character who displays too much kinship with the spirits of Swedenborg for his direct descent from the book *Heaven and Hell* to be doubted. This is Svidrigailov. We will grant that he has capti-

vated many readers and scholars who sensed in him a somewhat exotic element previously unencountered in Dostoevsky's
novels. While a good deal of symbolism is involved in the
name, appearance, and behavior of Sonya, we feel in Svidrigailov still another dimension, as though he had just arrived from
and were returning to the beyond, in spite of his palpable presence and his presumed biography. Everything about him—the
way he visits Raskolnikov for the first time, his physical features, his gestures, his speech, and his dreams—qualify as
Swedenborgian correspondences; viewed from that angle he is,
though alive, a melancholy inhabitant of Hell. In parenthesis,
the strong identification of Dostoevsky with Svidrigailov has
been noted by critics, but nobody to my knowledge has pointed
to the origin of that hero's name to back the assumption. Dostoevsky was not indifferent to the past of his family and he liked
to refer to his ancestors, nobles who had owned an estate, Dos-
toevo, in the Grand Duchy of Lithuania. One of the Lithuanian
rulers of the fifteenth century was Duke Svidrigaila, a well-
known historical figure. No other character of Dostoevsky's is
endowed with a Lithuanian name.

But unraveling the author's little secrets is more or less an idle
game. What is important is that love of self, as a central theme,
appears in *Crime and Punishment* in two forms: the one represented by Raskolnikov who gradually becomes aware of its
power, the other by his double, Svidrigailov, who has nothing
to learn for he knows his evil nature and has a feeling of eternal
damnation. Love of self, according to Swedenborg, character-
izes all the inhabitants of the infernal realm that remains, however, infinitely differentiated. To quote: "Every evil, as well as
every good, is of infinite variety. That this is true is beyond the
comprehension of those who have only a simple idea regarding
every evil, such as contempt, enmity, hatred, revenge, deceit,
and other like evils. But let them know that each one of these
evils contains so many specific differences, and each of these
again so many instances of particular differences, that a volume
would not suffice to enumerate them. The hells are so distinctly

arranged in accordance with the differences of every evil that
nothing could be more perfectly ordered or more distinct. Evi-
dently, then, the hells are innumerable."[7] Raskolnikov is an intellectual of the nineteenth century who has rejected Heaven
and Hell as depicted in Christian iconography and rejected im-
mortality along with them. The conversation between him and
Svidrigailov on that subject is one of the strangest in world
literature:

"I don't believe in a future life," said Raskolnikov.
Svidrigailov sat lost in thought.
"And what if there are only spiders there, or something of that
sort," he said suddenly.
"He is a madman," thought Raskolnikov.
"We always imagine eternity as something beyond our conception,
something vast, vast! But why must it be vast? Instead of all that,
what if it's one little room, like a bathhouse in the country, black and
grimy and spiders in every corner, and that's all eternity is? I sometimes fancy it like that."
"Can it be you can imagine nothing juster and more comforting
than that?" Raskolnikov cried, with a feeling of anguish.
"Juster? And how can we tell, perhaps that is just, and do you know
it's what I would certainly have made it," answered Svidrigailov, with
a vague smile.
This horrible answer sent a cold chill through Raskolnikov.

How could we assume that this image of a private hell does
not come straight from Swedenborg? Spiders, tarantulas, scor-
pions as symbols of evil return so persistently in Dostoevsky's
late works that they deserve the appellation of correspondences.
A passage from Swedenborg enlightens us sufficiently as to the
hells which are built out of correspondences to things perceived
by the senses: "Some hells present an appearance like the ruins
of houses and cities after conflagrations, in which infernal
spirits dwell and hide themselves. In the milder hells there is an
appearance of rude huts, in some cases contiguous in the form
of a city with lanes and streets, and within the houses are infernal spirits engaged in unceasing quarrels, enmities, fightings,

[7]*Heaven and Hell*, p. 588n.

and brutalities; while in the streets and lanes robberies and depredations are committed."[8] Of course, in view of the infinite variety of hells, there is room also for a country bathhouse with spiders.[9]

Svidrigailov suffers from the systematic visits of specters, but he does not dismiss them as delusions. He is inclined to think that "ghosts are, as it were, shreds and fragments of other worlds, the beginning of them." The dreams he has shortly before his suicide are so vivid that they resemble visions more than sequences of blurred images loosely bound together by an oneiric logic. Their horror surpasses even Raskolnikov's dream after the murder. One would not be far wrong in considering *Crime and Punishment* a novel that deals with Raskolnikov's self-will on one level only, while on a depper level there is another crime and another punishment: Svidrigailov's rape of a child and his suicide. But is there any reason to think that Svidrigailov had really committed that crime? Not necessarily. The coffin in which a fourteen-year-old girl lies among flowers, like Shakespeare's Ophelia, may lead us to believe that he had debauched an adolescent who then committed suicide. If so, he is a very sensitive devil indeed, for in the next dream the victim changes into a five-year-old child and he is terrified when suddenly she opens her eyes and looks at him with "a glowing, shameless glance." Faced with Svidrigailov's presumed misdeeds the reader is more or less in the position of Dostoevsky's biographers, aware of his obsession and uncertain whether he had in fact once raped a little girl.

Just as in *Crime and Punishment* the very core of evil had to do with the rape of a child, so in *The Possessed* Stavrogin, though he harbors in himself all the devils of Russia, accuses himself in his *Confession* of precisely the same sin. Yet his conversation with Tikhon leaves the reader perplexed. It is impos-

[8]Ibid., p. 586n.

[9]In Swedenborg's system there are no angels and devils except the saved and the damned humans. To this Dostoevsky refers in his notebook of 1875-1876: "Are there devils? I could never imagine what satan's would be like. Job. Mephistopheles. Swedenborg: bad people...about Swedenborg." [*The Unpublished Dostoevsky*, ed. Carl R. Proffer, Vol. II (Ann Arbor: Ardis, 1975).]

sible to be certain that Stavrogin once behaved as he says he did. The purpose of his confession, reflected in the ugliness of its style, is noted by Tikhon: this is an act of defiance by Stavrogin, not of contrition; he does not ask for forgiveness, but tries to provoke hatred and scorn. If this applies to the style, it may apply to the content as well and the whole story of the rape might have been invented. It seems as if Dostoevsky's feelings of guilt were constantly searching for expression through one symbolic event which returns again and again as a fixed correspondence. That symbolic reality has the same substance as do Swedenborg's hells; it resides beyond commonly accepted notions of the existing and the imaginary, the objective and the subjective.

A literary parentage going back to Gogol and E. T. A. Hoffmann is sufficient to explain the fantastic elements in the young Dostoevsky's fiction, for instance the pranks of Golyadkin Jr. in *The Double* which are still explained away in a rational manner by Golyadkin Sr.'s mental illness. Beginning with *Crime and Punishment* the rational cover for these extraordinary, bizarre occurrences grows very thin and thus they are elevated above mere phantoms. A rational explanation is contrived in the form of a state between dreaming and wakefulness, as experienced by Svidrigailov on the night before his suicide; of a confession written by Stavrogin; of falling asleep in *The Dream of a Ridiculous Man*, though his travel through time into the remote past of mankind has nothing dreamy about it; or, in *The Brothers Karamazov*, of the sober, psychiatric title of a chapter: "The Devil. Ivan's Nightmare"—while neither Ivan nor the reader is convinced that the Devil was merely a product of Ivan's sick brain.

DOSTOEVSKY AS A HERESIARCH

It is more than likely that Dostoevsky read Swedenborg when working on *Crime and Punishment* and that he was emboldened by a theology which assigns such a prominent place to the imagination. Whether and precisely what he borrowed from Swedenborg remains uncertain, with the possible exception of Svidrigailov's bathhouse full of spiders. But Dostoevsky's strategy as a religious thinker is of more consequence than possible borrowings of details, and Swedenborg's writings may offer some clues in this respect.

Anna Akhmatova used to call Dostoevsky and Tolstoy "heresiarchs," as we learn from Nadezhda Mandelstam's memoirs.[10] This is true enough. Their extraordinary minds, their fervor, and the gigantic stakes they played for did not save them from preaching fuzzy or even wild doctrines. Although basically dissimilar, they were alike in their effort to adapt Christianity to what they believed to be the needs of modern man. Yet Tolstoy's "true" Christianity, diluted by Rousseauism, resembled more and more a nontheistic Buddhism, as Solovyov noted. In Tolstoy's copious output as a sermonizer the metaphysical meaning of the Gospels evaporated and only the moral meaning remained. It would hardly be an exaggeration to say that Tolstoy ended where Dostoevsky started, and to locate the latter's point of departure during his fourierist phase, at the time when the belonged to the Petrashevsky circle.

The Christian vocabulary of utopian socialism should be kept in mind, whether its spokesman be Saint-Simon, Fourier, or George Sand. In its rejection of Christian churches and in placing itself under the sign of the Gospels, utopian socialism was to some degree the inheritor of such populist Christian movements of the past as the Hussites or the Anabaptists, who had proclaimed a return to the original purity of the early Christian communes. Yet the vocabulary veiled a profound change in belief, a result of the eighteenth-century *Lumières*. A social utopia now occupied the first place, not Christ: he was admired only as its announcer, as the most sublime teacher and reformer. Dostoevsky, as we know, was shocked by Belinsky's derogatory and scornful words about Christ. When he joined the Petrashevsky circle, it was different; discussions on Fourier or Considérant did not threaten his personal attachment to the

[10]Nadezhda Mandelstam, *Vtoraya kniga* (Paris: YMCA Press, 1972).

figure of Jesus as a moral ideal, for the precise reason that they
focused upon the Kingdom of God on earth as something not
very remote and easily attainable. Subsequently Dostoevsky's
whole life, beginning with his stay in the penal colony of Omsk,
would be marked by the incessant struggle in his mind between
two images of Christ; one, a model of perfection never equaled
by anyone else, yet still a mortal man and thus subject to the
law of death; the second, a God-Man triumphant over death. A
contradiction, overlooked by the humanists and socialists of the
Petrashevsky circle, gradually was to take shape in Dostoevsky's work, up to its most poignant presentation in *The Legend
of the Grand Inquisitor*. For the argument of the Grand Inquisitor with Christ is nothing more and nothing less than that of a
utopian socialist with his supposed leader who refuses to serve
as such and, what is worse, shows that his disciple had mis-
understood him. Christ says in fact that his Kingdom of God is
not of this world—and the freedom he offers man does not lead
to any perfect society. No one but the God-Man intending to lift
man up to his own divine level can ask for acceptance of this
freedom. The utopian in Dostoevsky yearned so much for the
Kingdom of God on earth that he sided with the Grand Inquisitor; it is this that explains the forceful speech the author, himself
internally divided, puts into the mouth of his tragic old man.
The divine nature of Christ appears as a major obstacle to
human happiness on earth and therefore should be denied. But,
by a dialectical countermovement, as soon as the earthly happiness of man is chosen as a goal it becomes obvious that it can be
attained only at the price of the total annihilation of human
freedom. Thus the argument expresses Dostoevsky's despair at
the thought of the erosion of Christian faith—in himself, in the
Russian intelligentsia, and in Western Europe. And it was this
that forced him to resort to arbitrary and unrealistic remedies.
In that big either/or—either a Christian civilization or the totalitarian society of Shigalev and of the Grand Inquisitor—he
paradoxically hoped to find a third way, and clung to his Holy
Russia with the peasant below and the tsar above as the only

possible mainstay of Christianity and consequently of human freedom.

THE HUMAN AND THE DIVINE

The problem of the two natures of Christ underlies Dostoevsky's whole work, and it also determines his journey from a socialist utopia to a nationalistic one. To say that at some given moment he became an atheist (whatever that word may mean) under Belinsky's influence is not truly relevant, for he was haunted by the figure of Christ the teacher perhaps no less in the forties than later on, when in the penal colony. Yet undoubtedly he underwent a change of heart in Omsk, in the sense that now the necessity of an act of faith became clear. His much quoted letter of 1854 to Fonvizina, written upon his release from the prison camp, contains the nucleus of those internal contradictions which torment his major heroes:

I will tell you regarding myself that I am a child of the age, that I have been a child of unbelief and doubt up till now and will be even (I know it) until my coffin closes. What terrible torments this thirst to believe has cost and still does cost me, becoming the stronger in my soul the more there is in me of contrary reasonings. And yet sometimes God sends me moments when I am utterly at peace; in those moments I love and find that I am loved by others and in such moments I have constructed for myself a symbol of faith in which everything is clear and sacred to me. This symbol is very simple: to believe that there is nothing more beautiful, more profound, more sympathetic, wiser, braver, or more perfect than Christ; and not only is there nothing, but, as I tell myself with jealous love, there *could not* be anything. Even more: if somebody proved to me that Christ is outside the truth, and if it were *a fact* that the truth excludes Christ, I would rather remain with Christ than with the truth.

This last sentence is potentially that of a "heresiarch." Who could *prove* to Dostoevsky that Christ was beyond the truth? A scientist, a philosopher, for whom everything is submitted to deterministic laws and who would shrug at the story of Christ rising from the dead as an offense to our reason? That sort of proof, through the universal order of Nature, is accepted by those characters of Dostoevsky's who are, more or less, the spokesmen for his "intellectual part"—Ippolit in *The Idiot*, Kirillov in *The Possessed*, and Ivan Karamazov. "And if Christ be not risen, then is our preaching vain, and your faith is also vain," says Saint Paul (I Cor. 15:14). Ippolit, Kirillov, Ivan, and the Grand Inquisitor have their negative proofs that it is really so, but they also realize that if it is so, if Christ deluded himself in foretelling his resurrection, then the world is a devil's farce. Dostoevsky himself, or that part of him which turns against his skeptical characters, "would rather remain with Christ than with the truth" and thus yields the field in reality to the so-called scientific Weltanschauung. The opposition of faith to reason has behind it an old tradition, but the opposition of faith to truth is a desperate novelty and dangerously favors any self-imposed deception.[11]

There is perhaps also a second layer of meaning in that enigmatic sentence. Since the Gospels are not a treatise on ethics and their message is often self-contradictory, many Christian mystics counseled clinging to the person of Christ as opposed to norms or values. A well-founded counsel—but at the same time a precept cherished by every sectarian, for it authorizes transforming the image of Christ as suits a given man or community. The suspicion arises whether "the Russian Christ" of Dostoevsky is not connected with such an exalted arbitrariness.

[11]Here Dostoevsky comes close to Kierkegaard, but the dichotomy is resolved by Kierkegaard who tips the scales in favor of "inwardness," "subjectivity," and thus identifies faith with truth: "The truth is precisely the venture which chooses an objective uncertainty with the passion of the infinite." "But the above definition of truth is an equivalent expression for faith." "Faith is precisely the contradiction between the infinite passion of the individual's inwardness and the objective uncertainty." [*Concluding Unscientific Postscript*, (Princeton University Press edition), p. 182]. A saying of Meister Eckhart's may be recalled here: "If God were able to backslide from truth I would fain cling to truth and let God go."

THE ONSLAUGHT OF PHILOSOPHY—
AND OF GNOSTICISM

A brief digression is necessary here. Christianity has in modern times, beginning with the Renaissance, been forced to renew its quarrel with philosophic thought. At one time, in the Roman Empire, it had been Greek philosophy; assimilated and tamed by the Church, it tended nevertheless to recover its autonomy and at last—thanks to so-called humanism—it grew in strength, inspiring modern science. Or to be more precise, one side of Greek thought was now taken over and turned against the other, which had been fused with the Jewish heritage. Quite symptomatic was the revival in the sixteenth century of the Anti-Trinitarian heresy also known as Arianism, though Arius had been condemned by the Council of Nicaea long before, in A.D. 325. Perhaps one should call it *the* heresy and trace it down through the history of Christianity in its various contradictory guises. At first sight the "luminous" rationalistic trend in the Renaissance (and undoubtedly Arianism with its dislike of incomprehensible dogma belongs here) had nothing to do with its contemporary "dark," more esoteric counterpart. Yet the two were just the two sides of the same philosophic coin, much as they had been before in the Hellenistic world. The origins of attacks upon the Trinity should be traced back to Gnosticism, which had already by the second century A.D. introduced a duality, a separation between Christ on the one hand and the God of the Old Testament on the other. The very dogma of the Trinity—of the three *hypostases* designated the Father, the Son, and the Holy Ghost—was elaborated as the response of the early Church to that Gnostic cleavage which broke the continuity of the Revelation through history. From its birth the Gnostic heresy, in its various ratiocinations, had at its core a resentment of the evil world: a God responsible for such evil could not be a supreme Being, while Christ was—or represented—the true deity.[12] Then the Manichaeans stepped in and followed a well-blazed trail. Ever since, Christology has been a territory for which heretics have had a predilection; they have tended to oppose Redemption to Creation, the Savior to Jehovah, or even to exult in the human nature of Christ, who, through *kenosis*, "emptied himself" of his divine attributes. In Dostoevsky's major novels all these problems are present implicitly or explicitly.

The theology of Swedenborg, who was both a modern Christian and a scientist, was a major attempt at wrestling with the dogma of the Trinity as recognized by all three branches of Christianity: Roman Catholic, Orthodox, and Protestant. He accused them all of teaching the faithful to imagine three gods, and thus disguising polytheism under a formula incomprehensible to the human mind. At the same time, however, he disapproved of the solution offered by the Arians, for whom Christ was not of the same nature as the Father and for a large number of whom he was merely a man. Swedenborg's system is dominated by a Christ who is *the only God*, not in spite of his

[12]"The following may be noted as the main points in the Gnostic conception of the several parts of the *regula fidei:*

a) The difference between the supreme God and the creator of the world, and therewith the opposing of redemption and creation, and therefore the separation of the Mediator of revelation from the Mediator of creation.

b) The separation of the supreme God from the God of the Old Testament, and therewith the rejection of the Old Testament, or the assertion that the Old Testament contains no revelations of the supreme God, or at least only in certain parts.

c) The doctrine of the independence and eternity of matter.

d) The assertion that the present world sprang from a fall of man, or from an undertaking hostile to God, and is therefore the product of an evil or intermediate being.

e) The doctrine that evil is inherent in matter and therefore is a physical potence [*sic!*].

f) The assumption of Aeons, that is, real powers and heavenly persons in whom is unfolded the absoluteness of the Godhead.

g) The assertion that Christ revealed a God hitherto unknown."

[Adolph Harnack, *History of Dogma*, English translation (New York: Dover Publications, Inc., 1961), I, 257-259. Harnack also lists other, additional points.]

having been born a man but precisely because he was born a man. Absolutely Christo-centric, Swedenborg's system is also absolutely anthropocentric. Its most sacred books are the Gospel of Saint John and the Apocalypse; by coincidence these were also the most sacred books for Dostoevsky. Swedenborg's credo is embodied in the exclamation of Thomas the Apostle when he touched Christ's wounds: "My Lord and my God." Man was created in the image and semblance of God, for Our Father in Heaven is Man; Heaven, as I have already quoted, is according to Swedenborg the Greatest Man.

To compare Dante and Swedenborg as writers would be hazzardous, but their respective visions of "the other shore" constitute two decisive testimonies to the imaginative life of our civilization. Dante's cosmology is medieval and his theology is based upon Thomas Aquinas, in whose syllogisms Greek philosophy was put to a Catholic use. The importance of Man, created and redeemed by God, is guaranteed in Dante by the Earth's central place in the universe. But by Swedenborg's time the universe is resolved into a motion of whirling planets and stars. If it were not for one man, Christ, God incarnated, mankind would dwindle into a speck of dust, into an accident in the incomprehensible mechanical order of things. Perhaps for that reason Swedenborg emphasizes God-Man as preexisting, the Creator and Redeemer in one person. It would be incorrect to classify Swedenborg as an Anti-Trinitarian, for all he wanted was to propose a new concept of the Trinity. Yet his disciple William Blake, occasionally a rebel against his master, hardly modified the Swedenborgian doctrine when he chose the Human Form Divine as the key to all the secrets of existence. And, unlike in Swedenborg, Gnostic affinities are obvious in Blake's multiple reversals of religious concepts: God the lawgiver equated with Satan, Elohim with inferior demiurges. The creation of the world, presented by Blake as an act of divine mercy *after* the Fall has already taken place (or simultaneously with it, which is the same where there is no time) is purely Manichaean. In the teachings of the founder of Manichaeism, Mani

(d. A.D. 277), after the Kingdom of Light was contaminated by the Kingdom of Darkness, the Kingdom of Light allowed an inferior demiurge to create the world in that zone so that it might be purified through the action of time.

Swedenborg (and Blake) humanized or *hominized* God and the universe to such an extent that everything, from the smallest particle of matter to planets and stars, was given but one goal: to serve as a fount of signs for human language. Man's imagination, expressing itself through language and identical in its highest attainments with the Holy Ghost, was now to rule over and redeem all things by bringing about the era of the New Jerusalem. Man was again at the center, even though his Earth and his galaxy were not. The Christian strategy of Swedenborg (and Blake) perhaps parallels that of Thomas Aquinas, who felt that philosophy (or at least Aristotle, *the* philosopher) must be absorbed by Christian thought. In the eighteenth century the Christian strategist was confronted with a more difficult task: philosophy was to be absorbed in its two derivatives, in the rationalistic trend and in the more somber heretical tradition of duality, of a chasm between Creation and Redemption. It was made possible by affirming that the Divine is eternally Human and that the Human is potentially Divine.

But Swedenborg (and Blake) teetered on the very edge, where the equilibrium between Christian faith and its anti-Christian denial was constantly threatened. The divinization of Man was already in the offing, accompanied by the advent of "European nihilism" as foretold by Frederick Nietzsche. Our era, the second half of the twentieth century, is marked by a tragicomic escapism, namely a "death of God" theology which proceeds from the idea of Divine Humanity and subjects it to an imperceptible alteration, so that it changes into its opposite. It is enough to read a book on Blake by one of the chief "death of God" theologians[13] to observe how this can be accomplished—obviously by enlisting the help of Hegel. To Dostoevsky's

---

[13]Thomas J. Altizer, *The New Apocalypse: the Radical Christian Vision of William Blake* (Ann Arbor: University of Michigan Press, 1967).

credit, let us recall here that, while the dialectics of God-Man and Man-God were present in his novels, he desperately struggled against blurring the basic antinomy between the two.

DOSTOEVSKY'S ATTEMPTS TO SOLVE THE PROBLEM

When describing the books in Dostoevsky's library, Leonid Grossman admits the probability of Swedenborg's influence upon what we may consider Dostoevsky's last word in religious matter, namely upon the discourses of Father Zosima on prayer, love, Hell, and contact with other worlds.[14] Grossman's hint has not, to my knowledge, been taken by anybody and a study of the subject is lacking. Father Zosima in many of his pronouncements indeed sounds like Swedenborg, particularly in his talk on eternal damnation. A man's life, according to Zosima, is "a moment of *active living* love" and is given to him as a gift of time and space, where love can be exercised. The drama of eternal life resides precisely in the brevity of this encounter with time and space, which soon are no more and then everything one has lived through becomes part of his interior states. The flames of Hell are within the damned and correspond to the quality of their love on earth: "For them hell is voluntary and they cannot have enough of it." "They cannot behold the living God without hatred and demand that there be no God of life, that God destroy himself and all his creation."

In Father Zosima's thinking, a Manichaean hatred of creation is characteristic of the damned. Yet Dostoevsky, like Swedenborg and Blake before him, tried hard to absorb the heresy and integrate it into a Christology of his own. In a novel this is, however, more difficult than in theology and poetry. Dostoevsky seems to say: if the concept of God-Man free from sin is to have any validity, then human nature should allow us at least an inkling as to how it might be possible. That is why Dostoevsky spent so much energy striving to create a perfect good man

[14]L. P. Grossman, *Seminarii po Dostoevskomu.*

as a hero of fiction. And he failed. Prince Myshkin is a living negative proof, for his acts show to what extent love of self is at the root of human nature and how insufficiently human someone is who lacks it. Myshkin, who is completely selfless, devoid of aggression and sexual drive, is no less a monster of emptiness than is Stavrogin with his excess of self-love. Father Zosima comes straight from the lives of the saints and eludes our questioning, for he is protected by his prestige as a repentant sinner. As for Alyosha, he is convincing only as one of the Karamazovs, united by their dark, violent blood. His missionary activities among schoolboys and the resulting brotherhood are, to be frank, melodramatic and outright *schmalz*. Artistic falsity reveals here the falsity of Dostoevsky's self-imposed collectivistic belief, his heresy which he propagated especially in his journalism. Alyosha, a Christlike leader, suggests the future Russian Christ and is surrounded by twelve children-disciples, but by a strange twist of stylistic fate (there are stylistic fates), the presumed Church changes into a Boy Scout unit. It is a doubtful proposition that one can achieve the Kingdom of God on earth by converting mankind into boy scouts, and that is why those chapters of *The Brothers Karamazov* read like an unintended parody. Shatov in *The Possessed*, who loves the Christlike Russian people but does not believe in God, might, however, have been a sarcastic jab intentionally directed by Dostoevsky against himself.

In the history of the rebellion of Man against God and against the order of Nature, Swedenborg stands out as a healer who wanted to break the seals on the sacred books and thus make the rebellion unnecessary. By revealing that God is Man he was convinced that he had fulfilled Christ's promise to one day send a Comforter, the Spirit of Truth; that Spirit spoke through him. Swedenborg's serene Christology may help in elucidating Dostoevsky's tormented and tortuous Christology. At the same time such a study would uncover some Blakean elements in Dostoevsky, who never heard of Blake.

Dostoevsky's rebels are invested with a false, exaggerated

moral sensitivity: the order of the world should be rejected because it offends Man's moral judgment; this world is full of the suffering and agony of creatures tormenting one another. The ideal man, Jesus, must stand in opposition to that natural order; unfortunately, he was for the rebels merely a man and his mistakes had to be corrected; hence the only logical conclusion was to postulate the advent of a Man-God. But Dostoevsky's "positive" heroes fare no better. His failures in drawing them probably testify to his utopian (Fourierist) vision of the ideal man as perfectly meek, perfectly humble and deprived of selfhood. William Blake knew better: he distinguished between Imagination enslaved by the Specter—by the Self—and Imagination making use of the Specter which is a permanent component of human nature. Such an appraisal of human faculties is more realistic. But Dostoevsky's failures, even more than his successes, pay tribute to the permanence of the dilemma which, some eighteen centuries ago, emerged in the guise of a quarrel between the early Christian churches and the Gnostics. The divinization of Man, when one abhors the order of the world as essentially evil, is a risky and self-contradictory venture.

1974

10
On Thomas Mayne Reid

In Chekhov's story "Boys," written in 1887, twelve-year old Volodia coming home for Christmas vacation brings with him his freckled schoolmate Chechevitzyn. The boys' behavior is strange, conspiratorial: they do not take part in family activities but instead keep aloof, whispering to each other. At last Chechevitzyn reveals to Volodia's little sisters who he really is: "I am Montigumo, the Hawk's Claw, chief of the invincible people." He lets this confession slip out in spite of the scorn he feels for creatures who have not read Mayne Reid and who are not aware of the big plan being discussed in secret talks by the two plotters.

"First to Perm," said Chechevitzyn in a low voice. "From there to Tiumen...next to Tomsk...next...next...to Kamchatka.... From there the Samoyeds will carry us in their boats across the Behring Strait.... Then we're in America.... There are plenty of fur animals there."

"And California"? asked Volodia.

"California is below.... Once you're in America, California isn't far. We can get food by hunting and robbing."

Volodia lives through internal agony. He worries about his parents but yields to the promptings of the Hawk's Claw and they escape, only to be caught at the first railway station.

The true instigator of that adventure, Mayne Reid, fired the imaginations of youthful readers in Russia as he did nowhere else; and in no other place have several generations remained so loyal in their maturity to a beloved writer of their school years. Today Mayne Reid is the rather rare case of an author whose fame, short-lived where he could be read in the original, has survived thanks to translations.

I was ten when I discovered a coffer of my father's treasures gathered in the years when he had attended a Russian high school. It was filled with Mayne Reid's books in Russian. Struggling with the Cyrillic alphabet I deciphered inscriptions under the illustrations, and this became the first text that I read in Russian. The editions from before the Revolution were far from the last, however. Quite recently some American friends told me about their embarrassment in Moscow when they learned, in a conversation about authors translated from the English, of the wide circulation of Mayne Reid's books. They had never heard his name in America. They are not to be blamed: in English-speaking countries with their rich literature for young readers Mayne Reid was overshadowed by his literary successors and utterly forgotten, so that even the best encyclopedias dedicate to him no more than a few lines.

Thomas Mayne Reid was born in 1818 in Northern Ireland. He was the son of a Presbyterian minister and, himself destined for a career in the ministry, received a very thorough education (to his bored dismay). Of a martial temperament, he dreamed of glorious deeds. Moreover, he sympathized with suffering Ireland and detested the monarchic establishment. In 1840 he migrated to America where he soon became convinced that his Latin and Greek were of no great use; thence his continuous attacks upon the obsolete (in his opinion) training of students in classical languages. Hunting was his passion, and his participation in trapping expeditions often became his means of subsistence; besides this he was in turn a teacher, an actor, and a merchant. His wanderings through the wild expanses of the continent, from Louisiana to the prairies and forests west of Missouri —Indians, buffaloes, grizzly bears—all this became material for his novels. At a given moment he hit upon his journalistic and poetic vein. A romantic poet, he published his works in the periodicals of Philadelphia, where he had settled. At that time one of his closest friends was Edgar Allan Poe.

When the Mexican War erupted Reid volunteered. As political questions were to play a considerable role in his life, a few words on the events of 1846 would be appropriate. The war against Mexico was a war of conquest. Its goal was to take California, but not limited to the area of the present state, for the name also represented Nevada, Utah, Arizona and New Mexico, as well as parts of Wyoming and Colorado. Now the war appears to be the logical consequence of a movement not unlike that which is created when two vessels, full and empty, are joined. On the territory at stake the Indians, a few Spanish settlements, and actually only one town—Santa Fe—were like grains of sand scattered on La Place de la Concorde. And it is precisely that feeling of empty space reaching to the Pacific that found expression in the slogan: Manifest Destiny.

Writers who brought fame to American letters of the nineteenth century—Melville, Emerson, Thoreau—did not have much sympathy for the commercial-industrial explosion. They were not pleased with plebeian money-grubbing, swindles, thievery, rapaciousness bearing a Colt or a bribe, a morality profiting from cotton grown by the slaves on Southern plantations. In their opinion, since the state condoned such evils, to keep his hands clean a man had a duty to limit his contact with the authorities to a strict minimum. War waged by such a state was "dirty." The writers of that decade hit upon solutions which are being chosen by American intellectuals to this very day. Melville constructed a legend of withdrawal into unspoiled nature, into the primitive. (His successors in Europe would be Loti, Gauguin, the near-folkloric motif of Tahiti, isle of bliss, and American beatniks were, most likely, simply a revival of that same nostalgia.) Melville ushers into literature the figure of the Protestant minister as a destructive force annihilating the joy and happiness of primitive peoples. His first novel, *Typee*, appeared (let it be pure coincidence) precisely in 1846. Thoreau found his own Polynesia in the woods of New England. And since only the individual is able to pronounce a verdict distinguishing between good and evil (in which, indeed, Thoreau was very far from the self-sufficient existence of peoples without technology, who are always subordinate to the strict rules of their small society), he advised the individual to disobey the state if the state were immoral. He had a deep faith in the moral instinct of the people. In his famous essay on civil disobedience he wrote: "Witness the present Mexican War, the work of comparatively few individuals using the standing government as their tool; for, in the outset, the people would not have consented to this measure." Is that true, or just an intellectual's delusion? Rather the latter. As for Emerson, he deplored corruption resulting from the fact that "things are in the saddle and ride mankind" but he knew how to keep his distance from unpleasant reality and consoled himself by forecasting the advent of an "eternal man"—which activity, let us be somewhat malicious, was facilitated by a beautiful house and three servants.

When the anthill swarmed westward, thrust forward the Indians (as well as the Mormons, forcing them into an exodus across the prairies), and quickly rushed into the war with Mexico, the noble-minded literati of New England such as Margaret Fuller (dear to the heart of the Polish poet Adam Mickiewicz) saw the salvation of mankind in socialist joint ownership. Having founded a commune—Brook Farm—they mowed hay, milked cows, and zealously read Fourier. No less zealously did they write; their opinion of the Mexican War as put forth in their periodical, "The Harbinger," demonstrates the possibility of both having one's cake and eating it too, or: how to preserve one's virtue by letting others do the dirty work.

There can be no doubt of the design entertained by the leaders and instigators of this infamous business, to extend the "area of freedom" to the shores of California, by robbing Mexico of another large mass of her territory; and the people are prepared to execute it to the letter. In many and most aspects in which this plundering aggression is to be viewed it is monstrously iniquitous, but after all it seems to be completing a more universal design of Providence, of extending the power

and intelligence of advanced civilized nations over the whole face of
the earth, by penetrating into those regions which seem fated to im-
mobility and breaking down the barriers to the future progress of
knowledge, of sciences and arts: and arms seem to be the only means
by which this great subversive movement towards unity among nations can be accomplished. . . . In this way Providence is operating on
a grand scale to accomplish its designs, making use of instrumentali-
ties ignorant of its purposes, and incited to act by motives the very
antipodes of those which the real end in view might be supposed to be
connected with or grow out of.

The text deserves reflection. Perhaps we are used to such
arguments, and have so completely absorbed them into our
blood that we are not struck at once by their strangeness. Providence has its plan in respect to states and political systems. That
plan is obviously good, for God cannot desire evil. He slowly
increases good on earth, and for that purpose He uses history
(which is not in itself a very clean business). People acting out
of low, egoistic motives do not realize they are only instruments
in His hand. Their thrashing around fits into the movement
which works toward a goal set in advance. Here we catch in the
act the lay idea of Inevitable Progress as it emerges from Christianity. The act had been prepared by stages throughout the
whole of the eighteenth century. At a given moment it would be
enough to replace Providence by another will and person,
History—and we would be in modern times.

The average American did not, like the Fourierists, make distinctions. He was not concerned with sublime goals and the
means to him did not seem dirty. Democracy, expansion, and
the empty continent to be taken combined in his mind and
emerged in one form: Manifest Destiny. The superhuman toils
of settlers perishing from starvation, from Indian arrows, called
for support. What fictitious borders traced on the map could be
recognized as valid in such cases? Upon increased contact with
the Mexicans, an additional cultural conflict ensued. Unrefined
Yankees straight from work in the fields wondered at Spanish
sophistication, gallantry, at their convoluted rhetoric in speech,

their feudal hierarchies, and popish superstitions. Scorn seasoned their amazement. Those American writers who shared
the feelings of the street and approved of the turbulent life of the
Republic nourished no scruples. Young Walt Whitman, a
printer and a journalist in Brooklyn, openly called for war. His
argument: nobody can stand up to us, we build the fastest ships
in the world. To accuse him and others who thought in similar
manner of simple-mindedness would not be very sound. Hegel
was being read then not only in St. Petersburg and Warsaw but
also in New York, and belief in a self-justifying movement
could back any type of optimism. Some, setting their sights for
the future, concluded that Holy Russia had the right to conquer
and oppress other nations because the Spirit of History had
assigned her a mission. Others on the contrary saw in the future
the reign of Freedom and were ready, for its sake, to spill the
blood of tyrants. Still others, in America, openly and boldly
(unlike the reticent Fourierists) proclaimed that the Mexicans
were not worthy of being spared if the exigencies of Progress
demanded action. Wherever this point of view prevailed, supported by a collective climate and chauvinistic bellowing,
democracy was identified with giving hell both to the Mexicans
in America and to the monarch-tyrants in Europe. Not only
Walt Whitman, admirer of European libertarian upheavals,
could be quoted here. A similar double-tracked tendency is
illustrated by the adventures of Mayne Reid.

The war of 1846-1847 consisted less in battles between men
than in battles fought against space and against the logistic mess
which arises when troops move whole weeks through unin-
habited territory. Although the exploit of the tough raggamuf-
fins' army *was* unbelievable—marching from Fort Leavenworth
to Santa Fe and then deep into Mexico (on foot and horseback
for thirty-five hundred miles, a true "Anabasis in homespun" as
it is called by historian Bernard de Voto)—nevertheless, no victory was in sight. Reid happened to take part in a decisive operation: the landing of troops under General Winfield Scott. The
young chauvinistic journalist Walt Whitman proved to be right:

the Yankee ships, though not insuring victory, did tip the scales.
Reid, one of five thousand soldiers put on board and disem-
barked near Vera Cruz, found himself in a tight corner. The
landing was ill prepared, and although the Americans got some
reinforcements, their forces were insufficient. They marched on
Mexico City via the road of Cortez, but the enemy's army
closed the circle behind them and there was no retreat. In
August of 1847 they reached the capital defended by strong
forts, first of all by Fort Chapultepec. It was there that Lieutenant Thomas Mayne Reid lived the day of his glory. To believe
the testimonies, not only his own but also those of other partici-
pants in the event, his impulse tipped the scales in the fierce
fighting. In his memoirs Reid states that everything appeared
very clear to him then: to go forward under the artillery fire
meant certain death, but not to take the fort also meant certain
death a little later. He gathered a squad of volunteers and led
them to the assault. He fell, wounded, but his men climbed over
the rampart. Chapultepec was taken and the city soon sur-
rendered. News of Reid's death spread in America; newspapers
published the hero's obituary, and poems about him were written. Meanwhile, the hero (according to newspapers "a combination of Adonis and Apollo Belvedere, with a touch of Centaur")
pulled through and was doing well enough, judging from the
name "Don Juan de Tenorio" which he earned with the *señori-
tas.* He explored not only that kind of fauna and flora in Mexico, however. He belongs to those amateur naturalists of the
nineteenth century who rendered serious services to science.

Upon his return to the United States, Mayne Reid was invited
by friends to their farm in Ohio. There he wrote his first novel,
The Rifle Rangers: or Adventures in Southern Mexico. This is
no more than a slightly fictionalized account of the campaign,
and some of the humorous episodes foreshadow Mark Twain.
A sentimental romance is rather unskillfully woven into the re-
portage. The narrator, an intrepid knight, saves two beautiful
maidens from the attack of an alligator by rushing forth with a
cutlass. He falls in love with one of the women and throughout

the novel is exposed to the intrigues of a rival, a somewhat dark character.

Before Reid managed to give final touches to the script of his novel, events ensued which again inspired his martial fervor. From Europe one heard of revolutions in Germany, Poland, Hungary. The year was 1848. Reid decided to go to Europe and enlist in the Hungarian revolutionary army. Let us be fair to his personality and not say that he only liked the smell of gunpowder. As mentioned earlier, he had his convictions: he loved the republic and detested the monarchy. He also had his own idea of war, of which we learn more from his poem "War" than from his journalism. These are his lines:

> Let pale lips abjure thee, and prattle about peace:
> For this is the fashion of times, as they go.
> Let the king on his throne, as he sits at his ease,
> To his minions and millions preach up "statu quo."
> "Statu quo," to a slave!
> Peace apostles, ye rave!
> Tis the peace of the gibbet, the jail, and the grave!
>
> And this is the gospel to peoples ye preach,
> While you tell them by "reason" their freedom to gain.
> How long might the slave to his master beseech,
> Ere he'd list to such suasion, and strike off his chain?

And the poem ends with an exclamation:

> For so long as on Earth, its fair features to mar,
> There's a despot not humbled,
> A throne that's not tumbled,
> A crown that's not crumbled,
> We'll welcome thee, War!

It is true, the poem was printed in 1869; but Reid had always thought thus, and therefore he felt close to the Hungarians fighting for the independence of their country. As for the Mexican War, it never seemed to him a shameless aggression, as it did to the New England intellectuals. In his writings we notice a considerable political interest in Latin America, which was for him a kind of "heart of darkness." While Europe was ruled in his opinion by a gang of diamond-studded scoundrels oppressing its peoples (he branded, as arch-villains of the nineteenth century, Lord Palmerston and Louis Napoleon), the Spanish colonization in America left as an inheritance only the rule of the Catholic clergy allied with the white aristocracy, obscurantism, exploitation, and inefficiency. He considered Mexico an unfortunate country in which the Church owned three-quarters of the wealth and in which dictators such as Santa Ana ascended to power thanks to the backing of the "clerical party." According to Reid, Santa Ana—an embodiment of cunning and cruelty—should have been called, rather, Satana. But what could a population kept by the clergy in the clutches of abominable popism do? Reid tells somewhere how once, in a street of Mexico City taken by Americans, a crowd in tatters with a priest at its head tried to force him, the conqueror, to take off his hat before the Host transported in a carriage, an act "which is intolerable to our religious feelings." He managed to protect himself only by drawing his saber. In his subsequent journalistic career Reid enthusiastically greeted Benito Juarez' presidency. At last justice had triumphed, for now the ruler was an Indian, a descendant of the Montezuma murdered by Cortez (as often happens, Reid loved Indians, but only "their" Indians). Did the Americans have the right to take the territories officially belonging to Mexico? Reid answered: yes. If a given country does not know how to use its resources, it loses its title to the property.

Nations, however highly civilized, upon whom chance has bestowed too large a territorial limit—that is, too large for them to turn to account, either through want of energy or inclining—such nations may be stripped of the superfluity without infringing one principle of human justice. Nay it is justice that they should be stripped.

After the Civil War, in accordance with that view, journalist Reid urged the United States to seize Haiti, as Uncle Sam had a moral obligation to prepare a spacious home for hundreds of thousands of refugees from Europe fleeing despotism; besides, the coffee plantations established by French Creoles had been completely destroyed by the unskilled Negro population, while the Americans needed coffee and they would know how to cultivate it.

In the year of the European Spring of Nations, 1848, Captain (it was with this rank that he had returned from the Mexican campaign) Mayne Reid met a revolutionary, Haecker, and together they began to organize in New York an expeditionary legion. Preparations took quite some time, though, and just when their unit was sailing to England the Russian troops were finishing off the Hungarian rebels. In London, his military plans a flash in the pan, Reid began to look for a publisher. The success of his first novel inclined him to choose writing as a profession. He discovered his genre, novels for young readers and, even though he was not ranked very highly in literary circles, he gained renown and a considerable income. In spite of the fact that he settled in England, he should be called an Irish-American author; he was attached to America and detested John Bull. He was angered by the English caste system, the arrogance of the rich, and the misery of the masses.

Reid's political passions did not die out in the years of his stabilization and well-being. In London he became acquainted with the ex-leader of the Hungarian revolution, Kossuth, and became his admirer, friend, and assistant. Kossuth was then being slandered by English conservatives, and the *Times* attacked the British government for having given asylum to a dangerous rebel. Reid engaged in pen battles with the damned *Times*, perhaps not quite successfully, for he was carried away by his temperament and his style showed too strong a penchant for grandiloquence. But Reid was ready to serve the Hungarian cause not only with his pen. The defeated revolutionaries were constantly on the lookout for "a change over there," and at one such moment of high expectations Kossuth intended to force his way back to Hungary under an assumed name with the help of

Reid. Captain Reid was supposed to go there as a gentleman tourist, Kossuth as his servant. Another revolutionary cause also preoccupied Reid, that of Poland; he was active in the British-Polish Society. That activity did not remain without reward, as at one of the meetings he noticed a young girl—no more than a teenager at that time—who was to become his wife. Elizabeth Reid was, it seems, quite a personality. Her book *Mayne Reid, a Memoir of His Life* (1890) is, considering that nobody else has written a monograph on the subject, our main source of information on Reid. I have taken my material mainly from that work. Another source of information, particularly in regard to Reid's political opinions, is the monthly "Onward" ("For the Youth of America") edited by him in New York in 1869-70 during his short stay there. Reid himself filled this magazine with stories of adventure, geographical descriptions, zoological curiosities, poems, and commentaries on the international situation. His was always a rare capacity for work; when he died in 1883 the list of books written by him was imposing.

I have allowed myself this discussion of Mayne Reid for a very personal reason: he fascinated not only Russian but also Polish readers. I remember climbing a steep street with a strange name, Mała Pohulanka (Little Spree), in Wilno with a book by Reid under my arm: the sleeve of my sheepskin coat, the belt clasping my sheepskin, gray winter weather, boys in the middle of the street gliding down stretched out on their sleds, steering with one leg. Such details are fixed in our memories as if at the moment of perception they were colored by a strong emotion. What I carried under my arm excited me then: a promise of delight. At that time I considered versified writings to be plain stupid and did not guess that over Reid's novel about the Amazon River, *Watery Wilderness*, I had acceeded to a poetic initiation.

To explore Reid's influence in Russia and Poland would call for a special study. Here I will only enumerate topics that such a study might develop. It was probably he who introduced a new approach to Nature, more, so to say, precise. Nature for his young readers ceased to be a projection of anthropomorphic images or a pretext for indefinite pantheistic transports. His mania for providing the name of every plant or animal with its Latin equivalent (in brackets), and the care he showed in describing the climate and the milieu proper to a given species, all made Nature less uniform and stimulated attention.

Włodzimierz Korsak, a Polish author of books on hunting for young people, was Reid's imitator in this respect. If I may judge by my own case, I would indirectly ascribe to Mayne Reid: my ability to name in Latin many species of birds, my Korsak cult, and my emotional responses (even today) to names of Polish hunter-naturalists such as Taczanowski or Sztolcman. Besides, the triumph of Reid's books occurred at a time when purely humanistic education was breaking down and when zoology and botany lessons in school inspired the zeal of youthful, rather cruel, naturalists—collectors of beetles, butterflies, and birds' eggs. Another topic would be the romantic appeal of America. Even if we were to trace it back (in continental Europe) to Chateaubriand's *Atala*, and later to Fenimore Cooper's novels, Reid's contribution was particularly significant. Chekhov and other writers take for granted the reader's familiarity with the scenery of Reid's novels. The poem "The Headless Horseman" by the Polish poet Antoni Słonimski, for instance, assumes the reader will remember Reid's novel of the same title and will respond to the words "prairie," "mustang," and "the banks of Leona" in the same way as does the poet.

After Reid the America of virgin forests, prairies, mustangs, and buffalo undergoes a peculiar, autonomous evolution in the literature of continental Europe thanks to the pens of authors never known in America itself. A German, Karl May, invented his megalomaniacal yarns of adventures in the far West while sitting in a debtors' prison. The superman narrator, undaunted Old Shatterhand, is a sharpshooter who never misses and who kills grizzly bears with a knife. He is at the same time noble-minded, kind, purehearted, and generous. Only in Europe did Karl May's *Winnetou, a Redskinned Gentleman* attain the status of a classic adventure novel. The novel, typical of May's compensatory dreams, reminds us of the compensatory self-idealization of a miserable young painter, Adolf Hitler, an assiduous reader of May. We can also assume that May, who had never been in America, borrowed the scenery and human types from Reid, reworking and blowing them up as was his wont.

It was rather late (only in the beginning of our century) that in Russia the image of Siberia acquired for some the seductive power of American-like prairies and forests, with its own natives acting as Indian counterparts. Then the appetite for imperial adventure was whetted by the books of Kipling and Jack London. If as grown-ups Volodia and Chechevitzyn from Chekhov's story traveled eastward (stopping for a reasonable time in Kamchatka and not attempting to cross the Behring Strait in a native's canoe), they owed their passion for traveling to their childhood readings. After finishing his studies at the Politechnical School in Riga (this was shortly before World War I), my father obtained his first appointment and found himself on the River Yenisey. He became well acquainted with that part of Siberia, from the Saian Mountains to the Arctic Ocean. I penetrated the secret of those travels when I opened the trunk filled with his school books. Thus, one more topic: how Mayne Reid acted as a guide to the exoticism of Russian Asia.

1963

11
Joseph Conrad's Father

Because Joseph Conrad's father was a writer (and together they create a dynasty) it might be rewarding to look for a continuity of emotional tone, if not of philosophical outlook, in their lives and works. Few of Conrad's biographers have studied the history of his family; among these, foreigners have obviously been hampered by linguistic difficulties. In order to understand the vicissitudes of the Korzeniowski family, moreover, one must enter into the historical complications of a little known part of Europe. The prospective biographer finds himself confronted by a mass of dates which roughly coincide with the time of the Crimean War. The aim of this article is to select certain details that will make the father writer more familiar to the Western reader.

Throughout the nineteenth century Russia was busy assimilating those territories which fell to her after the partitions of the Polish *Respublica*. The largest of these provinces was the part of the Ukraine situated on the west side of the Dnieper River. Because of the fertility of its soil and the bad conditions for agriculture in the rest of the kingdom, this area became the tsar's most valuable acquisition. In official decrees the new territories first were called "adjoined lands," then "recovered lands," and finally "native Russian lands." The last nomenclature was confirmed by learned evidence that showed Ukrainian to be merely a Russian dialect. This argument was not well received by the Ukrainians, and it later contributed to the enmity between the two Slavic peoples.

The Ukraine was also inhabited by a significant number of Poles. The class structure was based on social origin and religion. To be a Pole was to be a nobleman and a Catholic. The landowner, leaseholder, petty clerk, doctor, or lawyer in a small town all belonged to the same social class, internally stratified in that it embraced both the rich and their "clients." All occupied a superior position in relation to the illiterate masses of Orthodox or Greek-Catholic peasants. "New times," which brought speculation, development of the beet sugar industry, and the increased export of corn from the port of Odessa, were also destined to gradually weaken the code of custom that had knit the Poles together.

Theodore Korzeniowski, a resident of the Ukraine, was a nobleman and—true to the tradition—a soldier. During his youth Poland had identified Napoleon with its hopes for pushing Russia back to her former boundaries. Korzeniowski discharged his patriotic duty: decorated with the Cross of Valor after the Battle of Raszyn,[1] he was promoted to officer's rank. He served with Napoleon's Polish army through 1812, and many years later he participated in the 1830 uprising (during which he was again decorated for bravery).

Military exploits are, however, only a part of Theodore's biography. We should also imagine him as a *pater familias* and a landowner who inspected his fields on horseback or in a rustic carriage. Contemporaries relate that Captain Korzeniowski was inclined to lying and boastfulness, all of which was overlooked in view of his past exploits. He was a tyrant at home and given to outbursts of unrestrained anger. According to an old custom his sons had to kiss his hand. Yet Theodore was incredibly fond of his three boys. After one of them (Apollo) went away to study Oriental languages, the captain soon assured his neighbors that he had received a letter from his son in Arabic.

The wealth of the Polish nobility in the Ukraine has often been exaggerated. Korzeniowski had a penchant for speculation and tried thus to acquire a fortune—with just the opposite result.

[1]The victory of the Poles over the Austrians in 1809.

Having lost the entire estate in the Winnica district brought by his wife's dowry, he administered for the government the large village of Korytna, confiscated from Jagełłowicz. Although the village was prosperous and the rent assessment moderate, and although he was an entirely capable and hard-working manager—because of his propensity for giving himself over to illusions and living by them, he lost the rest of his capital there.[2]

Toward the end of his life, Korzeniowski experienced a misfortune that was shared by many Poles of that time. Two of his sons were deported—one, the youngest, to Siberia; the other, the middle son, to northern Russia. The eldest perished in the new insurrection. When the captain himself died, the commander of the local Russian garrison sent his orchestra to play for the funeral of this enemy who had fathered enemies.

We are concerned with the second son, Apollo. He was born February 21, 1820 in Honoratka (Bracław District). He went to school in various Ukrainian towns: Kamieniec, Niemirow, Winnica, and Zhitomir. He was constantly expelled from school for "free-thinking." This meant not so much Voltairian tendencies as it did "a complete lack of social and political conformity, and an innate violence which was later to characterize his writing."[3] The authorities' low opinion of Apollo's spiritual condition prevented him, once he had finished school, from going to Berlin— a mecca for the educated youth of that day. In 1840 he entered Petersburg University, where he studied Oriental languages and law. The letters in Arabic, however, belong to his father's legends. He received no diploma, and it is very likely that during the four or five years when he spent winters in Petersburg and summers in the Ukraine he occupied himself with everything but his studies. "Everything" meant chiefly literature and affairs of the heart.

"And he had his Beatrice," writes one of his critic-contemporaries, "she was full of charm and intelligence, a refined Ukrainian girl with the heart of an angel, who was later to be our poet's guiding star, the source of his inspiration, later his

[2]Tadeusz Bobrowski, *Pamiętniki* [Memoirs], 2 vols. (Lwów, 1900).
[3]Ibid.

betrothed, and finally his wife and the mother of his only son."[4]

Beatrice was called Evelina Bobrowska. Her brother, Tadeusz, was to become the author of memoirs valuable to any historian of the nineteenth century (he was also Joseph Conrad's patron and friend). Bobrowski asserts that Apollo Korzeniowski "was firmly reputed to be ugly and intolerably malicious." He qualifies this with the observation that Korzeniowski was only merciless (in conversation and in print) to the rich. Otherwise he was indulgent toward humble folk and pleasant enough in everyday life "for the sake of equilibrium." Buszczyński concurs in this opinion: "All that was honorable and good elevated him and inspired a kind of ecstasy in him. When he spoke at those times his eyes glistened with tears, and his countenance, usually marked by irregularity of feature, assumed an expression of strange beauty and incorruptibility in those moments of tenderness or rapture."

Although the girl's family found this gloomy and sensitive youth socially acceptable, they could hardly take him seriously as a suitor. The penniless Apollo had no profession and was supported by his father, whose own financial situation was thought to be less than brilliant. The young man furnished no guarantees for the future. Efforts were nevertheless made to marry him off within the neighborhood but he always managed, by the timely use of his malicious tongue, to alienate those families into which he had been introduced as a prospective suitor. Apollo finally overcame the older generation's resistance and, in 1856, brought about his marriage with Evelina. We can, on the basis of his literary work, conclude that these protracted sufferings shaped the poor but idealistic Apollo's relation to the caste.

Apollo Korzeniowski spent most of his life in the Ukraine, where he administered other people's estates. He was a leaseholder in Łuczyniec, then a manager and plenipotentiary to the Sobańskis in Derebczynka. This external respectability served

[4]Stefan Buszczyński, "A Little Known Poet—His Position before the Last Uprising, His Exile and Death," *Czas* (1870).

as a coverup for his literary occupations. He was in fact one of the last squire-writers who used to practice their art in a rustic corner. All of which could scarcely have helped him to maintain equilibrium. The cleavage is evident. The theme of a mask worn by someone who only outwardly conforms to accepted opinions predominates in his plays.

Korzeniowski was a rebel not atypical of his times. Confronted by the "swinish life" around him, which seemed to result from the very structure of the universe, he oscillated between extremes of mockery and despair. His poetry implies a tendency to divide humanity into the "sensitive" and the "swine"—a romantic division which lies at the foundation of most revolutionary movements created by intellectuals. He looked for help from the "sensitive," who were represented by Evelina and a few of his poet friends. In his translations, which were much admired at the time, Korzeniowski turned to writers who shared his aversion for the established order of things. He translated into Polish Vigny's *Chatterton*, parts of Hugo's *Légende des siècles*, as well as almost all of Hugo's dramas. Only some of these translations were actually published. We know that he used to return to this work at the most difficult moments of his life; thus during his last years, as a deportee in Chernigov, he translated Shakespeare's *Comedy of Errors* and Dickens' *Hard Times*.

Korzeniowski was primarily a poet, and as such he belongs to the "second wave" of the romantic movement. His writing is derivative; his incapacity for taking images directly from reality makes his work interesting only in terms of its contribution to the spirit of the epoch. Some of his works did enjoy great popularity at the time. *Words from the Cross*, written after the defeat of revolutionary hopes in 1848, circulated in anonymous versions, paradoxically enough attributed to Krasiński.[5]

"The most distinguished part of his poetry," says Buszczyński, "remains in manuscript. These manuscripts circulate in

[5]Zygmunt Krasiński (1812-1859) was, after Mickiewicz and Słowacki, the third most important Polish romantic poet. See chapter 4.

numerous copies from hand to hand throughout the country.
They are eagerly copied and often distorted. Because of its ignorance the reading public arbitrarily attributes them to different
authors." Buszczyński adds: "...all his manuscripts are in the
hands of the author of this article and are awaiting a publisher."
That was in 1870. They have not been published till now.

The cycle *Detached Stanzas*[6] is prefaced with the motto "Ubi
Crux, ibi poesia" ("Where there is a cross, there is poetry"). The
same motto recurs in Korzeniowski's later writings. Poetry is, in
his opinion, a function of suffering. "Crux" has a double meaning: personal and collective. The author's tone of despair expresses his total isolation amidst people who are only concerned
with buying, selling, and the idiotic diversions of snobbery and
social rank. We are led to suppose that his unhappy love for
Evelina (he had then captured her affections but not her hand)
offers a key to much of his poetry. His poems are often hymns
to perseverance; without the strength afforded by religious
belief, the only recourse would be suicide. "Crux" also desig-
nates a collective fate: according to its bards, the Polish nation
was being crucified. Its tragic situation reflected the widespread
debasement of a Europe that had become indifferent to moral
values. Because of the tortures she had been subjected to,
Poland had purified herself and others; she was, then, a nation
of poetry. But the "swine," indifferent to the Cause, opposed
their calling. Korzeniowski reproaches himself with having
understood this very late:

> Oh, how long, how basely,
> I have closed my life
> To inspiration and ardor!
> . . . .
> In the oblivion of self-love
> Between death and sorrow
> Between groans and the death struggle
> When only graves illumined
> My youth's first dawning,

[6]Published together with his play *Komedia* in Wilno (1856).

> I had no tear in my eye!
> My breast heaved not with sobs
> A youthful heart did not grieve,
> Oh, God, God, forgive me!

Korzeniowski, already a well-known poet, established himself as a playwright when as a result of his "commitment" he began to portray in verse plays some of the specimens of humanity he had come to know so well. *A History of Polish Literature* (published in 1877)[7] evaluates him in the following terms:

Apollo Korzeniowski occupies a highly prominent place in the field of our dramatic poetry. The theme of all his work is a social idea, reflected through the prism of poetic feeling and his personality as a poet. In his works he attacks above all those elements of the nobility which have been demoralized by egoism and inertia. He is not at all concerned with the trivial social vices. He willingly treats the blackest stains on the human soul—fraudulence, perfidy, cunning, betrayal—and does each one justice with passionate fervor and eloquence. His wit bites down to the very bone; his irony is homicidal. His laughter resembles the growl that precedes a deep bite.

His first play, *The Comedy*, was suspected by some contemporary critics of being an adaptation of Griboedov's *Woe from Wit* (the author, by the way, vigorously denied it). The critics were offended by the brutality with which "good society" is handled as well as by the play's indisputably revolutionary overtones. Published for the first time in Wilno in 1856, this play was performed for the first time in 1952 (!), whereupon it was proclaimed by the Warsaw press "the most progressive, violent, and mordant literary work of the eighteen-fifties." The next play, *For the Sake of Money*, published in St. Petersburg in 1859, was successfully staged by Polish theaters in Zhitomir and Kiev during the author's lifetime.

The action of both plays takes place in the wheat capitals of the Ukraine: Odessa, and Kiev. There is a common hero, Henry,

[7]Based upon the lectures of Zdanowicz.

in both plays. A "proletarian" by virtue of his poverty—he has no estate—Henry is a pure, feeling person, a complete stranger to the milieu of landowners. The corruptive power of money is doubtless the central theme in both plays. Even the two plots resemble each other; a marriage is thwarted because of intrigues to which high-mindedness falls victim. Paradoxically, Henry in *The Comedy* spurns the hand of his beloved at the moment when their enemies' machinations have been unmasked. The explanation for this rejection lies partly in the fact that Henry has no respect left for his milieu ("he shook the dust from his feet") and partly for the simple reason that a happy ending would be incompatible with the author's pessimism.

In *For the Sake of Money* Henry, ten years older, is no longer a young enthusiast who plots against the social order. He has adapted himself, and now he wears a mask. He is even noted for his wit, which conceals contempt and horror. Here the plot motivation centers around the prospective marriage of a friend of Henry's, Joseph. The latter, a revolutionary who has returned form a six-year exile, falls in love with a young lady from a "good home." Henry hesitates as to whether he should help his friend win her or try to discourage a terrible misalliance; he knows that the girl feigns interest in anyone reputed to be wealthy, and contrary to her supposition Joseph is a pauper.

Most noteworthy in both dramas (which are disguised as comedies) is the violence of the poetic invective and the sharp repartee. Evidence of this may be found in the Henry-Anna dialogues in *For the Sake of Money*. In the following speech Henry attempts to cure Joseph of his delusions:

> You believe, you believe, then you are an utter
> fool!
> And when Anna betrays you? You will believe
> that virtue
> Resides in me. I betray you—you will believe
> in the cat,
> The cat betrays you—you will believe in
> the dog, the dog betrays—

> You will put your faith in the table, chair,
> desk, pipe, and old shoes,
> In the calendar and gravestones!—You can travel
> Through snow-storms without a fur coat—you are
> warmed by your faith!

The gentry, which periodically gathered in Kiev for the so-called Contracts (during these gatherings the Ukrainian nobility met in large numbers and transacted business) or which carefully supervised its own interests in Odessa, did not overly concern itself with national issues. On the whole these Polish gentlefolk even had reason to congratulate themselves: they had profited as subjects of the Russian crown. Their petty existence was of course intolerable for those who "believed." *For the Sake of Money* (which was extensively censored at the time) contains a drawing-room scene that seems to echo something similar in Mickiewicz's *Forefathers' Eve*. The political allusions are quite explicit:

> We shall eternally be in the shadow,
> In peace, as though behind the stove; we can trade,
> Tread the roads of progress, buy, sell—
> And we so live that in our dying hour
> No one will stop to think we even lived.

What does Joseph find upon returning from his Siberian exile? His love for Anna turns out to be a misunderstanding:

> . . .But I was mad
> To shatter the remains of faith and hope and love
> Upon that gilded tomb of vermin!
> Which is their world of falseness and emptiness!
> Upon that world where each one hurries to a new
> Colchis
> In search of the golden fleece, or crawls, or
> walks!
> He tramples the heart along his road! He
> rejects feeling!
> He mocks dedication, confuses faith with false-
> hood,

> Spits upon virtue! And rejoicing in his animal
> cunning,
> Laughs a stupid laugh—because he has one ruble
> more!

A world without honor. Balzac has familiarized us with the perfidy and depravity which spring from man's lust for gold. The female monsters are, however, quite unexpected in a verse play written in the middle of the nineteenth century. Korzeniowski's monsters are beautiful, charming, intelligent. They stop at nothing in order to secure themselves physical comforts through the wedding contract (read: legalized prostitution). In *The Comedy* one of these charming creatures forges a letter in order to protect her dowry at the expense of the happiness of one of her best friends. During his struggle with her, Henry finds an ally in a true "proletarian"—a miserable bookkeeper who lives in mortal terror that he will not get his monthly salary and who, in order to assure this salary, participates in the Chairman's shady activities. At a given moment, however, he rebels and challenges his employer: a heroic exploit in that he is risking death by starvation! In all of Korzeniowski's work this is the only example of a character who hails from beyond the circle of well-mannered people accepted by the caste. (Despite their poverty, Joseph and Henry *are* socially acceptable.)

During the years between his second and his third, and last, play (we shall pass over some of his stage works for children) Korzeniowski pushed his "commitment" one step further by joining a conspiratorial action. This ultimately led to his imprisonment. His third play appeared after he had succeeded in leaving the borders of the Russian empire (where he had contracted tuberculosis). He was living in Austrian Galicia when he saw *The First Act*[8] performed in Lwów. He expresses his gratitude to the actors in a preface wherein he reveals his views on the function of literature; he also apologizes that his own writings do not attain the kind of perfection he himself might have expected from them. "It is evident on the other hand," he writes,

---

[8]*Akt Pierwszy* (Lwów: Biblioteka Teatralna Lwowska, 1869).

that there are certain social situations where one cannot expect order, moderation, and rounded contours from any manifestation of life, especially Art. We have found ourselves in such a situation for the last hundred years. We are partially a society of helots, and these of the best and worst varieties: some have out of utilitarian motives agreed to accept a position of subservience in order peacefully to gnaw the bones they are condescendingly thrown; others naturally enough seek to tear themselves away from such a situation and to bring to their senses those who endure it in peaceful, embroidered, and betassled ignominy. Thus two divergent, self-contradictory and clashing tendencies left their separate marks on the forces within our society—on domestic life, on science, on art—that is to say on the Good, the True, and the Beautiful of everyday life.

Further on in the same preface he declares that literature is a substitute for action.

We see a generation of writers and poets holding their pen like a sword, a weapon used by them whether they are on the defensive or on the offensive. How can one criticize such a militant stance on the part of those who have nothing to lose and everything to gain? Questions of art must often give way to those of life. Hence the frequent sins against the indifferent azures of the Aesthetic. No one of the Art for Art's Sake camp would subscribe to our view—may God bless them. We ourselves, and many others, make no claim to the title of literati; we have nonetheless long and diligently held the pen in our hands—we repeat the words of the great Italian patriot and poet: "I write only because I cannot act now."

The First Act is a short tragedy. The title indicates that the author intended to write a cycle of loosely connected scenes in which fate was to play a dominant role. A happy nest of rural gentlefolk—joy, prosperity—and the blow which falls when least expected. The wife comes from a tribe contaminated by collaboration, Targowica.[9] She betrays her husband with someone from an equally contaminated strain. We can only conclude that for Korzeniowski, serving the enemy (the Russians) indi-

---

[9]Targowica—the town where the confederation that betrayed Poland to Catherine the Great was formed. This paved the way for the third partition of Poland in 1795.

cated a weakening of the moral instinct. Betrayal becomes an inherited, psychosomatic feature of the personality. If in many famous tragedies Fate works through an inherited predilection for murder and adultery, why then should it not appear in this form? (If we somewhat boldly assume that collaboration always stems from the same causes: weak nerves and an attachment to material gain.) In any case, exactly the opposite atavism asserted itself in the Korzeniowski family. When it came to issues of national importance they were loyal at any cost. We may therefore justifiably raise the question of Apollo's political thought, especially since he exemplifies a paradox central to the Polish revolutionary movement.

A Russian who found himself in revolt was obliged, if he wished to save himself from pessimism and impotent irony, to turn against the tsar and (the next logical step) destroy the patriotic myth that was so closely linked to the Crown and the Orthodox Church. This was not easy—as is shown by the vacillations of Pushkin or the cautious liberalism of Turgenev. A Pole in revolt encountered no such difficulties. Since the evil seemed to come from the outside, he was able to identify his own struggle for independence with the struggle for a changed and better world. Because the feeling of biological menace from the "Giant of the North" was strong, and because it had to be opposed collectively, the struggle for liberty gained priority. Russia was held accountable for every social evil; even the vapidity of the *szlachta's* way of life was attributed to the debasement caused by living under conditions of virtual slavery, whereas it actually resulted from the social structure and the peculiar development of early capitalism in Poland. All this meant that the moment of liberation played, in the minds of Polish revolutionaries, the same role which the moment of revolution was later to play for the Marxists. It was to be an absolute beginning and a total solution. The cause of radical reform was championed as the means to an ultimate end, namely, the complete mobilization of the masses to armed action. The leading militants, however, relegated social prospects to the future, contenting themselves with a purely emotional sympathy for the downtrodden. Therein lies the reason why the movement's cutting edge was so often blunted. Korzeniowski's psychology shows that a refusal to accept existence *in general* was the motivating force behind his actions. It was not difficult then for him to accomplish the leap to an earthly absolute which embodied itself in Poland, the Fatherland. Perhaps under other conditions he would have donned the colors of the People or Art.

Korzeniowski's attack on art was extremely eloquent: You cannot serve two gods. In his idealistic view the word *Fatherland* had to include brotherly love as well as virtue. But events took place in 1846 which proved that strong class conflicts did exist in Poland. Korzeniowski considered the slaughter in Galicia—a massacre of nobles by their peasants, secretly abetted by the Austrian police—not only as a warning for the future, but as an explosion of savagery that threatened national solidarity:

> Struggle with the enemy!...Oh, struggle unendingly—
> With the strength of sacrifices, with the bitterness of bloody tears,
> With no pride of *caste* or *birth*,
> The eternal cankers of a poor nation.
> Scorn criminal fratricide and butcheries
> Which await the night and fear the sun—
> Forgive each other.

A comparison of Apollo Korzeniowski and his brother-in-law, Tadeusz Bobrowski, will provide a valuable insight into the ideological extremes that were prevalent at the time. Well adjusted to his milieu, sober, and dead set against overly lofty spheres of the spirit, Tadeusz Bobrowski had nothing of the romantic revolutionary about him. He regarded rebels like Apollo with indulgent skepticism. Surprisingly enough, this liberal conservative had a much better grasp than Korzeniowski of the most urgent questions of his time. Bobrowski was an activist within the framework of the status quo: he signed petitions that were presented to the authorities and participated in various counsels which advocated changes through legal means.

The key problem of the era was the emancipation of the peasants. Here the nobility of the Ukraine and Lithuania took a more progressive stand than their peers in Russia and in the so-called Kingdom of Poland. In fact, within the Russian empire the greatest initiative for change came from the Ukraine and Lithuania. Those nobles well knew how to look after their own interests. Having realized that change was inevitable, they tried to make it as painless as possible. Bobrowski was especially active in drawing up memorandums which were preceded by complicated diplomatic intrigues at the local level. This explains the tone of friendly irony in his descriptions of Korzeniowski:

Although he thought himself a sincere democrat, while some thought him an "ultra" or "Red," he was a hundred times more of a nobleman than I whom, as I often pointed out to him, neither he nor others had suspected of democratic persuasions.

I have never gotten to the bottom of his political and social convictions. I see only a foggy attraction to the republic as a form, and in it something equally foggy *per modum* of the rights guaranteed by the Constitution of May 3, 1791, which has already become inadequate in our time. He hesitated about the emancipation of the peasants. He sympathized with my opinions (expressed as early as in 1854) on the question, but he also somewhat timorously maintained that only those who actually owned land were qualified to pass judgment. All this hardly surprises me, for I consider it an axiom that poets, who are men of imagination and ideals, cannot clearly formulate postulates of life. They would, moreover, be well advised to eschew such tasks, leaving them to less pure and ideal spirits who are more aware of the actual struggles and needs of worldly existence.[10]

This is not to say that Korzeniowski was contemptuous of the people. His interest in them was, however, limited to their capacity for national *élan*. As for the peasants in his district, he asserted that their lot had changed for the worse since they had come under Russian domination. Up until then they had not

[10]Tadeusz Bobrowski, op. cit.

been obliged to provide recruits, and the administration had at least been honest. Korzeniowski anticipated no difficulties in stimulating the peasants to fight.

The Crimean War sent Apollo into a state of exaltation. And no wonder! The war was fought at the very gates of the Ukraine, and while Polish exiles in Paris were feverishly lobbying in the diplomatic chancelleries, a Polish legion was being formed in Constantinople to fight alongside the Turkish army (not as extravagant an idea as it might seem—the Polish *Respublica* and Turkey had had common boundaries for centuries). In 1855 Korzeniowski lived in the hope of a popular uprising which in conjunction with military pressure from the Allies would deliver a decisive blow to Russia. And then something happened which reinforced his hope: a genuine peasant insurrection occurred.

Both Korzeniowski and Bobrowski give accounts of this event. Although they agree as to the essential facts, their interpretations differ somewhat. The Ukrainian peasants from many villages in Kiev province had gathered in a mob and locked up the taverns "so people might not say that drink speaks through us and governs us." Then they went to the manors and proclaimed their "will," setting down the following conditions: one-third of the harvests would be for them and two-thirds for the masters. Officials and Orthodox priests were set afloat in the ponds, but no one was killed or wounded. During the twelve days the peasants were in control they kept guard, maintained order, and worked the fields. The local Russian administration panicked and sought to demonstrate that this rebellion (which was really spontaneous) had been the work of Polish socialist emissaries from Paris. Using a time-proven stratagem, the administration stationed a contingent of recruits from the Kingdom of Poland (who knew no Ukrainian) in Biela Cerkov. A rumor was circulated to the effect that they were petty gentry who, dressed in uniforms by the lords, were to be used in a punitive capacity.

The attempt to blame the Poles for what ensued was not

entirely unsuccessful. Both Korzeniowski and Bobrowski indignantly recall that the estate owners took refuge behind the advancing Russian army. With the aid of cannon firing into crowds offering only passive resistance, the army quelled the revolt. The rebel leader was sentenced to 3,000 cudgel blows, while the others received from 500 to 2,000. Everyone caught in the action was sent to Siberia.

The whole series of events (which occurred in 1855) profoundly shocked Korzeniowski. Speaking in the third person singular he relates how he arrived on the scene too late: "He who hurried to participate in it could only suffer in his heart, weep, and hope one day to be able to offer the memory of these events to the conscience of Poland and of humanity in general." He testifies that the peasants asked the masters to assume command and strike out against the Russians. The leader said at the investigation: "There is nothing to hide. In 1831 we were wrong not to have sided with the masters, but now they are wrong because they did not stand by us."[11] Korzeniowski also asserts that the leader's last words before being sent to prison were an appeal to "good people" not to believe the rumors about the petty gentry disguised in uniforms. Korzeniowski himself could hardly have been present and no one today can verify his version. All of which simply proves that a legend persisted after the actual events.

Bobrowski, the conservative, offers an explanation strictly along the lines of class analysis: the revolt broke out because a rumor was circulated among the peasants to the effect that the tsar had issued a decree granting them the rights of "free Cossacks." If they had immersed the priests, it was because they thought the priests were being paid by the lords to keep the decree a secret. Bobrowski mentions no "national tendencies."

For Korzeniowski the past assumed the colors of lost virtues. His plays suggest that he felt nostalgia for those patriarchal times when relations between peasant and master were based

---

[11]Those pronouncements (in Ukrainian) are quoted by Korzeniowski in his memoir *Poland and Russia*.

upon mutual obligations rather than law. In wanting to join the peasants' revolt Korzeniowski was perhaps being true to the spirit of these lost virtues. His gesture seems doubly quixotic in the light of his firm belief that rescue would come from the Black Sea and Turkey.

After the Crimean War the Polish anti-Russian movement took on new strength, which steadily increased up to the rebellion of 1863. Here the paths of Korzeniowski and Bobrowski separate. The former devotes himself to revolutionary activity: he moves to Warsaw and there becomes one of the founders of the clandestine Central Committee that was later to become the revolutionary government. The latter regarded the movement with hostility and thought it had no material grounds for success. He also violently opposed an uprising planned in Lithuania and the Ukraine. After his predictions had been tragically confirmed, Bobrowski complains in his memoirs:

> For lofty political reasons it has been decided to mark our frontiers in blood; double insanity: first, because it proved the fallibility of our claims in the light of new historical and political tendencies; and second, because it all-too-eloquently revealed the secret of our numerical weaknesses in both provinces.[12]

The uprising of 1863 was a complicated phenomenon, and it had complicated consequences. It caused a furious outbreak of chauvinism in Russia. A small group of Russian revolutionary democrats who fought the system and expressed their views in Herzen's *Kolokol* were virtually alone in their solidarity with the Poles. Tsardom, as was always the case when it was necessary to keep the Poles in hand, sought a rapprochement with Prussia. To deal with the revolt the Russian government resorted to various kinds of propaganda (without which terror is ineffectual) which had proven useful in the past.

In order to fully understand the 1863 uprising we must briefly turn to the peasant question which the Russians so cleverly

[12]Tadeusz Bobrowski, op. cit.

exploited. In 1861, Alexander II had emancipated the Russian serfs as well as the peasants of Lithuania and the Ukraine. But in the autonomous province called the Kingdom of Poland, where since Napoleon's constitution of 1807 the peasants had been *nominally* recognized as free men, their economic status underwent no change. The liberation movement was national in character; therefore its leaders, who all advocated independence, proposed differing and sometimes contradictory solutions to the peasant question. For instance the Whites, a faction in which the landowners had the deciding voice, opposed the manifesto of January 1863 whereby the revolutionary government granted land to the peasants.

The decision to revolt was taken at a most unexpected moment. It was provoked by the tsarist government's announcement of a new levy of recruits, something roughly similar to a forced labor deportation today. The insurgents were mainly of humble origin, yet the Russian officials were able to isolate them from the villages by pretending that the uprising had been undertaken by the nobility in order to defend its own privileges; the tsar was portrayed as the peasants' true benefactor. Regular armies crushed the poorly armed insurgents in the forests. Very few Russian soldiers were drawn to the losing side by the slogan "for your freedom and ours." The peasants quickly obtained their economic freedom from the monarchy and they began (on Russian instigation) a series of Byzantine orgies of thanksgiving, burning incense in front of the tsar's portrait. At the same time gallows were set up all over the country and thousands of condemned persons were deported to Siberia.

The official report that appeared in the *Wilno Messenger* gives an excellent idea of the official line used to prompt demonstrations of gratitude from the villagers. The catchword was "liberation from the Polish yoke." "This was a most solemn and pleasing moment," says the report, "everyone broke into tears from an overflow of emotion. We—did not feel that it was merely the portrait of the divine father-tsar; we thought that the

All-Merciful himself had appeared to us to bear witness to our joy. We—did not know what to do; each of us rushed forward trying to press his lips to the portrait, if only to its very edge."

On international terrain the propaganda action was carried out in the same spirit. The Polish patriots whom it vilified reacted with incredulity. Their feelings of bitterness and shock are eloquently expressed in an article published in the emigré periodical *Ojczyzna* (The Fatherland).[13] Here are some quotations from this piece written in 1864:

If we were to believe the words of tsarist diplomacy, there is no other government on earth which is so concerned with the cause of civilization and social reform—no government which so assiduously guards the interests of humanity—no government which cares with such maternal love for its subject peoples.

A high-minded conception of social needs, the noble feeling of the mission that Russia must fulfill in regard to the human race, the defense of order and healthy progress; in a word the most perfect philanthropy is synonymous with Moscovy's every action. Its royal edicts exude a peculiarly sincere good nature and sweetness; the notes of the tsarist diplomats can soften even the hardest heart....

In those Russian newspapers published for Europe, the series of atrocities perpetrated in Poland is represented as an unbroken chain of good works.... The tsar inquires with fatherly concern about the rebellion's suppression; he gives heartfelt thanks to his faithful servants who so well understood his lofty intentions with regard to the Poles and so adroitly accomplished the labor of pacification; he rejoices that his Polish subjects once again will begin to enjoy peace and blessed happiness.

Generally speaking the rebellion of 1863 has been harshly appraised by Polish historians. No critique on the subject, however, is more biting than that contained in Tadeusz Bobrowski's memoirs. Although Bobrowski's post-defeat hindsights are connected with the views of the Kraków school (conservative historians who criticized romanticism in politics), his sober observations give an unusually detached picture of the Polish debacle.

[13]Ojczyzna's home was Dresden, a longstanding haven for Polish exiles.

Bobrowski points to the hopelessness of a rebellion whose leaders allowed themselves to be dominated by an emotional chain reaction of their own making.

They successfully used falsehood as a tool, some consciously, in order to realize those would-be-lofty ends the attainment of which is permitted to lofty intellects; others served involuntarily, convinced by the repetition of slogans and exaggeratedly optimistic reports that went in two directions: from Paris to Poland and vice versa. Falsehood was used unscrupulously, whether it was offered to a secretary of Napoleon II's cabinet and Prince Plon-Plon or whether it was disseminated through every layer of Polish society right down to the humble alcove of a rustic clerk who was attracted to the revolution by false representations concerning forces that were to come to the rescue from abroad. Without exaggeration it may be stated that the events of 1861-63 were begun in falsehood and that they ended in falsehood.[14]

Bobrowski, whose brother played a prominent role in the revolution, was a strong antirevolutionary and therefore hostile to all "illusions."

No simplistic explanation, however, can accurately encompass the play of social forces that made up the revolution. Warsaw, where Korzeniowski had taken up residence in 1861, had become an arena for the factional struggles of various conspiratorial groups. Korzeniowski's position was close to that of the left (the Reds) but little is known about his exact views on the intrigues of that time. We do know that while he was founding a newspaper and working on the formation of the clandestine Central Committee, he miraculously escaped death at the hands of the Stilettists (an ultraradical terrorist group). Soon afterward, in October 1861, he was arrested and incarcerated in the Citadel. There he suffered from scurvy and rheumatism; he also managed to write a book of hymns and prayers entitled *In House and Temple* with the motto "morituri te salutant." In April 1862 his sentence was pronounced: deportation to Perm (in accordance with Korzeniowski's own wishes) where a former schoolmate was governor. As it later turned out, however, the governor was frightened by the prospect of such a

[14]Tadeusz Bobrowski, op. cit.

troublesome prisoner and intervened with his superiors, with the result that Korzeniowski was instead exiled to Vologda. Apollo's comrades in the conspiracy offered to help him escape, but he refused on the grounds that they should not all risk their lives for the sake of a single individual.

The trip to northern Russia was made in a horse carriage under police escort. Apollo was traveling accompanied by his wife and little Konrad, aged five, the future novelist.[15] It was a harsh trip for the woman and the child. Just as they were approaching Moscow Konrad fell seriously ill but their guards would not allow them to stop. When they reached Moscow they paused in order to change horses; here Konrad's mother, standing in the window of the posting station, began to shout "Save my child!" One of the city's inhabitants offered his assistance and brought them a Polish doctor whom Apollo had known many years before in Winnica. The doctor diagnosed Konrad's illness as meningitis, intervened with the authorities, and managed to save the patient.

Evelina was the next to fall ill. Near Nizhny Novgorod her condition became so grave that, after a stop, the guards carried her, wrapped in bedclothes, to the carriage. At this point her husband threw himself upon them; his determination must have been desperate since, in the battle of one against many, a cart shaft was broken. A Russian officer who arrived on the scene bawled out the guards and gave the family permission to stay ten days in Novgorod.

While in Vologda, Korzeniowski learned of the rebellion's outbreak. His impassioned appeal—"Not by this road! Not by this road! It is always this way with us! Either too late or too early! But God is great!" —shows that even the movement's most active leaders had not foreseen the revolt in the form which it actually took; in fact the whole thing had slipped from their hands altogether.

When in 1899 Conrad's friend, Robert Cunninghame

---

[15]Doubtless the father-poet was inspired in his choice of a name by two of Mickiewicz's heroes: Konrad Wallenrod in the dramatic poem of the same name, and Konrad the main protagonist in *Forefathers' Eve*.

Graham, invited him to attend a pacifist meeting in London,
Conrad replied that he viewed "the future against the background of a very dark past" and that he wanted to preserve his
"faith in a hopelessly lost cause, an idea without a tomorrow."
He refused the invitation:

Il y aura des Russes. Impossible! I cannot admit the idea of brotherhood, not so much because I believe it impracticable, but because its
propaganda (the only thing really tangible about it) tends to weaken
the national sentiment, the preservation of which is my main concern.[16]

When H. L. Mencken uncovered Slavic elements in his work,
Conrad reacted angrily. In his protest he reveals a typically
Polish antipanslavist view. He denies any affiliation with Russian literature, asserting that if he has read a few Russian
novels, he has read them in translation. "Their [the Russians']
mentality and sensibility were always abhorrent to me, in view
of my inherited inclinations and my personal disposition." Conrad's eccentricity on this subject seems much less pathological in
the light of some of his father's literary work.

During his exile in Vologda, Apollo Korzeniowski wrote a
treatise-memoir *Poland and Russia*, which he managed to
smuggle abroad. This little opus appeared anonymously in
installments in *Ojczyzna* (1864). The author here views the relations between the two countries in the context of a universal
threat to all of Europe. Speaking as "a man from the border-
lands," Korzeniowski stresses the Russian Imperium's gradual
and constant march westward. He sees his whole life in terms of
a struggle against Moloch; he discusses the approaching extermination of European civilization, heretofore only perceptible
to the unfortunate inhabitants of those lands that had already
gone under. His critique of the Eastern organism is reminiscent
of that contained in Karl Marx's essay on the history of Russian

[16]Conrad's letter was written on February 8, 1899. Part of the original is in
French. See *Joseph Conrad's Letters to R. B. Cunninghame Graham*, ed. C. T.
Watts (Cambridge, 1969), p. 116.

diplomacy. Both works were written more or less at the same time; moreover there is some evidence suggesting that Marx got some of his ideas from Polish emigrés. Korzeniowski also expresses some of the same ideas expounded by Mickiewicz in his course on Slavic literatures (given at the Collège de France 1840-1844). Korzeniowski's tone is exceptionally passionate. Here, in brief, is his reasoning:

The Tartar yoke has shaped Moscovy. It should be still considered a horde. Everything belongs to the Tsar, every subject is liable, from one day to the next, to be raised to the heights or cast down from them. Murders and palace plots are the principal means of government. The Tsar unifies in his person the functions of leader, lawgiver, and priest. Religion is state controlled and idolatrous; it propagates fatalism and fanaticism. The Russians are unsuited for free institutions: they feel that "in the fire of freedom they would go up in smoke like dry manure" and cease to exist as a nation.

Moscovy is such that it must, out of fear of its own annihilation, seek expansion on the outside. No matter how long Europe evades the conflict, the time will come when a clash will be inevitable. The time, moreover, will be that of Moscovy's choosing; i.e., the least convenient time for Europe, which will stand to lose half her strength.

Once and for all, in consideration of the Polish uprising, let it be stated as an article of faith for Europe that whosoever in his dealings with Moscovy believes her Tsars, even for a moment, or whosoever, even in passing, considers the Moscovites capable of freedom, must be deceived—and then conquered.

At the same time it is dreadful to think that barbarism has spread its carcass from the Black Sea to the Pacific Ocean; that it weighs down upon sixty million people, that it can field an army of a million men, that it has a fleet, and that, above all, like a burglar it importunately thrusts its will upon the governments of Europe. The whole thing is so monstrous that, if it did not exist, no one would believe in it.

According to Korzeniowski, the fear of Russia was a motivating force behind European politics in the nineteenth century. "At the Congress of Vienna those European powers which had just disposed of the threat offered by Napoleon, a man of destiny, now trembled before that fearful and destructive machine that called itself the Russian *Gosudarstvo*. The word 'peace' had acquired a special, arcane meaning: Europe was exhausted by twenty years of war; her governments were willing to defer to the most frightful acts of criminal violence in order to keep the peace. Their slogan 'Peace at any cost!' had a hidden and agonizing meaning—'Repel Moscow at any cost.' Peace is a good, a true and a beautiful thing, but give it to the Moscovite and he will forthwith transform it into falsity and ugliness."

The reason for Europe's weakness perhaps stems from Britain's policy of equilibrium during the Crimean War.

In order not to let France become too strong she abstained from supporting the rebellion in Poland. The recognition of national rights that would have been implicit in such support would have dealt Russia a death blow. The Russians perhaps best of all knew how many oppressed peoples would, following the Polish example, rise up in arms. They also knew that their empire was held together in the worst possible way: by force. Moscovy, furthermore, would lose with Poland—not only for the moment, but for all eternity—the best half of its military strength, the surest half of its financial resources, and those particularly European characteristics that it had gained from Poland's annexation.

By "Poland" Korzeniowski understood the entire extent of the occupied territories: Lithuania and the Ukraine as well as the Kingdom of Poland.

Thus, during the freezing northern evenings, the exile wrote by the light of a kerosene lamp. The above quotations well indicate the nature of the worldly absolute to which he was committed. Perhaps the vision of his father's hand moving over the paper lingered on in the son's memory. Later, Conrad must have read his father's treatise, which begins with his reminiscences of imprisonment in the Citadel. Russia was, therefore, not just another nation to the son.

Exile spelled disaster for the Korzeniowski family—Volgoda's harsh climate undermined Evelina's health—and it was only after many unsuccessful attempts that they finally got permission to leave. Chernigov was designated as their next settling place. There Evelina died in 1865, which meant that Apollo lost his main *reason d'être*. This misfortune signified to him the defeat of all his national and political aspirations; henceforth his loneliness was to be irrevocable. He tried not to betray signs of his despair. "The lie of serenity in my eye and on my countenance," he writes to a friend, "all my fear remains within, heretofore it has not appeared on my face; for *she* is looking at me. No matter what happens, *she* will surely know that we can never part—for otherwise I should not have the strength to continue."

The widower's son was now to be his only bond with life. Brooding, unhinged, and withdrawn, Apollo was able to force a laugh only with the greatest effort. What sort of companion was he? In 1866, he wrote with some trepidation about the nine-year-old Konrad:

If I could singlehandedly put Konrad upon native soil among honest men, I should desire nothing more. Then I could unite that living body and awakening soul with the body of our society and I could transport the dust that lies in a foreign cemetery to a familiar village graveyard; I could touch my homeland with my feet, breathe its air, gaze into the eyes of those loved ones and cry "Now, Oh Lord, free thy servant, for I am very weary!"[17]

Korzeniowski's religion was neither shallow nor ritualistic. It was based on a kind of Christian stoicism rather than reasoned belief. "Everything that surrounds me," he writes from Chernigov, "bids me doubt the existence of a divine omnipotence, in which I nonetheless place all my faith and to which I entrust the fate of my little one."

On the first anniversary of his wife's death, Korzeniowski suffered a tubercular hemorrhage. This human wreck no longer

[17] All quotations referring to that period of his life are taken from Buszczyński, op. cit.

presented a threat to the tsardom; freed in 1867, he received a passport to leave Russia. He went to Galicia with his son by way of the Ukraine and Podolia (where he was allowed to remain only a few days). During the trip he tortured himself for having deserted his wife's grave and found justification only in terms of his obligations toward Konrad. "My main task is to bring Konrad up as neither a democrat, aristocrat, demagogue, republican, monarchist, nor as a flunky or servant of any of these—but only as a Pole."

They spent a year in Lwów. Here the attitude of nonacceptance which had molded Korzeniowski's personality resurfaced. Just as in the days of his youth, ardor and enthusiasm elicited no response from the "human snails." Their somnolence astounded him: "They have forgotten how to feel—they do not know the gift of speech—they read nothing. Custom, language, and religion count for naught with them!" Contact with such people must have been even worse than imprisonment for Korzeniowski. Only his literary projects seem to have kept him going. He thought of publishing a collection of Hugo's plays in his own translation; he contemplated "a great Polish novel" about Moscovy's corrupting and cynical influence upon every level of Polish life. Finally he moved to Kraków to join the editorial board of a new journal called *Kraj* (*Home Country*).

Had Korzeniowski been well off financially he would perhaps have heeded his doctors' advice and migrated to a milder climate. Even this is doubtful, however, since any preoccupation with his own person was contrary to his inherent asceticism. His tuberculosis progressed quickly and, in the spring of 1869, he had to abandon all of his literary plans. In the last few weeks of life his pronouncements lost their accustomed acerbity. "I forgive people," he said to a friend, "and I wish people would forgive me. —I was bitter and angry because I loved. I intend to burn my poems, perhaps not all of them...but those which seem unnecessary today. There is too much bitterness in them." As he was taking leave of his friends after receiving the last sacraments, his smile did not come from self-enforced discipline.

He gave the impression of a happy man. "I have finished every-thing . . . I have settled my accounts with this world. Now I no longer belong to it." He died on the twenty-third of March 1869 in Kraków, at 6 Poselska Street. The twelve-year-old Konrad became an orphan. Under the care of relatives, he studied at Saint Anne's High School. Has Apollo Korzeniowski deserved a memorial? He has, for the sake of love. Who knows, perhaps there should be a monument in Kraków portraying the man with the boy who owed him so much, especially his "inherited tendency."

"He never wanted consolation," they wrote after his death. The same could have been said of Conrad himself. Both father and son, uncompromising, strict toward themselves as well as others, marched through an era of strident and crass material-ism. Romantics they were; but how much harder it is, instead of merely contrasting the real with the ideal, to acknowledge the inexorable tragedy of intentions doomed to defeat and yet not stop at the boundaries traced by irony and dandyism.

Perhaps Apollo Korzeniowski's goals were too narrow, too limited. But do not those who abstrusely reason about humanity tend to become victims of their own abstractions? To each is given the nearest, the most tangible sphere; in Conrad's case the deck of a ship. It is not improbable that the ship *Patna* (a somewhat blotted version of the word *patria*) in *Lord Jim* symbolizes the home country. The father stayed on deck until the very end. For him the only way the people of his milieu could attain real dignity was through disavowing the power of money. His notion of duty was that of the sailor whose ultimate concern is the fate of his ship.

The father's character does much to explain why Conrad was so wounded by an article by Eliza Orzeszkowa (a celebrated "positivist" novelist who wrote about many contemporary social problems) denouncing his "betrayal." In her opinion the betrayal consisted in writing in English, bestowing his talent upon another country. Conrad never heeded the advice of Tadeusz Bobrowski, who asked him in 1881 to contribute travel correspondence to the newspapers at home. His uncle praised his literary style in Polish and concluded his appeal thus: ". . .you would in this manner [i.e., by publishing in Poland] strengthen your ties with Poland, and it would be an act of veneration toward the memory of your dead father who desired to serve and did serve his country with his pen."[18]

Conrad did remain faithful in his own way to "an idea without a tomorrow." A memorandum on the Polish question, which he presented to the British Foreign Office in 1916, hardly testifies to his indifference. In 1919 he wrote Sir Hugh Clifford a letter in which he expressed sarcastic pleasure in the fact that not one English or French life was sacrificed to his country's cause: "The weight of the obligation would be too heavy." Like his father, Conrad was totally untouched by nineteenth-century optimism; they both despised the greedy and self-seeking bourgeois who enslaved poor wretches in his factories and derived faith in progress from the gold watch chain on his stomach. They witnessed this character or prototype undergoing a metamorphosis. In Apollo Korzeniowski's play *The Comedy* he appeared as the good-natured Chairman who pondered various base intrigues while ambling along the streets of Odessa; in Conrad's *Heart of Darkness*, which starts with a description of those white buildings that house the "Societés Anonymes" in Brussels, he has evolved into the demented half-English, half-German Kurtz, who acquires ivory by murdering people.

Both father and son measured these thieves (who were so highly esteemed by their fellow citizens) by the same standard of decency and honesty which binds together a ship's crew in its fight to the death with the dark element. For Apollo the crew was the Nation or Europe, the dark element Russia. For Conrad, the crew perhaps signified humanity in its struggle with destiny. Conrad inherited from his father a quick temper (which he was, however, more adept at disguising) as well as the stoic virtue of postulating values by sheer effort of will—against

[18]Zdzisław Najder, ed., *Joseph Conrad's Polish Background: Letters to and from Polish Friends* (Oxford, 1964).

chaos and destruction looming menacingly from all sides. He was, at the same time, always ready to admit the illogical nature of hope. Both men were fanatics of persevering tenacity. And if they may be reproached for appealing to lost virtues amid a world of commerce and industry, we may reply that there is a kind of greatness peculiar only to Quixotes.

1956

12

A One-Man Army:
Stanisław Brzozowski

[These are two chapters from a book, published abroad in Polish on
the fiftieth anniversary of Brzozowski's death, which had some influence upon his revival in Poland. Always a controversial figure, he was
boycotted at the end of his life—something which can be explained by
his rare gift of antagonizing both the right and the left and by the accu-
sation of cooperation with the tsarist *Okhrana* leveled at him by his
political enemies. From the end of World War II to 1956 he was taboo
in Poland for ideological reasons. Since that time some of his writings
have been republished there; but in spite of several studies dedicated
to him and his thought, no overall assessment of his philosophy seems
to be in the offing. In this study the American reader may find that I
make too many references to local names, institutions, and movements. Taken together with what is outlined in the preceeding essay
(on Joseph Conrad's father), however, this one should serve the purpose of introducing Slavists and others to unsuspected attitudes and
conflicts in that part of Europe. Even if some details are felt by the
reader as dispensable, the picture that emerges will probably be worth
the effort as it is far from being of mere local or provincial interest.
This applies even more so to the chapter composed mainly of Brzozowski's pronouncements. His verbalization (often irritating) notwithstanding, it is the story of a quest which might have been ours.]

> "Our life, our self, is a sentry post;
> when we abandon it, the whole of humanity
> loses it forever."—Brzozowski.

Stanisław Brzozowski died on April 30, 1911, in Florence of
tuberculosis or (it would be more correct to say) of poverty, in

the thirty-third year of his life. In the course of the half century which elapsed since that moment there has been hardly one literary discussion in Poland in which his name has not figured. Yet there has not been even such a memorial as a posthumous edition of his collected works in his native country.[1] The majority of his books today are already collector's items, and whoever wishes to acquaint himself with them must rummage them out one by one in the catalogs of large libraries.

Brzozowski's truest friend was his wife Antonina, née Kolberg. Thanks to her, a monument designed by the sculptor Roberto Passaglia bearing the inscription "Stanisław Brzozowski, poeta e filosofo" was erected in 1928 in the Trespiano cemetary in Florence. Another faithful friend was the Lwów critic Ostap Ortwin. In the final period of Brzozowski's life, when the author was hastening to finish as much work as possible, the Polish press and publishing houses put him under a boycott. Had it not been for Ostap Ortwin, Brzozowski's most mature books would have remained unpublished and the manuscripts would perhaps have been lost, especially since the boycott remained in force long after his death. Ortwin was a literary counselor for the publishing firm of B. Połoniecki in Lwów, which issued *The Legend of Young Poland* (*Legenda Młodej Polski*, 1909); *Ideas* (*Idee*, 1910); and later, after the author's death, the novel *Alone Among Men* (*Sam wśród ludzi*, 1911); *Voices in the Night, Studies of the Romantic Crisis of European Culture* (*Głosy wśród nocy, studia nad przesileniem romantycznym kultury europejskiej*, 1912); a volume containing *Phantoms of My Contemporaries* (*Widma moich współczesnych*) and the unfinished novel *A Book About an Old Woman* (*Książka o starej kobicie*, 1914); a selection of the writings of Cardinal Newman translated and introduced by Brzozowski (1915); and also, financed by Antonina Brzozowska, his *Diary* (*Pamiętnik*, 1913).

Twentieth-century Polish literature has no other writer of

[1]A collective edition was initiated shortly before World War II, then started many years later, in 1973.

comparable scope and seriousness. Intellectually he towered above every celebrity of his time, and this fact determines his special position today. Writers like Żeromski or Reymont became "established," planted in their own period, classified; it would not occur to anyone to censor their works. Editors and critics always approach Brzozowski with alarm and trepidation, although the reasons for their attitude change according to fluctuations in political circumstances. This means that he is always our contemporary, and that he has not yet become a subject of literary-historical research. Simply by taking pen in hand every critic comes out for or against Brzozowski. Granted this partisanship, it ought not to be concealed; it is rooted in the very nature of the problems preoccupying Brzozowski in his own time.

The overall theme of his writings was an upheaval in the history of mankind which had begun at the threshold of the modern era, at the time of the French Revolution. Each of his books might be described as an excursion into some area of the century which was undergoing more rapid transformations than any century before it had undergone. This applies also to Brzozowski's novels. *Flames* (*Płomienie*) is built around the activities of the Russian revolutionaries of Nechaev's group as well as those of the Paris Commune and of *Narodnaya Volya* in Russia. *Alone Among Men* depicts the years 1830-1848 in Poland and in Prussia, including the milieu of the Hegelian Left in Berlin. What we have of *A Book About an Old Woman* shows that it would have been a moving novel about the "official rehabilitation" of a 1905 revolutionary killed by his own party. The explanatory subtitle *Studies in the Romantic Crisis of European Culture* given by Brzozowski to the volume of his essays on French, English, and Russian writers underscores his view of the crisis as something continuous and continually assuming new forms.

The turbulent era which fascinated Brzozowski and was conceived by him as a continuum, as something in flux, became still more tempestuous soon after his death. We are separated from him not only by World War I and II and the Russian Revolution but also by a development still difficult to grasp because it is even now in its initial stage: a development toward a universal concept of man which would apply to all civilizations. A new terminology has grown out of experience; many endeavors, postures, modes of thought have since acquired at least provisional and approximate names; on the map of history in flux, orientation points have since been set. Because Brzozowski ventured into regions of thought which in his time hardly anyone either in Poland or elsewhere had explored, he had to devise his own instrument, his own terminology. Today we would say he conducted "an existential analysis of historical structures," that in his work everything revolves around the problem of "alienation," although he did not define it thus. Moreover, his desperate thrashings give the impression that he was a man who was trying to speak to the deaf. The deafness of his audience was due to its complete unfamiliarity with dialectical thought, to its demand that the answer to any arising problem be *either* "yes" or "no," that in examining an intellectual current, or this or that work, the "bad" and the "good" be discoverable. Hence the stupefaction caused by Brzozowski when in the same breath he would say "yes" and "no" (for example, his whole attitude toward Romanticism); hence also the outcry against his frequent self-contradictions.

No doubt we read Brzozowski today in a way different from that of his contemporaries, which is no merit of ours but a result of collective experiences which have melted the wax in our ears. We are less prone to take him literally; his elusive, protean thought appears to us to transcend itself all the time, continuously rectifying its own errors and yet moving in a clearly defined direction.

How is it that despite Brzozowski's conviction that he was rebuilding the consciousness of his people, he remains a writer unaccepted by those on whose behalf he lavished all his strength? Why is it that although so much has been drawn—and is in fact still being drawn—from the heritage of Brzozowski, it has been taken as if by stealth, without public acknowledgement? Why is this surreptitious borrowing the sole recompense for love? How does one become an *écrivain maudit?* Perhaps it is time for us to try to discover some answers to these questions, taking advantage of the perspective that a period crowded with historical events provides. Let this essay be the wreath which no pilgrim from among Polish men of letters will bring to the Trespiano cemetery on this occasion, the fiftieth anniversary of his death.

THE LINE OF FATE

There is a great deal of printed testimony—pronouncements of critics, memoirs—which convinces us that the public that read Brzozowski either did not understand him at all or understood only every third line. There were exceptions, of course, but they were not numerous. What were perfectly understood, however, were Brzozowski's attacks on individual writers. Because his readers usually skipped over the intricate argumentation, his sarcasm and eccentric passion appeared even more glaring. Brzozowski had the reputation of a young lampooner, defaming the good name of the worthy and the deserving, such as Sienkiewicz or Miriam Przesmycki. It is unfortunately easy to review his battles as if they were taking place today, to forget that they did not have the same meaning in his own time. Today his sharp judgments seem well motivated; back then they seemed paradoxical, exaggerated, tactless. When Brzozowski said he blushed from shame for Polish literature because it had produced a Sienkiewicz and such a masterpiece of falsity as *Quo Vadis?* even the opponents of Sienkiewicz winced in disgust. This does not mean that Brzozowski's critical campaigns did not increase the number of his enthusiasts among the young. In general, however, his youthful admirers were only sentimental allies declaring themselves for Brzozowski because he was "progressive"; he himself had little faith in them.

But what was most difficult for his contemporaries of any age to understand was the man himself, for he treated intellectual questions as though they were matters of life and death. To his countrymen this earnestness was strange indeed. In spite of all the revolts of Young Poland, the intellectual climate—that is, those permanent characteristics of the Polish intelligentsia regarded by Brzozowski as the heritage of the gentry (*szlachta*)— remained unchanged. And one of the main afflictions of that intelligentsia (and does it not persist today?) was its conviction that arguments concerning a *Weltanschauung* were something impractical, a social pastime entailing no consequences. The embodiment of this attitude was Mr. Podfilipski[2] (a figure whom, Brzozowski believed, Weyssenhoff had created without conscious satirical intent). In 1904 Brzozowski wrote his imaginary conversation with Podfilipski. Here is a fragment:

"—And I was thinking that convictions—"
"—Convictions? Who ever speaks about convictions?—why, only in Parliament. You have no convictions in society, and above all you do not force them on anyone. I, for example, prefer baccarat, sir, or what do you say to lansquenet?—Is that a reason to be at each other's throats? isn't it all the same? And just look around: there is an aristocrat, and there a democrat, and already disputes, quarrels."[3]

Perhaps few people realize the relationship between this code of tactfulness and the cordiality, hospitality, and warmth of the nest of gentlefolk that smoothed everything over in forbearance of human follies. Brzozowski was aware of this relationship. But only because he was different, because he was treated as an outcast by the intelligentsia, even by those of its members who revolted against the philistines, though they were bound to the latter by a tie stronger than they supposed. Therefore, in order to explain his "adventurism," people early in his lifetime started to circulate rumors about his peculiar origin.

Leopold Stanisław Leon Brzozowski was born June 28 (the sign of Cancer!), 1878 on the farmstead Maziarnia, parish

---

[2] The hero of Józef Weyssenhoff's novel *Życie i myśli Zygmunta Podfilip-skiego* (*Life and Thoughts of Zygmunt Podfilipski*) (1898).
[3] *Phantoms of My Contemporaries.*

Wojsławice, region of Chełm. His father, from a formerly wealthy but now impoverished family of the gentry, was the manager for the owner of Wojsławice, Count Poletyłło. This Count Poletyllo had a reputation of being a "weirdie"—why, it is difficult to discover. According to a whispered rumor he might have been the father of Stanisław Brzozowski: the weirdness of the father could then explain the weirdness of the natural son. There is nothing to confirm this story, however. When Brzozowski was born, the Count Poletyłło was already aged; Brzozowski's mother hardly knew him and lived in neighboring Maziarnia leased by the family.[4] Yet Brzozowski's father had a free hand in the estate of Wojsławice, and addressed Count Poletyłło as uncle; and it is for this reason the neighborhood maintained it was the manager himself, and not young Brzozowski, who was the son of the owner. Even if this had been true, aristocratic parentage would have given Brzozowski no financial security. Who knows, perhaps Count Poletyłło served Brzozowski as the prototype of the figure of the splendid eccentric, the castellan Ogieński, in the novel *Alone Among Men.*

At first Brzozowski went to the Russian gymnasium in Lublin (he had bad memories of it), then to the gymnasium in Niemirow in Podolia, where his family had moved. At the Niemirow gymnasium he underwent a crisis foreshadowing his further fate.

The "crisis" of Darwinism, as it was then called, ran its course among the Polish more mildly than among the Russian youth. Most often it was absorbed and to a certain degree diluted by the patriotic-Catholic tradition. Exactly this inclination to intellectual compromise—the reasons for which can probably be explained only by reaching far back into the structure of the old *Respublica*—hardly allowed a Polish youth to swallow even a modest dose of intellectual equations since these, once formulated, would be ruthlessly binding. But Brzozowski by temperament, and here we touch on a secret of his individual destiny, was an intellectual and from childhood a glutton for the printed

---

[4]As is affirmed by J. Al. Gałuszka, *Wiadomości Literackie*, no. 234 (1928).

word. The whole of his life was a series of philosophical dazzle-
ments induced by a book, a page, or a single line. The crisis
therefore had a more radical impact on him than on either his
Polish or his Russian colleagues. He notes in his *Diary*, written
in Florence:

I remember how naively my colleague Nikolaev was surprised that
someone could seriously concern himself personally with questions of
logic. "Basically all knowledge is induction," I, a Darwinist at that
time, said, "if man is the outcome of an evolution, knowledge, which
the entire human species finds ready within itself, was acquired induc-
tively by our animal forefathers." "Well, if you will be thinking about
such things!"—and we were then in the eighth class and N. must have
been 20.

Darwinism drew the young Brzozowski—he admits it himself—away from the Poles and toward the Russians. Here Russian literature made the difference, taken up not as it usually
was by Poles—the reader constantly bristling defensively—but,
on the contrary, with complete abandon and devotion. It is sufficient to cite the *Diary* once again:

In leafing through written pages, the name of Mikhaylovsky caught
my eye. How beautifully young I was when I read him. Nothing will
change the fact that so many of my freshest emotions, the youngest,
most sincere of my thoughts, merged with these names. Besides, we
wrong these men. Pisarev is worth no less than Stirner, very likely
much more. One may read Mikhaylovsky alongside Proudhon and
Carlyle; Belinsky, Dobrolyubov, Chernyshevsky, though undoubtedly of lesser genius, of lesser intellectual brilliance (now I may be
wronging Belinsky), are no less deserving of attention and study than
the English or French essayists. And my dear Gleb Uspensky! It would
be a grievance to my soul were I to allow them to be silenced and were
I to forget these first teachers of mine. I still remember my impression
on reading Turgenev's *Fathers and Sons*. What a book! There is nothing so harmoniously tragic and human in literature of this sort. Then,
when I was fifteen, it seemed to me that I had for the first time encountered the speech of adults. "The Brain," as Meredith says—for the
first time I met this element in reading. Until then, thought was something which I had not found by myself in myself, something solemn,
boring, and I had submissively accepted this state of things.

Intellectual emancipation for Brzozowski, a pupil at the gymnasium in Niemirow, took the form of a protest against his home environment, that is, against the Poland of sentimental tradition and customs, of a little Catholic village church, the cult of national martyrdom, the ritual gluttony on holidays, and the programmatic anti-intellectualism. Should one be a man, or a Pole whose humanity is diminished by the very membership in a national group and submission to its injunctions? Apparently for Brzozowski this question was a vital one, for in two of his novels the hero acquires internal freedom only by trampling on a national interdiction. In *Flames* Michał Kaniowski breaks with his aristocratic home and dishonors his family by becoming a nihilist, a *Russian* revolutionary; he joins the Nechaev group and then, as a member of *Narodnaya Volya*, takes part in plotting the assassination of Tsar Alexander II. In the course of his stay in Siberia he meets Polish deportees of 1863 who cannot forgive his collaboration with the Russians in their revolutionary activities: for them Russia is barbarian, corroded by bribery and syphilis, a colossus on clay feet.

In the second novel, *Alone Among Men*, the sixteen-year-old Roman Ołucki liberates himself from the customs and beliefs of his milieu by violating a moral-political taboo almost as strong as that in the state of Mississippi which prohibits sexual relations between a white woman and a Negro: he helps an aristocratic Polish girl to elope with a Russian officer. No other writer in Poland to this day has dared to violate the rule, shaped by a collective subconscious, which asserts that entry into the "Russian world," or agreement with that world, is tantamount to a moral collapse, to the eternal damnation of the soul.[5] In politics, yes, during the life of Brzozowski the left had already been torn asunder by the quarrel between the Polish Socialist Party (PPS) and the Social Democracy of the Kingdom of Poland and Lithuania (SDKP and L), a quarrel that was to divide the socialists from the Communists: on the one hand independence and socialism, and on the other, a revolution in which all national

[5]This tempted Tuwim in *Polish Flowers* (*Kwiaty polskie*).

jealousies would automatically dissolve. In literature, however, there was no counterpart of this quarrel on another, deeper level; the sources of the bad conscience universally perceptible in those who, for the sake of revolutionary principles, acknowledged the "Russian world" as their own have never been investigated. Only Brzozowski depicted the Polish-Russian knot *tragically*, that is, giving the arguments and the attitudes of the antagonists *equal* weight and attributing to Russians and Poles *equal* sensitivity and emotional strain. In his essay on Herzen, for example, he does not hesitate to view the insurrection of 1863 with the eyes of a Russian:

Herzen had a penetrating look, that of an artist; after a conversation with Giller he turned to Bakunin, speaking of Potebnya and other Russian members of *Zemlya i Volya*, who hastened to take their places in the ranks of the insurrectionists: "And their road seems not to be the same." Nor was it the same. General Mieroslawski even considered it proper and possible to speak of awakening agrarian movements in Russia as a simple strategic diversion: "Let those barbarians massacre each other." Potebnya and other members of *Zemlya i Volya* went to perish for the Polish peasant and the Polish worker; the diplomatic Polish gentry stole this blood, just as it had also stolen and wasted the blood of those heroic artisans, a significant number of whom were among the rebels.[6]

Brzozowski justified his fight against the gentry mentality, and especially against the mentality of the intelligentsia of gentry origin, by the claim that the year 1831 had spelled the end of the gentry as a class; that year witnessed its final real act, in the course of which it produced at least one great leader and thinker, Maurycy Mochnacki. After 1831 its flower went into exile, and the decay of what remained behind in Poland contaminated feelings and thoughts. Brzozowski's ire sprang from highly personal causes: he was menaced from within by his origins and by the environment of his early youth. In the *Diary* he keeps harking back to what, in his opinion, prevented him from attaining full humanity. This could be described as an instilled

[6]*Voices in the Night.*

mistrust in the efficacy of the intellect. The old habits of "good society," as well as the experience of political defeat, made the intelligentsia of gentry descent unconcerned with thought, for "in fact nothing ever comes out of it." This scale of values was inculcated in the younger generation unconsciously and as it were inadvertently; it became the very air they breathed. But Brzozowski cared little about instilling in his readers aesthetic feelings that, after all, they might reconcile with a frivolous conscience. He was basically convinced that his mind was drilling tunnels through which both his country and humanity might reach the light. This labor was, however, subject more and more to attacks of internal "nihilation"—a state in which it seems to the thinker that it is not worthwhile to follow up an idea, that it is doomed in advance, that there is nothing to warrant its importance. Brzozowski defined boredom as a state of vacillation between "for" and "against"; we become a prey to it when the thoughts conceived in our mind mutually cancel each other and no one of them acquires power over us—and here he probably diagnosed a serious disease of society. The great effort of will he expended in overcoming his own boredom led to aggressiveness, as if he feared that tranquillity was a trap, that it meant sliding into inertness. His opposition to the Polish tradition thus had the features of "moral hygiene"; it was a defense of the rights of eternal youth, with its courage and enthusiasm, against self-deceiving adulthood which mistakes apathy for wisdom. Many passages in his essays suggest certain concrete situations: we picture to ourselves a slender young man with blond hair and blue-violet eyes ("the eyes of a mystic," as one of his contemporaries said), biting his lips when one of his passionate perorations evokes nothing but indifference and yawning. When Brzozowski in his essay on Charles Lamb speaks understandingly of the misuse of time into which Lamb's father forced his son by demanding that he play cards by the hour, he reflects his own impatience over the theft of time by his father. His *Diary* confirms this; in it, he recalls his school years thus:

For me personally, one of the most attractive characteristics of my mentality—and in spite of the many falsehoods, stilt-walking, and contortions which disfigured my life I did not lose it, was my compassion and regard for those writers who healthily and powerfully felt themselves in their roles as writers: Balzac and Walter Scott, Dostoevsky and Carlyle, and the great workers of the pen of the eighteenth century. But in my life, through many long years, everything was trampled, obliterated, by the domestic atmosphere, with its skepticism and frivolity, and lack of any kind of discipline. In the year that I am now recalling, I remember endless, lingering evenings when my father would drag me and my brother to a game of *vint:* I remember the way he looked at me as he mercilessly circled around me, indifferent to whether I was reading or writing, and ignoring my pretense that I had not "seen" his attempts. I felt sorry for him and could not resist him. I reproached myself both for sitting down to the game and for doing it reluctantly.

We may suppose that Brzozowski's attacks on the Polish intelligentsia for its chief sin—the substitution of sociability for thought—were but generalizations of his own conflicts with people who thought that both the truth and the untruth of the currents, doctrines, and theories imported from the West were of no genuine concern, since Western ideas were used only for display in conversation. The pattern repeated itself later when he was launched on his literary career. "With what lordly calm, with what familiar offhandedness of judgments were ideas and men here patted on the back," he writes in *Flames.* "A solitaire-playing sage or a national martyr who was bored to death between one game of cards and another, one carnival booth and the next, with an indulgent smile would watch his son get up from his reading, excited by Darwin or Buckle." This aversion drove the adolescent Brzozowski to the Russians. In *Flames* the virtues of Old Poland are represented by the Bielecki family; in *Alone Among Men,* by the Kosecki family. In both novels the first stimulus of "antinational" acts is the reaction of the hero against emotional custom preserved in the domestic fortress. In *Flames* the town of Niemirow and its gymnasium are depicted—

many decades, it is true, before Brzozowski's own time. Nevertheless the "circle" of Russian pupils who passionately discuss principles is probably a fair counterpart of the circle to which Brzozowski belonged.

In his critical studies Brzozowski objected just as strongly to any conscious or unconscious connivance with the Polish gentry. In his treatise on Mochnacki he said: "In Poland, as someone put it drastically, a phantom nobleman, sitting on the shoulders of a working, creative man, is battling with a swinish nobleman." While Brzozowski regarded Sienkiewicz as the bard of the swinish gentry, in Young Poland he found many a phantom nobleman; and this is more or less the meaning of the blows which he meted out to Żeromski. "Żeromski is unable to overcome passivity, because for thought he substitutes sentimental illusion. He refuses to criticize the historical attitude from which his psyche grew, and that is why his inner life succumbs to a fatalism which frustrates freedom." Thus, for Brzozowski, Żeromski's undoing was a result of his own goodness, of his "sentimental illusion," or of a lack of enough courage to disengage himself from Old Poland and to see it as it really was. It is interesting to note that Brzozowski contrasted Żeromski's passive emotionalism to the dominance of the will in Dostoevsky. "When [Żeromski] senses *brutal* power, the *brutality* as such immediately screens from him the element of power. What matters to him is that this power offends his sensibilities." Dostoevsky proceeded in a completely different manner. For Brzozowski *The Devils* was a sufficient proof that "Dostoevsky accepts the moral responsibility for the entire terrible history of Russia, that he accepts Russia as she is as the concrete historical form of his own soul. 'It is myself and it is mine—this whole world of blood and crime: out of it we shall build the future.'"

Is it, then, appropriate to say of Brzozowski, as has often been said, that in several of his works, and especially in his novels, he revealed a tendency to treason? Perhaps it is not as absurd as it may seem. In human quarrels, each side requires clear and evident reasons for action. Whoever, like Brzozowski, explores the origin of these reasons weakens the compactness of the group; in other words, he does not possess the qualities of a good soldier. Yet there are circumstances in which soldierly qualities are needed, and without such qualities there is no morality. It is thus a vicious circle, peculiar to minority groups on the defensive, as may be seen in the example of the Jews, the Negroes, or the Algerians. An individual does not wish to carry the stigma stamped upon him by birth; he wishes to be a man just like those who received no stigma, but the choice before him is that of either betraying his minority group—thus we find such types as an anti-Semite Jew, a Negro who passes for white, an Algerian Moslem who is more French than the French themselves, and so on—or of identifying himself with those components and characteristics of his own group which are most hateful to him. In this sense, *Flames* can be interpreted as Brzozowski's duel with his own obsession to free himself from Poland. Besides, he himself admits (*The Legend of Young Poland* [2d ed.; 1910, notes]) that it was a necessary stage in his struggle to attain self-knowledge:

In *Flames*, and whoever wishes to read through the book without prejudice will confirm this, I endeavored to demonstrate that the lack of a creative national consciousness leads to the breaking away of the most independent individuals from the national community, to the vision of life in abstract, simplifying dogmas, to the impossibility of finding a bond with one's own nation without renouncing one's personal freedom. I intended the story of Kaniowski not to be taken as a mistake, but as a valuable, positive intellectual process in a given situation: the meaning of this process became more and more clear to me in the course of writing.

Somehow, this intricacy served Brzozowski the writer well. Tracking down in the history of the nineteenth century the reason for typical Polish attitudes, he succeeded in grasping the great collective unhappiness better than those who lamented over it as fully their own. Better, because pity, if it is not to be "self-pity" and if it is to act effectively through the word, requires a sense of detachment and even at times an irony that adds horror. In *Alone Among Men* Major Ptyś, an ex-officer under Napoleon, is an intellectually limited and comic figure, a survival like one of those residents of the Ekeby estate in Selma Lagerlöf's *Gösta Berling*. But through his great love for his fatherland, through his suicide at the news of the defeat of the insurrection of 1831, he is elevated to pathetic dimensions. In the same novel, men who are superstitious and little deserving of sympathy believe a miracle has occurred and arrange a procession with an image of the Mother of God: it is a collective psychosis, a transfer of politics to religious emotions. But they resist Russian troops and they die for their faith; for them Catholicism and Polishness are one and the same. To complete the irony the tsarist officer Reitern, although he is a liberal, massacres these illiterate and half-literate unfortunates.

Of all writers Brzozowski most fully describes the genesis, the causes, and the near inevitability of the Polish attitudes. Few authors, even in Polish literature, which was usually concerned with such subjects, succeeded in catching in so few sentences the grief of mothers who know that to have a son means to live in continual fear, for the hecatomb of insurrections and conspiracies occurs regularly in every generation. Here then, in *A Book About an Old Woman*, is the tale of a mother in the period immediately preceding the outbreak of the Revolution of 1905:

"I can't forget that morning. I am walking along the street. It is early, in the springtime. I want to surprise Alex; I got new radishes at the market. He was then preparing for an examination. I see some kind of paper pasted on a post; I had to go uphill, so I stopped to take a breath; I just looked, I read, my head spun, my legs trembled; a phrase was written out in large printed letters: 'Long Live Independent Poland!' Something there about arms, about a struggle. I lost my head: in a second Alex was standing before my eyes, I remembered the year '63. In a second and without thinking I tore the paper from the post; I reached home out of breath; I burned it. All that day I saw everything as in a dream; he studied, and like that dog, like a child who is afraid of the dark, I was sitting on a little stool at his knee."

Brzozowski explains, through the image of Russia in his novels, the reasons for the traditional Polish carry-over of politics into the sphere of moral evaluation, that is, the Poles' aversion to Russia as something impure by nature, something with which there should be no intercourse in any form. The story of Reitern, one of the most important characters of the novel *Alone Among Men*, is like a summary of all those Russian biographies in which there seemed to be no alternative but the path of the revolutionary or the rascal. Reitern, noble, enlightened, liberal, after years in a Ukrainian garrison town where he watched over the maintenance of the established order, changes into a hangman and a servile underling; but his awareness of his fall drives him to habitual drunkenness and psychopathic behavior. This same Reitern, always perspicacious and coldly intellectual, speaks thus of his country and the reasons for the anti-Russian sentiment among the Poles:

"I am not surprised, nothing surprises me. I do not understand how one can support Russia. We support her, we and the whole world, but what does that mean? I often thought, what would have happened, if in 1815 Alexander had gone mad, if he had suddenly let loose all his drunken hordes on Paris. I have dreamt about it. I dreamed that we were speeding through the night in a throng; the night was dark, as it had never been, coppery, and flashes of arms were visible and, above all, that speed. All around were horses; all of space was rushing, and suddenly I saw him, the Emperor; he was riding on some sort of wagon and shouting something, but it was not human. Then I understood that voice, I saw what it meant. It meant everything. When I awoke I forgot. I forgot everything. And then I knew: It was as if I knew for what man lived and that he would not be."

Brzozowski spoke most emphatically, however, against the traditional Polish contempt of Russia. Not only did he remind the Poles of Potebnya and the other Russians who had taken part in the insurrection of 1863, he also honored the memory of Perovskaya and Zhelyabov (later the Russian nihilists held the same fascination for Albert Camus); not only did he preserve

throughout his whole life a veneration for Russian literature but
even maintained that the future would assign to Herzen a place
beside Montaigne. According to him the anti-Russian complex
sterilized the Poles intellectually and artistically, since it veiled
from them the truth about the human condition. As a result, all
the evil and suffering with which the human species had to con-
tend was projected by them into a single, limited geographical
and historical frame of reference—in other words, blamed upon
Russia. The more Russia assumed the shape of a monster, of an
emanation of Hell responsible for all evil, the more accentuated
was the illusory idea of the angelic nature of man, if not real
man, then at least man as he is found in the dreams of Don
Quixote. That is why Polish writers were so often unsuccessful
in their attempts to probe the demonism hidden beneath the
surface of human affairs. Reitern, the *porte-parole* of Brzozowski, hits the nail on the head when he cries out: "Only a Musco-
vite, and but for him all of this world and man is fine! You Poles
are behind us as though behind a mountain: the Russians have
screened the sun from us, but it is there. Well, we *are* Musco-
vites, good only for screening the sun. Oh! I hate you, innocent
lamb's blood of Abel!" Another of Reitern's outbursts conveys
the same idea: "One must be courageous, honorable, noble;
then you are with him. You cannot understand the soul of a
base man. Base creatures!"

Another figure from the novel *Alone Among Men*, the German woman Gertrude, perceives the same thing: "I don't like
Poles: they want to be good, too good for the world, they want
to poison us with an evil conscience." She obviously does not
mean that Poles are distinguished by especially high ethics.
Simply, their culture teaches them that virtuousness as such
must receive a historical reward even when not accompanied by
reason and will. This Polish reluctance to face the tragic element
in life was loathsome to Brzozowski, who built his entire philosophy on the self-reliance of man in the face of the "ahuman," in
the face of chaos. Man has only that which he wins in the
struggle, overcoming resistance through work and technology.

And this struggle *is* tragic, for in it values are not guaranteed but must be continually created, through an "existential act" which postulates itself. It is for this reason that Brzozowski utters judgments so unflattering to Polish sensibility: "There are no castles but those of Macbeth, and everyone has his own Banquo";[7] or: "The Polish sacrifice, which takes the place of all accepted forms, is but a desperate attempt to create instantly what must be created incessantly."[8] And in the following statement he makes an even stronger case against using Russia as a scapegoat for all the sins of the world: "It should be remembered that the oppressive power which is crushing us must have been born of a tenacious and bravely maturing soul before becoming what it is."

Brzozowski solved the problem of national allegiance by becoming a socialist, that is, by testing the Polish past, by renouncing the parasite class that could not even maintain its own state. As the cultural model for the future he chose the Polish worker, who would extract from tradition all that was vital and consistent with the endeavor to transform Poland into a modern industrialized country. Brzozowski was far removed from cosmopolitanism. He kept stressing the responsibility of every individual. For him "action" was anything fraught with real social consequences, be it a line of verse or a solitary thought—anything as long as it was not daydreaming, as long as it could potentially overcome the resistance of reality and become invested with form. But this incarnation had to take place within the geographical, historical, and linguistic limits which mark the existence of a nation. History *in abstracto* did not exist for Brzozowski: there was only a history of nations. "*Nations are the unique organs of the historical emanation of the psyche*" (italics in the original), he wrote in *Voices in the Night*, "and the abstractly human, international attitude of the cultured intelligentsia is an illusion. I believe, I feel convinced, that *Europe* and *humanity* are not empty words, but I also believe that one may

[7] *Alone Among Men.*
[8] *Legend of Young Poland.*

work in them and for them only through one's own nation." It is probable that here his reading in the Italian "Risorgimento" was as decisive as that in his native Polish literature. Internationalism sinned, in Brzozowski's eyes, by an evasive flight from resistance, from the concrete: "Idealism in an alien context is an easy thing; there, the postulates are always apparent, but not the burden of their realization." One more quotation from Brzozowski should make his position clear: "Speaking in historical terms, all human thoughts and mottoes appear to be transformed into the increased or decreased energy of a certain group or human type. Only thus do they exist as moments of life, only thus do they remain in the life of the species."[9]

Foreseeing that the Polish as well as the Russian future belonged to the working class, Brzozowski, although he sought independence for his own country, did not doubt that the Polish-Russian knot of offenses and hatreds would one day be cut. Before 1914 one could permit oneself at least that much optimism. Besides, the difference between Poland and Russia, and therefore the differences in their future development, were for him unquestionable. He was a past master at finding endless hidden correlations, at recognizing the pattern of continuity in forms that were opposed to those preceding them and yet stemmed from them. He was interested in a *something*, barely palpable, which showed through the history of every nation. This *something* he attempted to seize hold of in his essay on Dostoevsky, in which he analyzed two parallel aspirations toward a "national faith," that of Dostoevsky and that of Towiański.[10] In opposition to the widespread notion that Towiański was a mere charlatan and the evil genius of Mickiewicz, Brzozowski the dialectician treated Towiański and his sect very seriously as a unique phenomenon, important for every investigator of nineteenth-century Poland: if one pierces the veil of its often maddening shibboleths one finds underneath an attempt

[9]*Voices in the Night.*
[10]Andrzej Towiański (1799-1878) founded a political-religious sect in Paris in the 1840s.

to discover a *novum*, an effort to elaborate a philosophy of history different from that which the "old sphinx" Hegel had imposed. Here Brzozowski's sympathy was extended to men who were trying to find a way out of an unbearable situation. Hence in his novels the fine figures of Towiański's followers, of emissaries from Paris stealing across the border into the Russian empire.

Reading the most recent works of Russian literature in the final period of his life in Florence, Brzozowski felt uneasy. Far from considering the Russian *Décadence* to be similar to the Polish one, he thought its significance lay in the fact that "the flesh of Russian history has merged with its soul, that to a certain degree the terrible graft of Peter the Great is just now coming to maturity." He explained this by the recent changes in the Russian intelligentsia's position in society. "The problem of the intelligentsia as a stratum or a group"—he wrote in *Voices in the Night*—"above all as a type of life, today occupies the thoughts of all nations. In *Russian literature* it must lead to a particularly acute crisis, because in no other society have certain specific features peculiar to the intelligentsia been so strong as to exclude all others." It is possible perhaps to speak of these features in terms which Brzozowski used in attacking the Polish *Décadence*: it is the "revolt of the flower against the root," the tearing away from the base (the daily work of the millions of humankind), the turning upside down of the hierarchy in such a way that what occurs in our minds is acknowledged as the law of reality. For Brzozowski the Russian intelligentsia was a "perfect example of the inability to be historically creative, masked as abstract Prometheanism." The actual consequences of this upheaval had to be wholly different from the illusory aims of the intelligentsia:

The conscience reached here a complete denial of life, an opposition to it: it often believed that it owed life nothing, that it was completely alien to real Russian life, and this foreignness was its criterion of worth; but at the same time, unwittingly it grew, in a more or less indirect, in a more or less hidden and complicated way, into just that Russian life which it despised. Aimed against the Russian state, the arguments became premises of historical syllogism whose ultimate conclusion always coincided with the *will* of the state, that organ which expressed the life of the people outwardly.

Brzozowski wrote this in 1909. From his reading of contemporary Russian literature, he was inclined to believe that the Russian state had significantly accelerated the process of securing its hold on the intelligentsia and making use of it. He closed his remarks on various writers by saying, "I have attempted to prove that the Russian state has always been the body of just this mutinous soul, which has now begun to express itself in Russian literature. Today this bond is even closer, the soul is merging with the body; its movements, when the crisis passes, will become more efficient, more elastic, dangerous." And, addressing his Polish readers with his accustomed moralistic passion, he concluded: "That is why we must realize that the force and the nature of the Russian pressure on our cultural and historical life will increase and change." Thus the most important commandment is: "Do not allow yourselves to be outstripped in your very maturity—the maturity of historical self-knowledge." Moreover, Brzozowski warns the frivolous-minded that one cannot simply ignore Russia:

For many years I have pondered over Russian literature and studied it: I think I understand what is happening in it today, and I deem it necessary, in view of what I said before, that we penetrate more deeply into the very pulsating center of this spiritual life, that we think of Russia as a great and terrible reality. In one way or another, we shall be encountering this reality on our historical path.

The confrontation with Russia that always preoccupied Brzozowski had had its origin in the intellectual experiences of the student at the Niemirow gymnasium. Later there were other confrontations. He learned French and visited the archipelagoes of Taine, Renan, later Georges Sorel, Proudhon, and Bergson. He learned German and became acquainted with Nietzsche,

Hegel, and Marx. He considered Italian influences as some of the most beneficial for himself; he worked on a selection of the writings of the eighteenth-century author Giambatista Vico, his avowed master. After he had learned English his admiration went to Blake, Lamb, Coleridge, Robert Browning, but above all to Newman and Meredith. In his projected history of nineteenth-century European literature, the first volume was to deal with the literature of England.

A historian of literature capable of comparing works in six languages is rare. Brzozowski followed the newest publications in the six languages, even though he lacked the money to buy the most essential books. In Florence he rebuked the German critics for overlooking the emergence of an outstanding new writer, Thomas Mann, who had just published his *Buddenbrooks*. Just before his death he began to write a study of Joseph Conrad. Although a knowledge of Russian and German was then much more widespread in Poland than it is now, and French was still considered indispensable for an educated person, there were many translations from foreign languages including the latest scientific works, for example treatises by Poincaré; nevertheless, Brzozowski was far ahead of the reading public. He continually cited authors who were completely or almost completely unknown to it. A few Polish poets did translations from the Italian but on the whole, with the exception of Dante and the poetry assimilated during Poland's Italianate Renaissance, Italian literature remained outside the sphere of Polish interests. In spite of acceptable translations of Shakespeare (even as early as the eighteenth century, Niemcewicz had affirmed that Poles were more sensitive to Shakespeare than to Racine or Corneille), and notwithstanding the popularity of Dickens, Wells, and Kipling, the Poles drew their knowledge of England mainly from Taine's *History of English Literature*. Perhaps Brzozowski offended his readers by pointing up their ignorance with his name-dropping. But there was in him a feverishness, a hurry, a premonition or even a certainty that he had little time left to him.

Polish literature was then under the spell of French Symbolism, Young Scandinavia, and Young Germany. Brzozowski did not conduct a campaign against borrowing ideas from Western Europe, for Poland had fed herself culturally there for many centuries. He campaigned against a Poland which, in Słowacki's words, was "a peacock and a parrot of nations"—that is, against the shallow and frivolous aping of foreign models which severed them from their national background. In the so-called Polish *Moderna* he saw above all a ferment of the unprepared and half-educated: from the not very fastidious kitchen of Sienkiewicz and Miss Rodziewiczówna the members of this movement turned straight to delicacies of the most refined modern taste. But these "schoolboys arrested in their development," so greedy for philosophical and literary novelties, annoyed Brzozowski by disregarding what was valuable in Western Europe and borrowing only what was gaudy and modish enough to attract their attention. Such disregard is, as a rule, born of self-deception. In actual fact, for the inhabitants of a country economically backward and deprived of independence, the grapes of Western technical and industrial achievements were too high and therefore sour.

Brzozowski, however, chose for his vocation the awakening of his countrymen's conscience; he believed that conscience and will are always able to master "the force of historical gravity." He did not wish to mask Polish misery. "Nothing wounds and pains me so much," he wrote in *The Legend of Young Poland*, "as this disregard, this bantering dislike with which independent, free, atomized Polish souls look on the collective lifework of other peoples. They are unable to feel the terrible effort, the ardent labor, the great moral beauty hidden beneath the rough, discouraging exterior of modern cultures." And further:

Currents reaching us from Europe are short-lived; we enervate ourselves from day to day waiting for the "socialist" revolution; we cannot shake all this off; we cannot understand that Western psychology has changed the socialist apocalypse into a means of frightening the *bourgeoisie*, into a justification of an opportunistic passivity; we cannot understand that these are all but symptoms of the more acute problems pervading the old European societies, that we must reach deeper than all this.

And so Brzozowski, born in the area between Russia and Western Europe, assigned to himself the task of acting within his complex society; by what was foreign he tested what was native in order to strengthen it. He wrote only in Polish. Another literary critic from the same part of Europe, who in his youth had some affinity with Brzozowski, was beginning his literary activity; but he did so in German. This was the Hungarian György Lukács, who for his German writings used the name of Georg von Lukács. Although later (having become a Communist) Lukács had to disavow those early writings of his, they exercised an influence in various countries and Lukacs found many disciples, especially among the "nonorthodox" Marxists in France. Because the range of Brzozowski's philosophical inquiries went far beyond the bounds of a single country and a single literature, he too might have become the founder of a whole school outside his native land had it not been for the language barrier.

IN QUOTATION MARKS

Summarizing any author's views usually turns out badly; especially if, as in Brzozowski's case, all "systems" are negated and a way of thinking and living is proposed instead. But even if shortcuts cannot render an author's thought in all its mutability, they have a certain practical value; the more so today because Brzozowski's writings are hard to obtain. I shall make use of his own words whenever possible, reserving for myself the place of empathetic reader.

Brzozowski himself would have readily agreed he was not a philosopher in one quite common (though not exclusive) sense, and that he should have been farmed out to a place where they indulge in such unscientific childishness as literature and art. For he offended the dignity of the profession, and the defenders of its privileges could rarely count on his support. He offended and wished to offend them thus:

> I often have the impression [he says in *The Legend of Young Poland*] when I compare the states of mind of the philosopher, the social thinker, and the politician to the psyche of the artist, that not only a formal difference, but also something like a moral nuance enters into account. Compared with the inner life of such an artist as Baudelaire, all other approaches to experience, to the very act of shaping it, *contain an elusive admixture of dishonesty.* [The italics are Brzozowski's.]

Perhaps this is the true reason: "While an artist talks about something he has experienced, a thinker looks first for an idea by which to become independent from his experience."

The revival of Kierkegaard and the full development of the philosophy of existence took place after Brzozowski's death. Giving fashion and apparent profundities their due, and also keeping in mind that there is no *single* philosophy of existence, it befits us to acknowledge some of these philosophers' achievements as lasting. While it is difficult to rank Brzozowski with those of his contemporaries who held university chairs, it is easy to place him among West European philosophers of the 1940s and 1950s. He penetrates to the very core of their teaching in one sentence:

"Each of my experiences has an undeniable value, each is a fragment of an infinitely important unique struggle; every moment I have to decide, and that decision persists throughout my life" (*The Legend of Young Poland*).

The tendency on the part of Brzozowski and his successors to disregard the boundaries between philosophy and art (also action), and their striving for unity, perhaps explains their respect for the artist—since in an artist's work (if it is fully responsible) the importance of the moment is clearly demonstrated. No subterfuges are possible here; the decision becomes immediately fixed, incarnated, already irreversible, and furthermore it springs from what the artist himself is in terms of all his previous experience.

But what struggle does Brzozowski have in mind? A struggle for what? What are the criteria for truth and for error?

An instinct for truth [consists in the feeling that] every experience, every action, every detail of behavior of a given individual will remain in his life in one form or another; that a given moment in the past will always have an indestructible meaning for a given individual. In other words, experiences and moments that are separated from one another by time are not isolated, but a part of a certain active continuity existing in life, defining itself in one way or another during every moment through which we live. (*The Legend of Young Poland*)

Perhaps this idea is not very new. In the middle of the twentieth century, however, it seemed new—for example in the Poland of the post-Stalin era it was willingly borrowed from Camus and Sartre.

A philosophy of human behavior so pertinent to the field of human ethics (after all, art solves the artist's ethical problems, too) cannot be deduced, Brzozowski assures us, from a "scientific world view":

The basic characteristic of the world of science or, more precisely, of scientific mysticism, is indifference towards human values. This confirms the general principle already established: not to allow subjective elements to interfere with research and reasoning is the basic rule of a scientist's activity. The world of naturalism, evolutionism, materialism, positivism, the world without man, is the hypostasis of methodological positions. For four or five years I have been trying to demonstrate that those "systems" have nothing to do with philosophy, that is, with the culture of self-knowledge. (*The Legend of Young Poland*)

If this is so, someone might say, Brzozowski is handing in his resignation; he is a pure intuitionist. Once we recognize the world as knowable, we can deduce some principles of our behavior from that basic knowability of the world.

Brzozowski was an enemy of the theory of knowledge founded by Descartes; he called it "a plague." According to him, this theory attempts to answer the questions: "In what zone are locomotives born?" or "On what trees do galoshes grow?" (*Ideas*). For the problem of the world's knowability is insoluble if man, conceived as thought, as consciousness, is opposed to the world, that is, if the "subject" is opposed to the "object." Here we have to follow Brzozowski along labyrinthine paths.

What he practiced may be defined as a *philosophy of time*, but of *human* time. Human time differs from the time of Nature in that man's acts become fixed through the only possibility he has to persist in the universe: work. These acts accumulate. Human time is the congealed work of generations. This means that man, in his cognition, is not an abstract "I" meeting a non-"I." He stands on the summit of a pyramid constructed by the efforts of all those who have lived before him, and is at the same time a part of the pyramid. Thence, instead of a "subject-object" juxtaposition, another juxtaposition appears in Brzozowski: "Human"-"ahuman."

We must exert ourselves in order to understand that Nature, a naturalistic world, and all such images and notions of an infinitely earlier reality larger than history and society, are *in fact* only crystallizations of certain human, historical processes, which are by their very character impoverished and fragmentary; for the historical reality sustaining them is incomparably richer. (*Ideas*)

The true causal bond of the "laws" of Nature is the industrial and scientific technology of that moment. (*Ideas*)

[Cartesianism] rejects all the premises and believes that it may thus obtain thought without premise, pure thought, an organ given by God himself; yet we saw that thought is dependent upon a multitude of premises thanks to which it exists. Thought maintains itself as a fragment of a certain historical reality, which endures; first of all thanks to the existence of a certain organization and religio-military discipline; secondly, thanks to man's productive capacity (once again, in other words, a moral-juridical discipline, internal and external, which brings forth the amount of will necessary to the existence and continuation of productivity). (*Ideas*)

Our relations with being are not established through abstract thought but through precisely that concrete, irrational, historical and custom-ridden collective process which creates all abstractions. It is interesting that William Blake continuously and forcefully expressed such an attitude toward abstract definitions of life, and his work as well as that of many English poets (Robert Browning, in particular) has great pedagogical value. We find expressed there emotions provoked by very modern, subtle, and involved philosophical experiences. (*Ideas*)

The present condition of humanity is the profoundest metaphysical work of man, the profoundest reality—above all reality. Our cities, wars, factories, works of art, science—this is not a dream beyond which there is something deeper, something capable of liberating us. This is sheer, irreducible reality. (*Ideas*)

We incessantly create and invent ourselves, and whatever is created in that fashion by any individual is created in a given manner once and for all, for the human collectivity; and this applies to every aspect of life. (*Ideas*)

I think that Marx's "theory of value" should be considered first of all from this philosophical, metaphysical point of view. If we assume that humanity is a certain continuity in time, a continuity sustained amongst other processes also going on in time, that is, never completed, infinite; in other words, if we assume that the world *is not* a closed, accomplished totality, but a sum of many processes, every one of which tends to organize the whole of being according to its aspirations, and that humanity is only one of those processes—then time will appear to us as a potentiality, then we can hope that the victory may be ours, that man will master "fate," "being," "will become the creator of the world" or its "redeemer." Every particle of time is then a part of that possibility and therefore a part of true human value: we measure the importance of that part by its relation to *a value already realized*, that is, to energy shaped by human will. I feel that Marx's theory of value is one of his deepest metaphysical visions, while its importance in a political economy depends upon the fact that, using this vision, we are able to grasp *the notion of the economic process as a whole*, as a reality created by man in the midst of spontaneous processes alien to him. (*Ideas*)

It is difficult to express and show the full magnitude of the change in the nature of our historical experience brought about by Marx. Thanks to him the revolt of the deepest, most elemental forces of human life against culture, against the constructive, promethean character of Western history became transformed into a striving to gain control over history to transcend it. (*Ideas*)

Work is the exchange of a certain amount of our time for some permanent, immutable or relatively immutable conditions of our subsequent life. By using ourselves in a purposeful way we transcend ourselves and create something upon which we may rely. *This is, for us, the most universal feature of the world—that it is commensurate with work: it absorbs our work, writes it down upon itself and preserves its results.* The most universal characteristic of the world consists in this: not in its convertibility into our own terms, nor its causality, nor in its qualitative character, but in its commensurateness and receptivity to work. Therefore, our internal gestures are commensurate with the world, and we are not deaf and dumb in the face of what lies beyond us. (*Ideas*)

Human collective life, maintaining itself against the universe which is eternally inhuman, eternally alien to us, weighing upon us with its enormous mass. (*The Legend of Young Poland*)

Everything is constructed upon an abyss, through the will and sacrifice of those now dead; and we can say nothing of the ahuman except that construction and sacrifice were possible upon it. Whoever is attached to religious symbols can find here the modern contents of Roman Catholicism. In any case, we encounter here an autonomous, profound, definitive meaning of history. (*Ideas*)

I personally believe that our life can subsist owing to an understanding established between our creativity and the creativity or creativities which operate beyond man. But here I am not concerned with imposing my metaphysical or religious faith. (*Ideas*)

Brzozowski says elsewhere: "I strongly and positively believe in the existence of forces and laws that are active in the world and that surpass man; yet in our spiritual life what appears to us as superior to our own thought and will and inaccessible to their workings, is merely our own disorganized psyche." (*Voices in the Night*)

Very well, but what about the knowability of the world and the discovery of its laws through science? Is it not true that man's domination extends itself precisely thanks to a better and better understanding of the laws of Nature and history? No, answers Brzozowski. On the contrary, the struggle is first. We must make a distinction between the enormous progress of science and a "scientific conception of the world," that pseudophilosophy which is rather an obstacle to science. This conception is also a product of history; it reflects the situation of European societies in the eighteenth and nineteenth centuries.

We live and breathe the consequences of the Romantics' creations, and a scientific conception of the world is, no doubt, a product of the romantic sensibility. (*Ideas*]

Cold reality is nothing but social existence created without the awareness that we have to postulate through our constant effort the source of all value for us: our human *patria*. Only in a consciousness torn asunder could something like that appear: a phantom of a life that is ours and yet not ours. Darwin's world is only one of the metamorphoses of Rousseau's world. (*Ideas*)

A mentality (naturalistic, intellectualistic, positivistic, etc.) marked by scientific superstition preserves the Romantics' reality which they already emptied of value; however it rejects their internal world, their unwordly spiritual reality. (*Ideas*)

For the essence of the Romantic sensibility is a split into an external world subject to ironclad laws, and man's emotional-intellectual life which is impotent in relation to that external world:

The products of human thought again start to rule over it (thought) and that which is *our attitude* toward reality appears to us as an immutable quality of the world and independent from us. (*Culture and Life*)

Contemporary progressive circles have been using an improper philosophy, a philosophy woven of elements of a culture based on social-
economic relations alien to these circles. (*Culture and Life*)

What Brzozowski has to say about empirio-criticism in *Culture and Life* is important to an understanding of his work. This
trend (empirio-criticism) was for him the highest phase of positivist materialism—a self-destructive phase, for it involuntarily
revealed its weaknesses. The notion of truth was ranged with
fact; therefore it is presumably enough to examine the conditions in which that fact emerges—or in other words, to examine
"the relationship between an opinion regarded as a fact and the
facts determining it, in order to assess whether a given opinion
should be recognized as true" (*Culture and Life*).

In other words, positivist naturalism through exploration of the
problem of cognition, had to realize its own relativity, and, consequently, to validate research which would define that relativity and
thus preserve thought from theoretical nihilism—an inescapable consequence of attempts to create a *relativisitc Weltanschauung*! (*Culture
and Life*)

but an individual who is a true genius, that is, who possesses the
power to adopt every idea to the extent that it becomes his own
destiny—Nietzsche—is destroyed in his desperate struggle with the
tragic consequences of naturalism thought out to the very end. (*Culture and Life*)

About the application of the methods of the natural sciences
to society (as by Marxists for instance):

Every ideal can be considered and defined as a result of class psychology, but this is not the only point of view and, what is more important, this ideal is not a result: it can only be considered such from the
point of view of a scientist. In a word, every value, whether cognitive,
aesthetic or ethical—can, indeed, be treated as a fact, although it is
not. (*Culture and Life*)

Something here is not in order. Is not the almost miraculous
progress of technology sufficient argument for the verification

of our knowledge, even if we agree that the builders of the scientific Weltanschauung move in a vicious circle? What does Brzozowski propose, after all, in order to surmount relativism, while he himself seems to profess complete relativism? We should remember, however, that technical progress at that time was no less miraculous than it is today. We forget, for example, how revolutionary the invention of the airplane seemed. It is easier to reproach Brzozowski with overabundant respect for man's cosmic dominion than with indifference to scientific achievements. If he combatted "scientific superstition," it was because he did not share the belief in the existence of *ready-made* laws of the universe which are independent of man and only *unveiled* by his reason. I am not certain I have grasped the author's thought, but I think he might have said the following: Let us imagine a species of creatures endowed with completely different organs from humans but equally intelligent. They would invent science and technology operating according to different laws which would be equally provable; for Nature (the "ahuman") is a store of infinite potentialities, but they are only potentialities, asking for conceptualization. He might also have said today: the physics of Newton were provable, and they did not become false just because of Einstein's physics. They simply corresponded to man's degree of mastery over Nature at that epoch.

Scientists should understand that the reality with which they deal is nothing but the functioning of their instruments, which constantly change and are constantly placed in new conditions. Until they realize that they deal with attempts to create newer and newer forms of mechanical, technical activity which leave a trace upon the ahuman; until they stop deluding themselves that they are defining something existing beyond man, science will make progress only through a revolt against its own petrified results. Science will remain a mystery to itself and will produce that most comical theology, which is the saddest, because it is devoid of content. Today it is called the theory of knowledge and it serves to solve the problem of how man knows and how he discovers in the external world the facts, which are merely rules of the functioning of his instruments. (*Ideas*)

Rationalism (and its descendants) proclaims that "being should be known in order that our behavior, based upon that knowledge, should lead us to desirable results. To be sure, the real logic of things is just the opposite. Work secures our domination over certain realms of being. Thought, generalizing the rules that make work possible, creates knowledge" (_Ideas_).

This kind of opinion cannot be popular because it opposes man's naively realistic tastes (or idealist concessions). In his hostility toward the theory of knowledge, however, Brzozowski is not alone. Lucien Goldmann, for example, a French Marxist developing the remarks of the young Georg Lukács on the essence of tragedy (written in Brzozowski's time), violently attacks the offshoots of Cartesianism. Pascal, Goethe, Hegel, and Marx successively represent for Goldmann the liberation from a vicious circle.

Had Brzozowski polemicized with Lenin the philosopher, he would surely have asked Lenin why he got entangled in epistemological quarrels completely alien to the interests of Marx; was that not an example of how "the new" is often caught and strangled by "the old" and was not Engels, who glamorized Marx with "scientific superstition," the chief offender here? Brzozowski would perhaps have concurred with Simone Weil's article (1937) on Lenin's book _Materialism and Empiriocriticism_. She says:

Here an objection can be raised: Marx never asserted that he did not agree with the doctrine expounded by Engels in his philosophical works. He read _The Anti-Düring_ in manuscript and gave his approval. This only means, however, that Marx never took enough time to consider what separated him from Engels. All of Marx's work is conceived in a spirit alien to the coarse materialism of Engels and Lenin. He never considers man merely a part of Nature, but always—since man develops freedom of activity—as an element antagonistic to Nature. In his study of Spinoza, Marx reproaches Spinoza straight out for having mixed man with surrounding Nature instead of opposing him to Nature.

And referring to Marx's *Theses on Feuerbach*, Weil adds:

Undoubtedly Marx does not recognize pure thought developing outside of any contact with Nature. Yet a doctrine which makes man nothing but a product of Nature, and thought nothing but a simple reflection, has nothing in common with a doctrine for which reality appears at the meeting-point of thought and the world, in an act enabling man to take possession of the world.

I shall probably not betray Brzozowski's intention by placing the following remarks side by side with the passages by Weil quoted above.

In the course of time it will be acknowledged as a general truth that Marx was, first of all, a powerful intuitive philosophical mind: but this will not be understood as long as the fable circulates about Engels the philosopher. (*The Legend of Young Poland*)

For Engels, freedom is a product of necessity: an identity knowing itself. Modern thought conceives the place of man in Nature more tragically: Man is alone in the face of chaos, and he is not to be a logical result of a that chaos. He must save himself, his irrational essence, in spite of it. Man is not a further continuation of evolution but, on the contrary, an opposition to it, a break in its pattern. (*The Legend of Young Poland*)

When we compare Brzozowski with French authors we should not overlook their differences. Brzozowski is a writer of optimism, of Prometheanism, intoxicated with the discovery *that man has a history.*

If we can regain a belief in the reality of our world we shall understand that there was no time when so much of the ahuman would have acquired a name. Shall we always be too weak for the flame of those revelations that we provoke? Modern man is pitiful and ridiculous when he does not feel that he has transformed himself, that he has grown up internally thanks to himself, that the wisdom of other ages was applicable to almost another creature. Our faith resides in our actions and those actions now seem alien to us because the spirit expressing its belief through words is outdistanced by the spirit that lives in the action, the will, the use and sacrifice of all our living being. (*Voices in the Night*)

Thus for Brzozowski everything is social: man is the work of man—"not in the knowledge of being, but in the creation of man, lies the basic problem for mankind" (*Stanisław Wyspiański*).

"Collective life is always deeper, more powerful, larger than the consciousness which grasps it" (*Stanisław Wyspiański*).

Our attitude toward Nature is a social product and even "our attitude toward our own body is a product of society" (*Stanisław Wyspiański*).

Social analysis of experiences expressing themselves in art is still in a very primitive stage. It looks for a tendency; it forgets that social life shapes that which is most personal in us—our physical and mental make-up—and it forgets that the structure, the most intimate life of a given society, is most strongly reflected in precisely these personal features. (*Stanisław Wyspiański*)

Until now every era had its own taste; we, on the other hand, possess a historical sense. (A quotation from Nietzsche used by Brzozowski)

What about the *foundation* for our activity?

Science does not make use of the notion of being, and one of the commonest intellectual fads (literally: "inconsistencies") is to apply scientific findings to solving problems of being. (*Culture and Life*)

Since mankind does not grasp the essence of being, however, we can not transfer our own responsibility upon that essence. (*Culture and Life*)

Man's existence is inexplicable; it is the work of his own creativity. (*Ideas*)

Mankind does not perceive the meaning of the world beyond itself, but creates it. (*Culture and Life*)

No value can be adduced from the notion of being, nor can such a value be adduced from consciousness, as historical psychologism would like to do: "If we admit that every value is only a state of consciousness, we solve this problem of value in a negative manner, and the very problem is then impossible" (*Culture and Life*).

We cannot delude ourselves that truth will be established through a doctrine. Thomas Aquinas belongs to the past. *We must understand that there exists another foundation for truth than intellectual coherence. Truth should consist in the fact that we are it, and not that we perceive it.* The entire multiform, individualized, infinitely diverse human world can be in *profound agreement with itself*, while preserving its infinite intellectual and spiritual *diversification* and knowing that this very diversification guarantees agreement. (*Ideas*)

A concrete, particular value, a self-establishing act, expressed in activity, in judgment, in feeling, and so on, is the only reality. (*Culture and Life*)

In every creative moment, an actual value, having been created, takes first place, sometimes opposing all other values. That opposition, sometimes reaching exclusiveness, is a necessary moment here. Through it, the value acquires force and distinctness. (*Culture and Life*)

Nothing, moreover, that is true value ceases to be such, and everything that has been a value must be found again in some higher synthesis, towards which creativity directs itself through all such oppositions, disruptions, and splits. (*Culture and Life*)

It is proper to say that Marx did not betray Kant, but developed his premises. (*Culture and Life*)

The future is given shape by the freedom to create.... Everything with which we have no creative rapport becomes *past history*.... The substance from which we separate ourselves and the extent to which we separate ourselves from it becomes past history.... But it should correspond to that substance which we actually create: In separating ourselves, then, we maintain a feeling of solidarity.... Through a historical point of view, we establish the present and the past in our creativity, while the present is only a geometrical point of the incessant realization of the future. (*Culture and Life*)

The main value for Brzozowski is the very multiplication of values or the growth of human freedom in their realization. In turn:

The only foundation of human freedom is the power of the human hand over matter. When that power diminishes, the power of cosmic necessity over us grows. In that way, we define the meaning of progress. (*Culture and Life*)

The basis of our human edifice is the strength of our species in the face of the universe: To the extent that our consciousness can master that basic irrational fact, making it possible; to the extent that man is able to live in the climate of his own law created by himself. (*The Legend of Young Poland*)

When he contemplated the life of contemporary Europe, however, Brzozowski wrote the following:

And our situation corresponds more and more to the following definition: the speed and intensity of the powerful movement which carries us increases from minute to minute. We are ignorant, moreover, of the movement's purpose or objective, although we ourselves create it. (*The Legend of Young Poland*)

Brzozowski holds mainly the philosophers responsible for this state of affairs. "The aim . . . of philosophy should be not the understanding of being but the creation of a consciousness which can transform history into a work consciously created by man" (*Ideas*). ("To create" is, as we may easily note, the most common and the most overused verb in Brzozowski's vocabulary.) Philosophers have been contaminated by the Weltanschauung of the natural sciences. This also applies to those who should have been immune, that is, the Marxists.

And I come to the conclusion that "scientific ethics" have not as yet gone beyond Spencer. (*Culture and Life*)

The ethics of Spencer could have also been called an apology of progress. Progress [in Spencer] is not something which can or can not become a fact. It is the result of forces acting together with the necessity of Nature in human relations. One cannot find happiness in acting against progress. "Volentem ducunt fata, nolentem trahunt." (*Culture and Life*)

Brzozowski saw something like a betrayal in the second half of the nineteenth century—a betrayal of the daring philosophical concepts of the first half. This can be illustrated by a passage from Rickert on Schopenhauer, cited by Brzozowski: "On the one hand, a weakening of historical interests in philosophy; on the other, an increase of interest in the natural sciences or at least a fondness for scientific phraseology, were conditions indispensable to Schopenhauer's posthumous success" (*Culture and Life*).

All progressives contaminated by rationalism reason thus, according to Brzozowski:

Nature (as well as society) is thought of as external being, completely ready in relation to man, found in its place by him, to use the language of the empiriocritics. This being is subject to laws, according to which it transforms itself. Nothing is left to man but to guess the direction of these transformations and to make his ideal from this. (*Culture and Life*)

As for the "historical monists," the Marxists:

The dialectical method gave their arguments the appearance of a larger, or, in any case, a different, more mysterious necessity than that necessity which would have been found there, had they been able to see what their arguments really amounted to—the result of applying a method from the natural sciences to the study of economic and social life. (*Culture and Life*)

In the dialectical method something remained from those times when it unveiled laws governing the development of universal Reason; and this imperceptible something imparted itself to everything that passed for a result gained by dialectics. (*Culture and Life*)

It would hardly be reasonable to make Brzozowski into an apostate of Marxism. We should not project in retrospect notions which were barely outlined then (before World War I). Then, the phenomenon of orthodoxy and heresy barely existed in lay philosophy. In order to bring about such a state of affairs a sanction, a power able to hand down anathemas as well as doctors busy with ferreting out deviations and errors, is necessary. It is true that Brzozowski sometimes speaks about the orthodox Marxists, among whom he does not place himself, but such distinctions had a polemical character and were rather loosely associated with sin or virtue. Whosoever disagreed with Marx on some points, or criticized Engels, was not on this account alone a scoundrel; nor was heresy considered to be an outward sign of moral decay. Likewise, any of Brzozowski's involvement in the later odious bickerings between reformists and revolutionaries, Socialists and Communists, would have missed its aim. His rapprochement with the PPS and then with the Social Democrats, when he cooperated with *The Voice*, were problematic, and historians would be guilty of inexactitude if they placed him among the writers of any of these parties. Brzozowski often made fun of French and German Socialists for their intellectual sterility, and he was sympathetic only to the Syndicalists of the Confédération Générale du Travail. There can be no doubt that he proclaimed the need of "commitment," but he understood even this in a very complex fashion. Perhaps those who deny him the title "philosopher" are right in the sense that he continually came out on the artist's side:

Whenever we ascribe to our life some absolute, infinitely correct meaning, we escape from ourselves and put a curtain of ritual between ourselves and truth. Humor is a religious state of mind and it levels down the ritual: it liberates our life from an internal priestly mumbo-jumbo which enables us to tell lies. (*The Legend of Young Poland*)

Neither Byron nor Shelley did as much for a real, maturing freedom as did, for instance, Browning or Balzac. And there is not the slightest doubt that precisely those are the educators of a nation, who cannot be classified from the point of view of political struggles. For they serve real life and not the purpose of organizing mirages, superstitions, and political fictions. (*Ideas*)

Yet in each of his books Brzozowski had the misfortune of returning to Hegel and Marx. Had he dedicated himself to the study of butterflies, or flowers or had he been interested in Schopenhauer, no one would have reproached him later. Those two names, however, act as an electric current and make one's hair bristle at their very sound; our century reminds us, in this respect, of the thirteenth when one's hair would bristle at the mention of Aristotle who was still two-sided, Arabic, yet acceptable to the Christians thanks to Thomas Aquinas. Brzozowski became a heretic retroactively, in accordance with the same rule that once gave to some scholastics the smell of pagan sulphur only because they had been attracted to Aristotle earlier than was Thomas Aquinas. Undoubtedly one day a study will be written on Brzozowski and George Lukács, his junior by a few years. Such a study will show the similarities of their beginnings and their subsequent parting of ways. Lukács, however, was more privileged than Brzozowski due to his coming from a rich family: he received a thorough education, first in Budapest and then at German universities where his professors were Max Weber, Rickert, and Simmel. Brzozowski was almost completely self-taught—which does not mean that he should be treated with indulgence or that we should bow only to those who have their diplomas in order. Now I pass to excerpts which may give some idea of Brzozowski's Marxist problems.

"Vico, the only thinker who really overcame ahistorical intellectualism" (*Ideas*).

This intellectualism, a feature of the modern era, could not have appeared in the military-religious order of the Middle Ages. Favorable circumstances arose in the period of the Renaissance and the first great figure in this respect was Machiavelli:

Carducci is right. The sky of Galileo is the extension of Machiavellian politics over the universe when it lacked room on earth. (*Ideas*)

When we look for the origin of rationalism in this way, we find the following approximate groups and tendencies which nourished it: (a) the diplomats and the lawyers who tried to find a common ground for debating questions otherwise solved by force; (b) the military man preoccupied with the technical side of war—artillery, the art of siege; (c) the financiers, men in direct touch with the material side of life; (d) all those who were striving to achieve a position in society, or to improve an acquired one, and had to look at *life* from the perspective of a goal to be attained, of a plan. (*Ideas*)

Now why at the time when the "Ancien Régime" was disintegrating in Europe did the aristocracy, too, bound to the old order by its interests, assimilate and propagate rationalism (interchangeable in Brzozowski's language with pure intellectualism)?

Rationalism sounded convincing to the bourgeois, *for they already had profited from it* and were well rooted in their habits, their customs; it began to sound convincing to the noblemen as soon as they were no longer certain of their customs, as soon as they no longer had *a typical pattern of life.* If in the life of a given class there is a pattern securing a good deal of success, that class is ripe for a victorious rationalism. If a class loses that pattern and success or failure depend upon chance, that class is ripe for a demoralizing rationalism. (*Ideas*)

In the eighteenth century "the process achieves its final stage: thought capable of clearly expressing itself becomes a model of life. Formulation in words resolves all enigmas. That dark will which may work itself out through concrete, infinitely varied forms of life here conceives of itself as sojourning in the domain *of freedom:* in language, in pure expression" (*Ideas*).

And then appears Hegel, the crowning conclusion of an entire era.

"Logic should be, after all, no more and no less than an unveiling of that thought which is Being, and Hegel's identification of logic with metaphysics is merely the consistent unfolding of premises accepted by intellectualism" (*Ideas*).

This is, however, a higher stage:

> *The idea* is different from other forms of thought in that *it contains in itself the whole world of culture as its content*, and our religious, aesthetic, and legal approaches to the world grow out of it, out of its movement, same as do our cognitive approaches. Hegel surpasses all proponents of intellectualism because he does not limit himself to concentrating upon cognitive aspects as the only real ones; if our life grows out of thought, thought should contain in itself whole life, and not only what can be grasped by the intellect. (*Ideas*)

For Hegel, a test of thought is already found in the "increase of human competence":

> *Many times* I had the opportunity to peruse whole treatises on Hegel's famous saying that "all which is real is reasonable." This saying testifies to Hegel's attitude toward life, expressed thus: our thoughts are correct only when they provoke consequences which are not destructive but favor growth in the collective life of our society. (*Ideas*)

> Hegel's philosophy was, so to say, *a repatriation* of the rationalists' abstract reason. *The idea*, thanks to its consequences, was to create *forms of life* able to exist in a given cultural and social framework. (*Ideas*)

Brzozowski was very much interested in Hegel as a man: it must have been a strange organism, indeed, which had nourished such an extraordinary mind. A main character in the final chapters of the novel *Alone Among Men* is a German philosopher wih an English name Truth—a malicious, though at the same time respectful, portrait of Hegel. In *Ideas* Brzozowski's critical method applied to Hegel seems to be fruitful; it consists in establishing links between somebody's philosophy and his body, his temperament, his surroundings. As far as I know no one else has looked at Hegel from that angle, going back from his philosophy to some features of his personality. Who knows, perhaps dialecticians really are born and only a certain psychosomatic constitution, when placed in favorable circumstances, can achieve skill in the art of dialectics? Perhaps all others who practice this art are merely following fashion, and are doomed to clumsiness. And did not Brzozowski make out many things about Hegel only because he transferred to him what he knew about himself through introspection?

It seems, indeed, that Hegel was saved by the immense counterpoise of his own *restraining and controlling centers;* that at the instant he was confronted with *any thought,* any tendency, any value, the inclination to reflect arose as to why exactly he should focus his attention on that form of life and matter. Every moment in which he embraced a given thought was closely followed by another moment dominated by all the thoughts which had been excluded and which now called for supremacy. In order to win authority in his consciousness, a given thought had to strengthen itself against those assaulting thoughts. It had, in a way, to maintain not only its own authority but to take over their authority as well, to embrace not only what made it at first attractive but also what had kept him back from it. Hegel had a need *to feel* that it was impossible to live in a manner other than the one in which he lived at a given moment. Every interest of his provoked *the power* of all other interests: *the lived moment itself* would not become concrete for it would then impart the feeling of concreteness to the other moments which excluded it. *All life remaining beyond its immediately given form* became real, concrete, more alluring and desirable than that form. It seems to me that this is the key to the intellectual biography of the author of *Phenomenology. (Ideas)*

Is it not perchance also a key to Brzozowski's intellectual biography, to all his Marxist-Catholic polarity? He wanted to embrace everything, to place everything in a balance of contraries. It is true, Brzozowski did not come from the same social class as Hegel and speaks of him thus:

I guess that there one should give due credit to whole generations of German bourgeois families living in constrained, difficult conditions, distrustful of momentary temptations and drawing deep satisfaction from little pleasures which were secured by many sacrifices and by long endurance—they felt the fullness of their good sense, in this pipe, this piece of furniture or that musical instrument, objects potentially containing all rejected greater pleasures. *(Ideas)*

Perhaps these excerpts concerning Hegel should be completed by Brzozowski's remark on the traps hidden in any philosophy of history:

Every philosophy of history, since it deals with laws of the development of humanity, must be, by its very nature, conservative or reactionary. It must have an admixture of conservatism, even if it takes on a revolutionary form. For every theory of historical development must be based upon a notion which embraces, in the best case, the sum of all past historical achievements, and, considering that the existence of such all-embracing minds is not probable—a part of those achievements. Such a temporary phase in human development is next hypostatized and taken for *the law* of development and of progress. (*Ideas*)

And Marx? How did he remodel Hegel? Who was Marx? In *Flames*, the scientist and philosopher Samuel Ast defines him as follows:

An extraordinarily organized head: it is simply impossible to understand this. After all, limits of our understanding are traced by the structure and the functioning of our brain. Whoever is able to coordinate two or three conceptual sequences at best, will not be able to follow the thought of somebody who coordinated six or seven sequences. He will always have only to choose between varieties of one-sidedness.

And Ast (in 1871) foretells:

They already make a religion out of him, a new kind of providence. Machines are being invented and perfected; in the end the whole world is a perfectly functioning pushbutton mechanism and men change into idlers who come each day to receive their mechanically produced portion immediately paid in kind. They will make a theology out of him, you will see!

According to Brzozowski, Hegel is consistent only if we accept his premise that man enters through cognition into a relationship with being. A revolution accomplished by Marx meant this in his opinion: "Marx hits the core when he attacks precisely that premise; *for man exists and persists in being as a self-maintaining activity.* Feuerbach's theses on the philosophy of the future, a number of aphorisms of true genius, provided Marx with a liberating vision" (*Ideas*).

Next, it is appropriate to quote from Brzozowski's pronouncements on the evolution of Marxism:

Theories known today under the name of historical materialism are fossils; they preserve concepts, methods, and attitudes bound in a most direct manner with a certain moment in the history of the European intelligentsia. Every philosophical *concept* hides in itself, in the secret logic accessible only to its inventor, a story of its life, and when a concept wanders from soul to soul, or even from generation to generation, it gradually changes its nature. Often even its inventor ceases to understand his own standpoint as the years pass; his views, detached from the life which created them, look all the more certain the less he feels their flexibility and mobility under the pressures of his internal effort. Now they are realities, something which cannot be changed any more and if he tries to prove to himself their correctness, his reasons often violate the very essence of his concept. I am convinced that Marx's thought underwent such a transformation. His life was sufficiently long, intense, and spent in those milieus over which he towered, so he was not submitted to the kind of pressure that invites incessant control; just the opposite was true: he was influenced by a multitude of small factors which slowly transformed his thought. His relations with people of very different mental levels, often of a very primitive, naive mentality, produced, through friction and coexistence, a dust and spontaneous vegetal growth which veiled from the thinker the very foundations of his thought, leaving only the final results.

All the more so, as *his thought always responded* to a need of ordering collective actions and therefore was always tempted to bypass those differences which did not lead to any divergences in political practice. Slowly his thought was losing its sharpness and grew insensitive to the subtleties of its own development. (*Ideas*)

Brzozowski, who did not know Marx's early manuscripts (which were to be published a few decades later), is, though, more akin to many Marxists of our day, interested as they are in the young Marx, rather than to the Marxists of his time. He dis-

covered problems latent for a long time and destined to surface
only gradually. They remained latent in the head of Marx as
well:

Certain philosophical premises were elaborated by Marx at the time
when he still had an intense and lively metaphysical "disposition,"
when Hegel's philosophy was for him not just a theory but like a part
of his organism with which he absorbed life, saw life. As the years
went on, those premises played a changing role, adapted to new pursuits and interests, and Marx did not pay attention to those subtle in-
flections in his psyche, those shifts in centers of gravity, the chemical
mutability in his intellectual structures; *besides, he always treated his
thought as an arsenal destined to furnish arms and instruments to all
those who, basically, were engaged together with him in a common
action at a given moment.* Gradually a certain *simplified structure*
typical of the majority of the minds with whom he cooperated, a certain average culture began to cloud his personal views and his *lofty
though untrained, visionary philosophical genius* perceived itself
dimly in that fog of standard habits and opinions which were pre-
dominant in the radical, revolutionary wing of the European intelligentsia. (*Ideas*)

When and where did Marxism receive a stigma of naturalism,
so that man and his subjectivity were taken out of the equation
as irrelevant? This is not clear for Brzozowski's readers. In his
Philosophy of Polish Romanticism, written in 1906 when he
had just discovered with amazement the richness of Polish literature, he accuses all of German philosophy including Hegel of
helplessness where it tried to solve the problem of human
freedom:

"German philosophy aspires to learn about freedom. Yet
man's freedom can be known only to the extent it becomes
reality in man." While for German philosophers "not he (man)
fulfills it, it fulfills itself in him; he is only perceiving the process
of that self-fulfillment."

And the following sentence:

"If the heir of German philosophy—the German Social Democratic Party—got bogged down in opportunism, it is a consequence stemming from German philosophy by inexorable logic."

In other books by Brzozowski his main attacks are directed
against Engels, for Engels made explicit what in Marx was either
a result of negligence or of resignation. It is also Engels who is
responsible for the views of the Social Democrats:

> An orthodox Social-Democrat is in fact a perfected model of a bour-
> geois "utopian" and of a bourgeois "rationalist." The latter waits till
> life matures up to the level of what he already bears in his thought, a
> Social-Democrat knows that in a proper moment the historical devel-
> opment will create in him the necessary, victorious, correct ideas, the
> ways of assessing life, the new attitudes. (*Ideas*)

> For Marx the victory of the working class was necessary as he con-
> vinced himself that he was able to create, to secure that victory and he
> felt his own direct participation in it. For Engels that whole structure,
> together with Marx's will which animated it from inside, was just
> knowledge, it changed itself in his thought into a cognitive totality
> which satisfied his requirements and embraced facts known to him.
> (*Ideas*)

> For Marx matters looked differently; the very moment he expressed
> his thought in any form, he was afraid of having been caught by a
> dead thing. (*Ideas*)

> This is the reason why a sort of bald self-satisfaction transpires in
> Engels' writings: man is for him a trifle, after all; he should be happy
> and free, that is, not provoke in Engels' mind any disturbances of a
> logical nature. (*Ideas*)

Brzozowski adds ironically: "The life of the world consists in
maturing up to the level of Engels."

The romantic original sin, which was rationalism in reverse,
left its traces in the "monistic concept of history." "It is precisely
an absolutely dualistic theory, for it conceives thought and
everything which is a direct content of life, as not belonging to
reality in the strict sense. Thought is here a kind of shadow, a
fog hovering over a mechanism which transforms and recreates
itself" (*Culture and Life*).

Therefore "historical dogmatism leads to destruction of value in everything and to changing what is our task and the object of our activity into an already written chapter of history, at best not yet deciphered." (*Culture and Life*).

Nevertheless: "All the branches of knowledge, which are used to combat Marxism, tend, in the final account, to transform society and its tools into the products of some independent and irresponsible Nature" (*Culture and Life*).

They signify a return to pre-Hegelian positions, while Marxists hadn't succeeded in going beyond Hegel's Idea:

Those well-intentioned gentlemen do not suspect that poor Matter is also an idea, a blind hen, not less but more abstract than the idea of Hegel. (*Ideas*)

In Hegel there is really a constant, demonic struggle waged by logic, by intellectualism against an acceptance of an attitude which, roughly, could be called a *Nietzschean* one. Nietzschean as pathos, for Nietzsche did not succeed in establishing any foundation for himself. It is enough to be aware that the *tragic* character of such an attitude cannot be overcome. The world is so ahuman, that man builds his life upon a ground which he himself creates by offering and, in a way, by sacrificing his own life. (*Ideas*)

The monistic concept of history would be a theory of progress only in the case it was proved that the weight of facts always corresponds, by the nature of things, to an ideal of good, that an accomplished fact always fulfills some law, that is, that the course of events is directed by an all-wise, all-benign Providence. (*Culture and Life*)

All the activity of Brzozowski as a literary critic bears the stigma of an anti-intelligentsia trauma, inclining us to suspect that he constantly belabored his own shortcomings. Brzozowski, not unlike Baron Münchhausen, tried to pull himself out of a bog by catching himself by the hair. The European intelligentsia was, according to him, suspended in a vacuum and the process of alienation (noticeable already in the first bourgeois clerks) was advancing throughout the nineteenth century. Brzozowski's hypersensitivity on the subject is understandable in the Polish conditions of that time: he had before his eyes (and in himself) somewhat of a laboratory. Phenomena mitigated in other countries by the pursuit of formal perfection in art, for instance, here appeared in their nakedness (the worst poems and novels of Young Poland are the most interesting from this point of view). Thence his inclination to explore the shameful background of their philosophy and of philosophy in general. His essay on Amiel, included in *Voices in the Night* and dated around 1910, already describes the alienation of an "objectified man." Elsewhere he generalizes from this and applies it to all schools and tendencies:

Social transformations bring to the surface a multitude of people who, *for one reason or another,* have access to a portion (and a quite considerable one at that) of produced goods. The less time and effort they use to participate in production or to submit themselves to any social discipline, the more resources they can dedicate to feeling and thinking. . . .

The classes which live an active life are unable to perceive their own faith and their own self-discipline, except when it has already been transformed into something made independent of those classes. . . .

The intellectual life of the century has been falsified in a most incredible manner, just because in all of the trends and all of the oppositions the center of the stage has always been occupied by a struggle for power, waged by various groups of the European intelligentsia. (*Culture and Life*)

Engels discovered a great secret: nobody should respect what he is able to create, for this is always no more than a fragment; life itself should be considered indifferent and alien by everybody, like a process of Nature. (*Ideas*)

For Engels, not to want and not to be able to live in any existing society is the best preparation for a society of the future. (*Ideas*)

Their looking at the economic need as if from the outside, calling it the only cement of society, is connected with the extraordinary cultural sterility of the Social-Democrats. (*The Legend of Young Poland*)

A misunderstanding which arose between socialism as a doctrine of the intelligentsia on the one hand and socialism as a workers' movement on the other, consists in this: the intelligentsia does not grasp the fact that economic production is not a purely mechanic consequence following some theories but an infinitely complex phenomenon of life, the outcome of long lasting labor, long lasting self-education, something which is kept together by an infinitely subtle equilibrium of opinions, needs, perceptions, and feelings. (*Ideas*)

What is today called socialism is an image maintained by those who want to wrench the direction of production from the hands of capitalists with no other intent than to offer it to the economically incompetent intelligentsia. I am convinced that they are sincere and really believe in a future universal incompetence shared equally by workers and aesthetes as well as political lazybones. (*Ideas*)

The very essence of work is not understood and this is the most unsound area of modern thought. Work is looked upon from the outside and not from the inside, where it appears as an unceasing, autonomous bio-psychic creativity, always defined, always concrete. Socialists most often do not notice the problem or they disguise it. They say that with the passage of time *work* will become much lighter, more enticing, that it will be reduced to a minimum. All that is possible, but we still remain on a superficial level. *First of all, we should keep in mind that even if technological improvements will make work infinitely lighter* (though all papers written by socialists of Lagargue's ilk show an absolute ignorance of modern machines and their new applications), *mankind would not cease* to be its own accomplishment, sustained, with difficulty, against the onslaught of the elements; for besides those elements which are resisted by technology, we have to deal with an element which is much closer and is much more dangerous: ourselves and life. Even if technology progresses in the most astounding way, its very existence will be dependent upon our life, upon biological features sustained by a strong, severe sexual and educational ethics. The more man will be free *from oppressive poverty*, the more he will need inward heroism and willpower, *which protects the biological basis of all his achievements.* (*Ideas*)

Brzozowski believed that only those who are in a direct relation to production, the working class, can liberate man, in other words, make him fulfill a maximum of values; yet he did not agree with the thesis that it is enough to chase away capitalists to achieve victory. Since he tried to define the prerequisites of victory and saw them in the qualifications of the working class, its readiness for self-discipline and self-government, he may be called a socialist-moralist. For the type of Marxists which he criticized, this must have been no more than sterile sermonizing. Much time passed before the quite real needs of countries with nationalized (though "from above") economies incited many people to ask the question most important to young Marx himself: how to accomplish "man's return to himself." Thus, for instance, Bronisław Baczko in an article "On the problems of alienation"[11] says that "in the very notion of alienation a judgment is already contained." If we think that sentence over, it rehabilitates all of Brzozowski's worries.

To socialists Brzozowski opposed French syndicalism because it preserved the workers' pride and the faith in their own competence. In his essay on Herzen (*Voices in the Night*), he attaches great hopes to that movement. Those hopes proved to be illusory, though we do not know as yet how the movement influenced the history of France and whether one day it will not be recognized as being of greater consequence than it seems today. In any case the following fragment applies not only to the French scene:

It is here that we see that "leap" where freedom and necessity are made one. Here man's eternal dream about his free will is fulfilled. The problem of free will, a central problem of philosophy, is solved today not in university chairs but in workers' unions. Things happen now which were not dreamed of in philosophy. Neither did Herzen dream of them, but in spite of that he, too, is much superior, in more than one respect, to those who are considered today to be the summits of philosophical thought. Current philosophy probably will soon be eliminated even from the margins of bibliographic surveys. It is not impossible to envisage a day when even the self-taught Proudhon will be recognized as more deserving of being ranked with Aristotle, Plato, Kant, Hegel, Marx, Labriola than those illustrious gentlemen Wundt, Cornelius, Oswald, Külpe, and company. Then in the history of philosophy there will be a place for Herzen, and right next to him the tragic figure of Nietzsche, and we cannot even tell which of those two figures will look more imposing.

[11]"Studia Filozoficzne," no. 6 (1959).

Was Brzozowski a socialist after all, did he place the necessity of nationalizing the means of production at the core of his philosophy? He touched upon that subject many times, but reserved the name *socialism* to nationalization fulfilling *certain conditions* only:

We do not ask for justice: nobody knows what is just; we do not promise and do not look for happiness: man will never be happy. There are some absolute values in suffering and we do not want to renounce them. But we believe that man should exist because he has learned to love his existence and to appreciate its worth, that he creates himself as that reality whose actuality he craves, that he creates himself as his own absolute meaning and the goal of the world. There would be nothing, there would be no psychological quality of time, if not for the large quantity of work, above all physical work, being done day after day. (*Ideas*)

If work cannot be free, [if] it is not liberated, if *external motives*— fear, pursuit of consumption—incite the working class at the expense of an ascetic love of their own dignity and freedom, then the amount of work organized from above will always outweigh the amount of work done freely. The working class will suffer visible defeats and even worse, hidden defeats, poisoning the soul; human dignity will remain a problematic concept. Man will not be a metaphysical being but a creature maintained in the habit of existence by fear and consumer's urges. Here, too, only struggle can solve anything; only coming together and gathering forces after every lost battle. When the working class achieves the capacity to produce freely an amount of work outweighing that which is produced without freedom—they will win. If you call this socialism, I am a socialist, if not, I am not. Neither collectivism, nor universal happiness, nor a just economic system are for me decisive factors; I believe in the importance of a workers' struggle and remain indifferent to formulas. (*Ideas*)

For we must understand that the working class remained for Marx a metaphysical symbol, that he handled that concept *as a whole* and never penetrated its hidden core. The proletariat was for Marx a solution to his philosophical problems, but *when he wanted* to formulate prerequisites for the liberation of the proletariat, he would stop at affirming that this liberation really resolves his problems. (*Ideas*)

Brzozowski, however, completes his assertion as follows:

After all he [Marx] asked himself what worthless people should think when they take power, as only such people could take power— and what the working class should know, be it in a merely abstract way, in order to be able to control those rulers of theirs and those leaders. (*Ideas*)

The automatic development in history which itself must lead to free work, without any of the two old stimuli *fear and consumption*, is according to Brzozowski a myth: a social myth as understood by Sorel. Defending Sorel against the attacks of Russian Social Democrats who branded Sorel's theory of myth as reactionary, Brzozowski writes a dangerous sentence (in our *ex post facto* judgment, for we have seen how the concept of myth was subsequently put to use by fascist movements). Yet the entrenchments against such use are sufficiently strong in his writings, and if he recognized the validity of myths to some extent, undoubtedly it was only as far as revolutionary myths of the left were concerned:

The Russian Social-Democracy, were it aware of the fact that thinking *in myths* is unavoidable in any social collective action, could say at best that for the Russian proletariat or for its intellectual leaders the myth or rather the legend of automatic progress is still a necessity. (*Voices in the Night*)

But how to reconcile this with Brzozowski's passionate assaults upon any myths and legends? If "thinking in myths is unavoidable in any social collective action," then (let us not carp at his terminology) he introduces the concept of truth useful "at a given phase," and he should have no quarrel with Engels who provided the revolutionary movement with a "scientific faith." Yet Engels' dogmatic historicism was, for Brzozowski, equal to moral nihilism. Does it mean that political leaders must sometimes make use of a false philosophy while others, once they discover its falsity, are forced to exclude themselves from any collective action? Was that not the dilemma later confronting Georg Lukács? If he renounced his early writings it probably was not because he recognized his mistake but because, desiring to take part in a collective action, he submitted himself to the Communist party as the incarnate consciousness of the proletariat, able to decide what at a given moment is needed in philosophy. His early books reached into a still forbidden sphere, and perhaps he hoped they would be rehabilitated later. Here we place ourselves amid a fluidity where all borderlines between truth and its transitory version are blurred. Let us but take notice of the (not so irrelevant) dilemma, as it may explain Brzozowski's inability to accept any collective party discipline.

A moralist is incapable of providing a clear answer to the question: what should be done? A moralistic trend, strong in the French literature of the twentieth century, abounds in examples of such helplessness. Albert Camus for instance chose for his rule not to reach further than one can, while his antagonist Sartre was ready to make spine-breaking acrobatic efforts to participate in politics (not necessarily successfully). Brzozowski could not have been declared a leader in any political action, and even then, before World War I, his sympathies for French Syndicalism did not offer Polish readers any practical solutions. For that reason, he was finally thrown out into the external darkness as "useless" (which in politics means "harmful").

Yet Brzozowski would have been in disagreement with himself had he, as did the moralists of old, established only general principles and rules. That would contradict his conviction that truth is lived, not learned.

"One should not believe Prometheuses who are fully convinced they are right. The message of every man under the sun is himself; he cannot prove his mission, for were this possible, he himself would be unnecessary" (*Ideas*).

Brzozowski's worship of work was often attacked as bearing some obsessive features. And certainly we would have good reasons for seeing in it a kind of self-propelling rhetoric, if not for his way of life, so that he bought the right to such worship by "using up all his essence." Whoever knows how much physical energy is needed to write one book must think with horror of that man who lived only thirty-two years, who would be immobilized for whole weeks and months by illness, operations, convalescences, and yet left behind several thousand pages important enough to turn upside-down the mental world of writers in his country. When Brzozowski thunders against the parasitical life of the Polish intelligentsia he stands on firm ground: the intelligentsia conceived of literature as the fruit of moods, of inspirations, of imbibing the Absolute, while he fulfilled himself as a worker at the writer's table just because he felt *it had to be done*—because if he didn't, it would not be done by anyone else. Conceiving of work in that manner he was overcoming the intellectual in himself, and the words "the working class" seem to acquire in his mouth a warm, personal nuance because he ranged himself among the workers, though not by origin. It is surprising that those who were sarcastic about Brzozowski's bowing down before the titanic power of human work did not care to associate it with his everyday life. Yet his own tenacity probably explains his respect for the professional pride of French workers and his scorn for those who "devaluated" life in the hope that the Revolution would solve everything. If the goal of mankind is free work, not work performed out of low motives, then a certain type of writer augurs the worker of the future. I allow myself to give here a reconstruction of his reasoning; it would be easy to back it with remarks dispersed throughout his literary criticism.

It was not an idealization of work as such, of work motivated by necessity, by fear of starvation. Aesthetes, cross at Brzozowski because he presumably asked them to glorify unskilled laborers, did not catch his distinctions. He saw in work the necessity burdening our species in its struggle against "the ahuman," and only as such (conscious and engaging all the strength of human will) work would mean freedom. We are not far here from Norwid's[12] "working in order to rise from the

---

[12]Cyprian K. Norwid (1821-1883), eminent Polish poet whose writings influenced Brzozowski.

dead." But Brzozowski did not advise any idealization of work in conditions degrading man.

He shaped his views *in opposition* to those of the contemporary Polish intelligentsia, and that is why we find in his writings so many messages that seemed unnecessary then in Western Europe, itself more opulent and carefree. He searched for the ability to resist, for stamina, for something steellike in people and societies. He was, in a sense, a product of the Polish tragedy; who knows whether features common to him and to some Western European writers active after World War II could not be explained by the fact that the Poles had discovered earlier the same tragic political issues. This applies to life and to the theater as well: Brzozowski is, in a way, Wyspiański's[13] successor. We have even read in scholarly works that of all the writers of Young Poland, he remained loyal to Wyspiański alone. This is not true, however, for being aware of how much he owed him, he still succeeded in overcoming his influence. It is enough to quote his words; he pronounces the following judgment on Wyspiański:

He turned the castle of thought into his stage; instead of thought he presents a tragedy of his own nonthinking, nonadvancing. If he makes progress, it is only in contemplating his inaction. Do not look to him for live truth: as the source of his creation he chose the act of meditating on how thought does not want to think, will does not want to will, cognition does not want to cognize. And when he dashes forward, as if suddenly awakened, unpreparedness is at the foundation of his thought, immaturity at the foundation of his will. (*The Legend of Young Poland*)

Does it not sound, too, like an anticipated picture of Poland of the years 1918-1939?

Brzozowski's opposition to the mores of his milieu also found expression in his frequent remarks on the social aspects of eroticism:

[13]See above in the essay on Stanisław Ignacy Witkiewicz.

It is significant that every variety of romanticism and individualistic spiritualism appears as hypocrisy, lie, or deceit when confronted with sex and as something immature when juxtaposed with death. (*The Legend of Young Poland*)

But if in a given culture love is treated with contempt, it is an unmistakable sign pointing to the fact that people who lack self-esteem play a significant social role in that culture. (*The Legend of Young Poland*)

The role of eroticism in our intellectual life, especially as far as products of cultural collective thought are concerned, is very important and has hardly been noticed. (*The Legend of Young Poland*)

If man's erotic life contradicts his vision of the world, if the world of his work is not the world of his love as well, such a disparity will, sooner or later, destroy the harmony of that culture. (*The Legend of Young Poland*)

Even now, when I write this, the problem remains obscure. What has been said about it by many people is not quite satisfactory. Then, at the time of Young Poland, the problem provided at best an opportunity for psychological divagations.

One thing, I hear someone say, is irritating in Brzozowski: his syncretism, his mixing contradictory trends and slogans, coupling philosophies alien or hostile to one another. Such a stew must have provoked the mistrust of the public, and thus Brzozowski himself was after all responsible for the resulting misunderstandings. Andrzej Stawar, criticizing Brzozowski from a Marxist position,[14] immediately chooses this very fault for his target:

What then was the sense of eulogizing, as a matter of principle, both revolutionary writers and reactionaries, intellectual explorers and clergymen, apologists of the Church? What made it possible to put together writers representing social contradictions and social classes opposed to each other? It is not difficult to answer. The unreconcilable contradictions merge in one cultural fact defined by the word: West. That is the premise of his thought and thence comes its main dichotomy.

---

[14]Andrzej Stawar, *O Brzozowskim* (Warsaw, 1961).

In other words, Brzozowski involuntarily fell victim to old habits and was a typical representative of the Polish intelligentsia kneeling before the West:

He approaches that world with the humble admiration of a barbarian and with a feeling not unlike that of a child who begins to discover the realm of ideas. That world oppresses, tortures him by its scope, by the amount of its achievements, of ideas already invented, books already written. . . . Somehow one need only get access to that treasure and take from it everything with both hands. Such are precisely the vulgar superstitions of the Polish westernizers whom Brzozowski combatted, but in his struggle he proved to be chasing the Devil only to introduce Beelzebub.

Brzozowski then, according to Stawar, did nothing else but modernize the superstitions of the Polish intelligentsia. And Stawar would not be disturbed by the following statement from Brzozowski, for whatever man says, hidden social determinants are there and act in a most surreptitious way:

No one is able to appreciate how much we would gain, if we could acquire the conviction that we cannot, for one reason or another, rely upon the West to provide us with basic cultural goods, transferable to the extent they can be intellectualized or practically mechanized. This is a paradoxical wish and only one road leads to a more virile attitude toward Western culture and toward one's own internal life: a full, complete self-awareness. (*Voices in the Night*)

Here it would be easy to say that Brzozowski foreshadows precisely what in Poland only the Communists were to propound. Stawar, however, does not want to spoil his hypothesis. This hypothesis does not stand up under closer scrutiny. Had the "West" been for Brzozowski a pantheon he visited with awe, he would not have attempted to make order in it according to his taste and so unceremoniously that he was breaking the noses of statues adored by the public, throwing them down from their pedestals and preparing room for his own candidates. His was not the humble attitude of a barbarian, rather the proud one of an equal. His essays on various Western writers do not serve the purpose of "transplanting" them to the native soil, that is, the author reveals all his violent loves and idiosyncrasies. Besides, that "Western" pantheon proves to be quite spacious if it is also inhabited by Herzen, Belinsky, Turgenev, Dostoevsky, Norwid, and Mickiewicz. Thus we notice that the "West" so irritating to Stawar is everything that is not the Poland contemporary to Brzozowski. Such a quarrel with one's own country can be (why not?) proof of a typical "intelligentsia trauma." Yes, Brzozowski practiced a self-castigation common in Poland, advising the Poles to recognize that the Russians were more *serious*, as he did in his novels *Flames* and *Alone Among Men*, or to compare themselves to their own past, as in his essays on Mochnacki, Norwid, and so on, or to the West as in the majority of his philosophical essays. Yet writers practice this today, too, often using it as a device made popular by reformers. Neither should we see in this a Polish speciality, as the tendency to make comparisons disappears only in countries prone to self-admiration. If, however, we affirm that Brzozowski felt an exceptionally strong urge to deprecate "Polishness" (and how strong that urge was before him in Słowacki, in Norwid!), we are no wiser. Stawar also refers to Brzozowski's own confessions in his *Diary:* didn't he himself deplore his lacunae, his lack of education? But such confessions, often desperate ones, abound in the diaries of most important writers. Rare are the cases like that of a Russian proverbial (second-rate) novelist who used to say: "I do not understand why others torment themselves so much, for I write much and well."

In truth, the matchmaking between philosophies, so characteristic of Brzozowski, offers too much food for thought to be dismissed with a reprimand. To make peace between contradictory visions of the world becomes an eclecticism deserving blame only if those visions are abstracted from time which leaves in them its imprint and works in them. Let us take as an example the little French town in Flaubert's *Madame Bovary*. The inhabitants of the town are divided into the followers of the vicar and those of a progressive apothecary, Homais. Either the ones are right or the others, *tertium non datur?* Yet there is also a *tertium:* Emma Bovary. She tries to escape from grayness and boredom by taking refuge in her "inward world," in her dream of perfect love, union of souls and bodies. Flaubert was neither on the side of the vicar, nor Monsieur Homais, nor Madame Bovary. For him all of that was life "as gray as the life of wood-lice." Flaubert was immoral. Being himself not unlike his heroine (with another kind of love, for his writer's craft) he reconciled contradictions through his generalized negation, his loathing of observed society. Antiprogressive, he lashed with predilection at Monsieur Homais' stupidity. He could not become the guide for a progressive bourgeois leader, though he was not an ally of a conservative, either.

Whoever reconciles contradictions one way or another may be suspected of immorality, and not without reason: man cannot wait for the political camps or ideologies of his time to reach the stage when what contributed to their mutual hatred will fall off as dry husks. Like the heroes of *The Undivine Comedy*, man, entangled in actual events, too often has a choice only between the revolutionary army of Pancras and the Ramparts of the Holy Trinity. Not so in time as seen in a vision. Pancras is a negation of Count Henry and he wins, but then in its turn appears a negation of a negation: a cross in the sky (this is, obviously, not a postmortem rehabilitation of the castle's defenders but a third link in the triad). Similarly, it is diffcult to conceive a more blatant contradiction than is Christ marching at the head of a Red army patrol in Alexandr Blok's "The Twelve." But for Blok that contradiction was to be solved in time, through the "music of history." Boris Pasternak's *Doctor Zhivago*, written in a similar spirit, should offend partisans of militant ethics: either one is for communism or against, while in Pasternak's novel the revolution looks the part of a Christological process in the life of mankind and, since it is an inevitable dark collision, a cataclysm, it redeems Russia through suffering, prepares its greatness and purity.

Historicity eats up everything that occurs at the present moment; a dialectical thought once put in motion cannot stop.

This is probably the source of anxiety for Marxists who read Brzozowski. They realize that while making use of such a method in thinking one must at last say "enough" and freeze it, otherwise all action would be paralyzed in advance. Were we to look at contemporary events from a historical perspective, as if skimming over a chronicle of the French Revolution, we would not be able to send to death any specific individual of blood and flesh; we would be visited by doubt. Destruction of a concrete individual is irreversible, while hatred between the Patriots, defenders of Virtue, on the one hand and the monarchists on the other, once very real, becomes quite a dusty past.

Where all literature is a kind of guidebook to distinguishing between friends and enemies, where it is supposed to incite fighting, a character like Yuri Zhivago should appear immoral, owing to his lack of passion, that is, his overabundance of imagination. What happens now is contemplated by Yuri Zhivago as if from the height of time already passed, when graves of friends and enemies will be undistinguishable. We sense here some very old conflicts between tragedy—or art, imagination, vision in general—and action. Any action calls for contradictions that would not be mitigated by anything, and the idealization of a goal that must be presented as final.

Brzozowski was familiar with that problem. Did he not say that value strengthens itself and ripens through opposition and exaggeration? Let us remember, too, his opinion cited above on Hegel's sentence: "everything which is real is reasonable." No value is lost, everything strong enough to subsist and to increase the competence of mankind in the struggle against the "ahuman" is preserved and incorporated into a negation of a negation, and such an ascent on a spiral has no limit. It occurs in time. Do we have the right to draw aside the curtain of tomorrow? He recognized his own right to such "eagle's flight." Simultaneously, in every book which fell into his hands he looked for signs indicating that man's consciousness had once more moved forward, announcing again the elimination of another set of the contradictory "yes" and "no." That penchant of Brzozowski's probably reaches its acme in the following passage:

> I wish to draw your attention to a thought which (long ago) appeared to me in vague outline. I find it clearly formulated by a writer whose book will become a source of great and calm strength to one who reads it with sincere devotion. I have in mind *L'Action* by Blondel. Work, says Blondel, is our appeal to life beyond us: we make efforts, moves, in order that something beyond us be created. Isn't it then true that we make signs to which the great world responds, a world which understands them? It understands and receives that which is our work; but, in turn, what is our work already contains the world's life. The organism of a given nation's labor is thus a live language of an ahuman but humanized truth. Therefore everything proper to that organism—customs, folksongs, law—comes from the same powerful source. Our Mickiewicz gives here his hand to Blondel, and the austere Marxist thought recovers the flexibility of life. We are able to see what Proudhon meant when he felt he was a providential announcer of truths elaborated by peasants and artisans of his country. Pragmatism which conceived of truth and cognition somewhat like a lottery game, is swallowed up here by a higher idea, disappears in it as an arrogant and garish one-sidedness. Cournot's *probabilisme*, Sorel's criticism, the ancient wisdom of Vico, Newman's theory of the development of ideas, everything grows into one great concept, which was grasped, we may say, in its general outlines by Mickiewicz, Norwid, Towiański, Wroński, Cieszkowski. (*The Legend of Young Poland*)

Brzozowski's Christian sympathies did not date from the last period of his literary activity. That activity starts in 1910 and *Philosophy of Polish Romanticism*, written in 1906, is already not unlike a confession of Christian faith, though we may assume it was an expression of a passing mood and was not sufficiently integrated into the whole system of his ideas. We observe in Brzozowski an ebb and flow, though every consecutive incoming tide has stronger waves than the previous. In his philosophical last will—in *Ideas*—both waves, of Christianity and of internal Marxist problems, acquire a considerable intensity.

In order to be just, one should forget for a moment about the peculiar role of Roman Catholicism in Poland, then used to consolidate the so-called national ideology—the program of the nationalistic right wing. Brzozowski, when he tried to cope with questions of a religious nature which he asked of himself, did not pay attention to that politicized Catholicism. On the other hand, since he lived by his reading, he reacted to the intellectual situation of Catholicism in two countries particularly, France and Italy.

The situation on the eve of World War I, as it is presented by the eminent Thomist philosopher Etienne Gilson in his book of reminiscences[15] was not very good. Overtaken by the ancient regime's destruction, a calamity which seemed like a violation of the natural order, the theologians attempted throughout several decades of the nineteenth century to exorcise the secularizing demon by entrenching themselves in a traditional fideism. Next, noticing that the adversaries' pressure was too strong, they endeavored to provide Catholics (in schools, seminaries) with rational arguments opposed to arguments of science. This, however, led, according to Gilson, to a rather sterile scholasticism which often blurred the borderline between rational cognition and faith; faith was destined, so to say, to supplement what could not be proved by reason—that is, the principle "credo ut intelligam" ("I believe in order to understand") was neglected. The encyclical of Leo XIII, Aeterni Patris (1879), advised a return to Thomas Aquinas. Yet a renewal took time, and Thomism truly reemerged only after World War I. In Brzozowski's lifetime the tasks of Catholic philosophers were not yet delineated—they hardly began the necessary revision. The main stimulus came from a non-Christian philosopher, Bergson. He seriously contributed to the appearance of so-called Modernism in France. Gilson speaks of Modernism with sympathy and compassion, certain though that the whole movement was justly condemned by the encyclical Pascendi in 1907. The Modernists, reacting violently against ossified scholasticism and defending "a religion of the heart," went in his view too far, which

[15]Etienne Gilson, La philosophie et la théologie (1960).

proved to be unnecessary as in their beloved field, biblical exegesis, they were soon surpassed both in daring and in scholarly rigor by more orthodox specialists. Bergson, however, influenced not only the Modernists. His students at the Sorbonne were future renovators of Thomism, among others Jacques Maritain and Gilson himself. This does not mean they should simply be ranked with Bergson's followers. From another Gilson pronouncement, an interview given in 1946 to a Parisian periodical *Le Littéraire*, we learn what philosophies he esteemed: "Thomism is bursting with life," he said. "It is the philosophy of the future. It will engage in a philosophical dialogue with existentialism and Marxism, because those are serious philosophies." It would be useless to try to guess how Brzozowski would have reacted to such a statement. He shunned scholastic philosophy such as he encountered, passed through Bergson, and had a feeling only for Catholic thinkers more or less "modernistic" (in Poland, Marian Zdziechowski also sided with them). All his dislike for the type of a "rational" Catholic, a scholastic and a totalitarian (for some reason totalitarianism and scholasticism used to go together), he discharged in the novel *Alone Among Men* by introducing as a character a Jesuit, Giava. This Giava is nearly a double of the Jesuit Naphta in Thomas Mann's *Magic Mountain*—though Mann, writing his novel much later, was probably unaware that Naphta's literary prototype already existed. In Brzozowski's novel, set in the Berlin of the 1840s, Giava engages in Machiavellian activity by backing the revolutionaries (the Hegelian left) in order to make the generalities of their ideas surface, to confront these ideas with reality, and to deflate them in that manner. At the same time Giava is a projection to the first part of the nineteenth century of much more recent attitudes, and is used by the author for criticizing the Catholicism of scholastics who offer ready-made proofs of God's existence, and so on. It is Giava who criticizes himself and all those who believe religion is founded first of all upon the argument and not upon the act of faith. Here are his confessions:

Aha, you notice now that we must not necessarily believe in that which is truth for our impotent knowledge, and that our lack of faith may be a disability in our own eyes. I concede, He won here, totally: I see most precisely, most distinctly, that all this is truth, I suppose I see more clearly than do believers themselves; too clearly; I should say I see with my posthumous, damned sight—and I cannot believe. Do you realize: here, this instant, I define my own state of mind, I know it cannot be anything else than what I said it to be, and, do you realize, I am certain and I cannot believe. And I know everything with me is like that: I am convinced that they are right, I know that His flesh and blood are in a chalice; I know as if I were present at their very becoming bread and wine, and I do not believe.

Giava is an extremely complex personality, no less than another priest in the same novel, Rotuła, a Jacobin, libertine, wencher, and together with that a man of childish faith (Brzozowski's best literary creation, the most profound figure of a priest in Polish and perhaps world literature). Both characters prove how much Brzozowski owed to Dostoevsky. Giava, after he has opened himself so thoroughly to Roman Ołucki, wants to make him his deputy in faith, a second half of himself:

"Wait! I want you to believe to the very core of your heart, to become His knight, to go and fight where today He is being scourged, where they spit on Him and strike Him on the face asking: guess, Jesus, who is hitting you, guess, because I myself do not know, I do not know who I am, whether I exist at all, I who see only darkness."

The writings of Cardinal Newman finally reconciled Brzozowski with Roman Catholicism. By "reconciled" I mean that he succeeded in integrating his meditations on history into an all-embracing Christian vision. I shall not attempt to show how this was possible. That stage in his evolution was suddenly interrupted by death; we can at best deduce something from fragmentary, often cryptic, notes mostly bearing an earlier date or, as far as the last period of his life is concerned, from his no less fragmentary *Diary*.

The entries in the *Diary* are so condensed that we may perceive in them materials for whole books he still hoped to write.

The basic orientation is the same as when Brzozowski castigated any entrapment of the "new" by the "old," by naturalism. Incidentally, that is why he felt he was in his right when denying that his ideological zigzags proved his lack of consistency. The following passage from his *Diary* contains the very essence of Brzozowski's historicism. Even allowing for the peculiarities of his style the wording is very intricate:

Coleridge speaking of Sir Thomas Browne says that he was a Spinozist without being aware of it; Sainte-Beuve says a similar thing of Montaigne. Now Spinoza's premise consists, in my view, in treating culture, in the broadest meaning of the word, as a consequence of a value unknown to us; culture is regarded then both as a product and form of being, the essence of which is unknowable. As to myself, I follow here Hegel, Vico, Newman, and consider all values and all qualities as products and forms of culture. Swedenborg says: woe to anybody who puts Nature at the beginning. Our relation to God is the sum and essence of all the relationships, attitudes, forces, aspirations which create culture. Culture transcends man as he is and thanks to this transforms him from outside. The superhuman creates man and defines him. All Nature is held by the supernatural. These are not my views but profound and undeniable facts. Our relationship to God should be marked by something which would prevent us from changing God into a part or even a sum of man as he is. God cannot be a concept. God-concept is the same as Nature. Such is the meaning of the Trinity. Did S. T. Coleridge perceive it in that manner? If we want to grasp the mystery of the Trinity, we should take for a point of departure the very essence of human coexistence. God is the foundation and the source of all interhuman relationships. Does it mean that by interpreting that dogma in such a way we deprive it of a religious value? Not at all. Human life is religion, as a fact and as a striving toward understanding; man in his striving creates religion as thought, faith, consciousness, he is so constituted that by desiring to know himself he finds God. But then God is nothing more than human? How wonderful! Why should truth be ahuman? By knowing himself man learns to know the structure of being, the structure of truth, he grows into it by his thought as much as he is integrated into it by his existence.

For Feuerbach, if man creates God, it meant that there is no God. For Brzozowski, precisely the fact that man creates God means that he was created unto God's image and likeness. As everywhere he attacks here reduction, the main principle of every scientism: "man is no more than . . ."

Thus in 1911 Brzozowski developed thoughts he had jotted down in haste in his *Philosophy of Polish Romanticism*. He spoke there of the Word, Logos:

> For such is the unity of the Word in mankind that wherever it is endangered, it is endangered in all men. And because of that the Word is one, indivisible, and mankind is not a multitude of individuals but a church, that is, a live communion of spirits in love and truth. . . . One cannot secede from the church. One may only work for the church without knowing he does. . . . The church is a communion of mankind in creative labor. It establishes a bond between the highest spiritual summit and utter dejection, a bond which cannot be broken.

At that time, however, he had not yet read Newman. In his *Diary* he judges his own books quite severely—with the exception of the "mature" parts of *Ideas*—finding in them too much lyricism and even demagoguery. In February 1911, not long before his death, he expresses his gratitude to Newman for having cured him of these faults and the tribute sounds like a prayer:

> Blessed be the name of my teacher and benefactor. I hardly dare to bring my poor soul near his lightness. I should not write on it any more. I should not use words in connection with this subject—I deposit my future, my soul in the care of his prayers, I ask his protective spirit for intercession, for understanding pity and enlivening strength. I believe that he exists, that he lives in a blessed whole of the all-embracing structure, I believe in a power of intercession, in the holy power of prayer and of communion.

Brzozowski read today is not what he was for his contemporaries, since we put his books on the table together with others which much later gave shape to similar themes. When citing various names, I am not necessarily trying to prove that Brzozowski was a pioneer. My intention is rather to counterbalance scholars' clichés according to which Brzozowski was a strange, purely local phenomenon—at best an impressionistic literary critic of genius, hesitant and unstable as to his philosophical orientation. Such clichés could implant themselves because his mind was lightning-quick in associating ideas remote from one another. Today many of these ideas are easily grasped, and not only by poets, though in his lifetime (and for a long time afterward), a stagecoach was used to travel between them. Besides, it is possible that some of his "leaps" are still too difficult for us to understand, due to the incompleteness of the works he left.

I have presented no more than a catalog of philosophical topics, separating them from his literary criticism and often even forcing myself to shun it, because Brzozowski the critic has fared better with the scholars than Brzozowski the philosopher. Every topic could become the subject of a separate chapter or even of a dissertation, and only then could one hope to succeed in elucidating the meaning of all those "too intricate" or even apparently perverse ligaments in Brzozowski's writings.

1961